De Gaulle and Churchill

De Gaulle and Churchill

The Foundations of a Perplexing Franco-British Relationship, 1940–1946

Evan McGilvray

Pen & Sword
MILITARY

First published in Great Britain in 2024 by
Pen & Sword Military
An imprint of Pen & Sword Books Limited
Yorkshire – Philadelphia

Copyright © Evan McGilvray 2024

ISBN 978 1 52678 646 3

The right of Evan McGilvray to be identified as
Author of this Work has been asserted by him in accordance
with the Copyright, Designs and Patents Act 1988.

A CIP catalogue record for this book is
available from the British Library

All rights reserved. No part of this book may be reproduced or
transmitted in any form or by any means, electronic or mechanical
including photocopying, recording or by any information storage and
retrieval system, without permission from the Publisher in writing.

Typeset by Mac Style
Printed in the UK by CPI Group (UK) Ltd, Croydon, CR0 4YY.

Pen & Sword Books Limited incorporates the imprints of After
the Battle, Atlas, Archaeology, Aviation, Discovery, Family History,
Fiction, History, Maritime, Military, Military Classics, Politics,
Select, Transport, True Crime, Air World, Frontline Publishing, Leo
Cooper, Remember When, Seaforth Publishing, The Praetorian Press,
Wharncliffe Local History, Wharncliffe Transport, Wharncliffe True
Crime and White Owl.

For a complete list of Pen & Sword titles please contact

PEN & SWORD BOOKS LIMITED
47 Church Street, Barnsley, South Yorkshire, S70 2AS, England
E-mail: enquiries@pen-and-sword.co.uk
Website: www.pen-and-sword.co.uk
or
PEN AND SWORD BOOKS
1950 Lawrence Rd, Havertown, PA 19083, USA
E-mail: uspen-and-sword@casematepublishers.com
Website: www.penandswordbooks.com

Contents

Acknowledgements		vi
Chapter 1	The Early Years: 1874–1940	1
Chapter 2	De Gaulle Arrives in the UK	22
Chapter 3	Into Africa	51
Chapter 4	1941: What to do with the Free French?	69
Chapter 5	North Africa: War and Politics	82
Chapter 6	1942	102
Chapter 7	1943	133
Chapter 8	Preparing to Return to Europe	168
Chapter 9	De Gaulle Triumphant	192
Notes		211
Bibliography		228
Index		231

Acknowledgements

This work is the result of a family holiday in Paris during the summer of 2006. On seeing a statue of General de Gaulle I mentioned to my wife, Ela, that I remember de Gaulle's death and his funeral. I was nine years old when de Gaulle died. I also mentioned that my father, as with many British people at the time, was less than gracious about de Gaulle's memory and legacy. Ela promptly said that I should write on the subject of de Gaulle and his wartime relationship with the British, notably Churchill. And so, this work was conceived.

As with all authors, we have literary debts – in my case with my publisher Pen & Sword. Namely: Philip Sidnell, my commissioning editor; Matt Jones, my production handler; and Richard Doherty, who edited this work and pointed out my blemishes and mistakes with great courtesy and grace.

I also have a huge debt to Allen Packwood, the Director of the Churchill Archive Centre at Churchill College, University of Cambridge. Allen, using the Jennie Churchill Fund, allowed me twelve months of unfettered access to the online collection of Winston Churchill's papers. For me this was fantastic as I was able to take my time to examine Churchill's papers from my own home – no expensive or inconvenient travelling!

But, overall, the main debt is to Ela for her prompting the subject of the book and for putting up with me always reading or writing while I perhaps should have been doing something far more useful.

So, thanks Ela – and I love you as ever!

All images used in the plate section for this book are courtesy of the National Army Museum, London.

Chapter 1

The Early Years: 1874–1940

The Making of Two Great Europeans

Winston Churchill and General Charles de Gaulle were two great Europeans whose leadership during the Second World War ensured their places in history but their relationship during those years was never easy – they were not easy men to work with. Both men were proud, determined and always wanted the best for their respective countries, the United Kingdom (UK) and France. Both were also geniuses in their own ways and far from conventional owing to their experiences of life. It is also a tale of stability and instability – the British since the end of the civil wars of the seventeenth century had enjoyed relative peace and prosperity in their homeland at least with, for them, a European peace lasting from 1815 to 1914.

France had had quite a different experience beginning with revolution in 1789 which led to many forms of government and change from then until 1870 with war with Prussia and defeat in 1871. This led to the establishment of the Third Republic which saw a reasonably stable France until the First World War in 1914. Both Churchill and de Gaulle were products of their national experiences. The Canadian historian, Jean Edward Smith, notes that Dwight D. Eisenhower, who spent a period in the 1920s in Paris, noted French history after 1789 and realised that France was a very difficult country to govern.[1] This realisation was to prove fruitful in 1944 when he met de Gaulle and worked with him on the liberation of France. British observers were also astute as Harold Macmillan, Churchill's representative in North Africa, observed that, owing to the upheaval in French politics since 1789 with various changes of regime, unlike a British or American officer, a French officer often had to decide where his loyalty lay.[2] De Gaulle was always certain – it lay with a free France and a free French people.

Churchill is the better known of the two leaders but without doubt in the francophone world de Gaulle has made his impression. Regarding post-war Europe, during the 1960s as the UK tried to enter the then Common Market, today the European Union (EU), de Gaulle opposed British membership of the trading bloc. The UK did not join the Common Market until 1973. Given the failed relationship between the EU and the UK; perhaps de Gaulle perceived something, perhaps a littleness, which his fellow European leaders had failed to see about the British and Europe.

As with all tales we start at the beginning with an examination of what made these men so different from others in 1940. As Churchill was born first in 1874 this narrative will begin with his origins. Compared with de Gaulle Churchill was certainly born with a silver spoon in his mouth; he was part of the illustrious Marlborough line and was born at Blenheim Palace on 30 November 1874, apparently two months premature, the son of Lord Randolph Churchill and Jennie Churchill, née Jerome. From this family background Winston Churchill was always able to access the great and the good but there was a fly in the ointment – there always is. Sadly, it was his own father, Lord Randolph, who enjoyed a short, yet spectacular life, mainly in politics, which had seen him at his zenith appointed as Chancellor of the Exchequer by the then British prime minister, Lord Salisbury. Lord Randolph, at 37, was the youngest Chancellor since William Pitt the Younger in 1782.[3] Nevertheless, Lord Randolph's career and life was cut short by an illness, about which some still speculate; he died in January 1895 aged only 45. Whatever the nature of Lord Randolph's illness was, it was clear that he suffered both a mental as well as a physical deterioration. Fifteen years later it was feared that the same fate had struck his son, Winston, who, when addressing the House of Commons on 22 April 1910, speaking for forty-five minutes without notes, suddenly broke down into silence mid-sentence. Amnesia, the horror of public speakers had struck. After a futile search of his mind and pockets, Churchill resumed his seat in silence. Some wondered whether it was to be the same sad tale of Lord Randolph but, as history knows, it was far from being so. On the day he was supported by his party as he sat down and never again did Churchill ever venture into the chamber without notes.[4]

Lord Randolph's death in 1895 was at the time when the young Churchill was just about to set out as an independent young man. Churchill began his career as a soldier after being educated at Harrow where he was placed in the army class, a place reserved for the less academically gifted taking three attempts before he qualified to enter the Military College at Sandhurst to train for a military career. Once at Sandhurst, the young Churchill did well. After just about getting into the college he passed out eighth in his cohort of 150.[5] Clearly, conventional education had done little to stimulate Churchill but something that he was interested in, the military, did and he also learned that he had a knack with horses. In February 1895, weeks after his father's death on 24 January, Churchill was commissioned as a second lieutenant in the 4th Hussars. His pay was a little more than £150 pounds a year. This was to increase almost immediately to nearly £300 as the 4th Hussars were about to embark for India. Service in the so-called jewel of the British imperial crown attracted a larger salary whilst expenditures were considerably less than those incurred in the UK. Nevertheless, Churchill needed another £500 per annum (equivalent to approximately £67,000 in 2020) to live up to the style of the regiment. But there was little left in the Churchill family coffers as his mother was a drain on them; but she was an able networker which was to allow Churchill to follow another line in his professional career – that of a writer.

Churchill and the 4th Hussars arrived in India, disembarking at Bombay (Mumbai) in early October 1896, and stayed on the subcontinent for eight and a half years but not Churchill who quickly became bored and stayed for a mere nineteen months with his regiment. During this time, he managed to include two London leaves of a few months each, three winter visits to Calcutta (Kolkata) which involved four days of travel inward and outward, and a trip to Hyderabad to take part in a polo tournament in which his team was successful. He also went on a hazardous expedition to the North-West Frontier which was one of the few places that British soldiers could find anything like combat as Afghan tribes frequently raided this unstable outpost of the empire which bordered Afghanistan. It also produced copy which served Churchill an opportunity to begin his career as a journalist and writer.[6]

Churchill was a born adventurer as, just after being commissioned into the Hussars, he went out to Cuba to observe the uprising against the Spanish as the Spaniards tried to hold their empire together. Indeed, Churchill was pleased to celebrate his twenty-first birthday under fire, an attraction which he never failed to get over. Using his mother's contacts, Churchill was able to send war reports on the conflict to *The Daily Graphic*. On his expedition to the North-West Frontier, Churchill was able to reports on the Siege of Malakand which were published in *The Pioneer* and *The Daily Telegraph*. He also produced his first book, *The Story of the Malakand Field Force*. To relax during this period, he wrote his only novel, *Savrola*. Nevertheless, Churchill remained bored with his service in India and sought adventure elsewhere.

The next phase of Churchill's writing and military career produced his next literary work, *The River War*. This was an account of the reconquest of Sudan in 1898. Since the beginning of 1898, Churchill had sought to be part of the Sudan campaign; indeed, he sought action anywhere and, as he was in India, also tried to be taken on the Tihar campaign, once more on the North-West Frontier. This proved to be a bloodless affair in which diplomacy played its part and a disappointed Churchill was back in Bangalore (Bengaluru) by mid-April 1898, and once more trying to get to Sudan before it was too late. As a result of the campaigning in Tihar, Churchill had again been granted home leave. Historian Roy Jenkins notes how extraordinary this was as even viceroys would normally have to wait nearly three years to get home leave.[7] Churchill just seemed to be well placed and lucky.

No matter what, Churchill struck lucky once more, owing to the unfortunate death of a subaltern from the 21st Lancers which meant that Churchill switched regiments and, by 24 July 1898, was on his way to Sudan to join Herbert Kitchener's expedition. Before he left London Churchill had negotiated a deal with *The Morning Post*, in which he reported from the Sudan campaign at £15 (just under £2,000 in 2020) a column. The expedition concluded on 2 September 1898 with the British victory at the Battle of Omdurman. However, by now Churchill was getting somewhat bored with his military career and was looking for a career in politics. It may have been that the slaughter at Omdurman of virtually unarmed fanatical Islamic fighters, followers of the Mahdi, sickened Churchill as well as the desecration of the tomb of the Mahdi as ordered by Kitchener.[8] Nevertheless, Churchill began to look around to find a way to pursue political ambitions. On 2 December 1898 he embarked for India to complete his resignation from the 4th Hussars.

However, Churchill's journalistic efforts and embryonic writing career did not go unnoticed, and it was not always positive as, within military circles, negative voices rose. In January 1899 a piece was published in the *British Pelican* which pointed to the advantages that Churchill already enjoyed as he was linked to the Duke of Marlborough and a 'high future' was predicted for the young Churchill who was 24 at the time of the article appearing. The author agreed that he had liked to listen to Churchill's father, but Winston needed to make up his mind which career he wanted to pursue – was it to be the army, politics or literature.[9] As it turned out Churchill followed all three.

Churchill was criticised for his journalism while serving as an officer in the British Army, but he remained defiant regarding his paid writing. On 11 February 1899, in the columns of *Army and Navy Gazette*, he replied with feeling to an earlier letter featured in the magazine from a correspondent signed only as 'A General Officer' who criticised the activities of a journalist who was still a serving soldier. This could have only been directed at Churchill, who replied that the writer's argument should not be with him, Churchill, but with the War Office (WO).[10] An article printed earlier in *Modern Society* accused Churchill of merely 'playing at soldiers'.[11] Churchill defended his activities strongly as he was, certainly not in his own mind, 'playing at soldiers' whilst he without doubt needed the income derived from his quite capable pen to support the lifestyle he wished to pursue. Furthermore, he gave to late Victorian society an insight into what was happening on the various fronts of the colonial wars being fought in their names. What should be recognised is that the Victorian era British Army was a stuffy institution and did little to encourage advancement, such as learning local languages or volunteering for Staff College.[12]

The turn of the twentieth century saw more frantic activity in Churchill's life. Soldiering had not turned out to be as interesting as it might have been in his imagination or indeed the collective mind of late Victorian society but, as most professional soldiers will testify, military life is largely mundane, with duties rather than action. Churchill was, in reality, a war correspondent but really wanted to be a politician even though at the time back-bench members of Parliament were unsalaried. This meant that MPs often had to find a sponsor or have an independent source of income. Churchill certainly had family background and influence in spades and was beginning to make an impression as a writer. He did not mean to sit on the backbenches for long. He was certain of his greatness while indeed a great many things seemed to fall into his lap.

Once free of his military duties Churchill was free to pursue his life as he wanted to once more. During 1899 war was brewing in South Africa between the British and Boer settlers there. On 11 October 1899 war began with the British government sending troops to quickly pacify the Boer republics and regain the upper hand. The war lasted until 1902 and the Boers were not defeated by military means but only by brutalising the civilian population and basically starving the Boers into submission, a method which did indeed cause outrage in the UK. Churchill quickly made his way to South Africa to cover the war for the *Morning Post*. He was swift to get to South Africa as, by October 1899, he was already near the town of Ladysmith which was besieged by a Boer army. However, Churchill was captured by Boers and interned in a camp in Pretoria. In December he escaped and, with help, finally got to safety in Portuguese East Africa. This exploit not only caused the Boer government to place a £25 (£3,000 in 2020) bounty on Churchill's head but created column inches in the British press. In 1900 he briefly re-joined the British Army as a lieutenant in the South African Light Horse Regiment and joined the fight to relieve Ladysmith and capture Pretoria. He was amongst the first British troops into both places. Churchill was not one to have any truck for the anti-Boer prejudice which swept the UK; he wanted magnanimity and asked for the Boers to be treated with generosity and tolerance. In July, after resigning his commission, Churchill returned to the UK. The *Morning Post* had published his despatches from South Africa under the title *London to Ladysmith via Pretoria*. It sold well.

In October 1900 Churchill was returned as a Conservative MP for Oldham. Another book of his, *Ian Hamilton's March*, an account of his South African experiences, was published in the same month. However, writing was not enough financially for Churchill and so he undertook a lucrative lecture tour of North America. The lectures focused on his time in South Africa. In 1901 he did the same in Paris, Madrid and Gibraltar. In February 1901 he made his maiden speech which was widely reported in the press. However, Churchill could not agree with his own party over several matters and in 1904 he switched his allegiance to the Liberal party who were in opposition at the time. In 1908 Churchill gained his first ministerial post when he was appointed President of the Board of Trade. At the age of 33 Churchill was the youngest Cabinet member since 1866. As a newly appointed Cabinet member Churchill was legally obliged to seek re-election but lost his seat on 24 April 1908. The Liberal party provided him with the safe seat of Dundee which he won easily on 9 May 1908. During the same year, in September, he married Clementine Hozier, his beloved 'Clemmie'. In a meteoric rise Churchill was made Home Secretary in 1910. In October 1911 he was appointed First Lord of the Admiralty which took his career to the outbreak of the First World War in August 1914.

Now we must turn to Charles de Gaulle, the other subject of this work, and note his life. To be honest, de Gaulle, born in Lille, northern France on 22 November 1890 into a modest conservative middle-class family, was quite unremarkable in his early years when compared with Churchill. Of course, Churchill was sixteen years older than de Gaulle and well connected, with the 9th Duke of Marlborough as his cousin; his father had been Chancellor of the Exchequer. De Gaulle had none of those advantages but, nevertheless, was an incredible man. In 1908 de Gaulle entered the St Cyr Military Academy; in 1912 he graduated well in his class and was commissioned as a second lieutenant into the 33rd Infantry Regiment. When war broke out in Europe in 1914 France was invaded by Germany. In the early battles of 1914 Lieutenant de Gaulle, as he had become, fought well and with distinction and was twice wounded. In 1915 he was promoted to captain. However, de Gaulle was about to become a victim of the war.

On 2 March 1916, de Gaulle was captured by the Germans after suffering a bayonet wound in heavy fighting before losing consciousness as a result of a gas attack. At the time it was thought that he had been killed. His commanding officer, Colonel Boud'hors, put de Gaulle up for the prestigious French award for gallantry, the *Légion d'honneur*. Colonel Boud'hors wrote:

> Although [de Gaulle] was badly wounded by a bayonet thrust after a furious hand-to-hand engagement, he organised a knot of resistance in

which his men fought until all ammunition was gone, the rifles shattered, and the unarmed defenders fallen. Although [de Gaulle] had been wounded by a bayonet thrust he continued to be the heart of the defence until he fell senseless from the effects of poison-gas.[13]

The sense of a French Army officer's honour at that time is clearly demonstrated when de Gaulle's father, a veteran of the 1870 Franco-Prussian War, who had been wounded at the Siege of Paris, on hearing that his son was missing went to see Colonel Boud'hors to ask of his son's conduct. He was informed that Captain de Gaulle 'had done his duty to the end'.[14] De Gaulle senior was satisfied. However, Captain Charles de Gaulle was not at all happy with his lot as he was to spend the remainder of the First World War in enemy captivity. De Gaulle, who had sought death or glory, kicked against his confines, but he also made the most of his time. He learned German and, from German newspapers, learned about the progress of the war as, curiously, Allied communiqués were published uncensored by the German authorities. De Gaulle also studied and pondered the military situation as it unfolded, as well as lecturing his fellow inmates on just about any subject. He also found the time to try to escape – five times in all. Consequently the Germans sent him from prison camp to prison camp until finally, as a recognised prolific escaper, he was sent to the Colditz of the First World War, Fort Nine in Ingolstadt, Bavaria.[15] A fellow captive at Fort Nine was a certain Major Catroux who, in 1940, as Governor General of French Indo-China, was one of the first senior French figures to rally to de Gaulle.[16] De Gaulle also shared a cell with a Russian officer, Mikhail Tukatchevsky. Later Tukatchevsky was to achieve fame as a Red Army commander before being murdered during the Stalinist purge of Red Army commanders during the 1930s.

However, one thing which de Gaulle was spared was the mutinies of the French Army during 1917. Prior to his capture, de Gaulle had protested against the huge losses being suffered by the French Army, but the high casualty rates continued after de Gaulle's capture and peaked during the Nivelle offensive of spring 1917. By 1917 the French Army was exhausted. Conditions, including billeting, were terrible, food was bad and scarce, while medical care was somewhat neglected, leave home was rare and often cancelled arbitrarily. Furthermore, French troops were being influenced by German sponsored peace propaganda which, incredibly, was encouraged by Louis Malvy, the French Minister of the Interior, an extraordinary state of affairs in wartime. In 1918 Malvy was charged with treason and exiled for five years.

Nevertheless, as the morale of the French Army continued to plummet; the Russian Revolution of February 1917 seemed to offer a radical alternative to the collective experience of the army. Throughout France, both within the military and without, it was felt that the war could not be won. By the end of April 1917 mutinies began to break out amongst French troops; the first refusal of French troops to obey orders occurred in the Fourth French Army on 29 April 1917. News of the mutiny spread rapidly while two Russian brigades serving on the Western Front removed their officers and introduced 'councils' or, to the use the Russian word, 'Soviets' and refused to fight any further. The Russian example encouraged French troops to take more radical action and entire units threw down their arms and deserted while shouting 'death to officers'. There were further abuses of French officers while two regiments began to move towards Paris. By June 1917 the mutiny had spread to five army corps and affected fifty-four divisions. This rendered the French Army useless – French troops still manned the front line but would do nothing except on their own terms. Amazingly, the truth of the mutinies never leaked out and the only hint of the reality of the French Army in 1917 reached Allied senior commanders. The British War Cabinet and the prime minister, David Lloyd George, had no idea what was going on as their own commanders did not tell them.[17] Overall, such was the serious nature of the munities in the French Army that, decades later, the British historian Geoffrey Hoskins noted that they were considered to be more serious than those in Russia in February 1917, which had heralded the first revolution of that year in that country.[18]

It is interesting to note that the future Major General Sir Edward Spears, who was to be so closely involved with de Gaulle after 1940, including plucking him from France during the summer of 1940, was well aware of the mutinous state of the French Army in 1917. In May 1917, then a colonel, Spears was part of the British General Staff and was liaison officer between the French Ministry of War and the War Office in London. During that month Spears was summoned into the presence of Lloyd George to report on the condition of the French Army. Spears was aware that Lloyd George had been putting out peace feelers, notably in the direction of Austria and, therefore, was aware that if he was to give a blunt assessment of the condition of the French Army as it stood in May 1917 there was a distinct possibility that Lloyd George might well pull out of the war. Prior to his meeting with his own prime minister, Spears had learned, and was convinced, that General Philippe Pétain, whom he knew, could reverse the pathetic situation in which the French Army found itself. Therefore, Spears gave Lloyd George a précised version of events regarding the French Army and, to his chagrin, was made to swear on his honour as a gentleman and an officer that he considered that the French Army would recover itself. But he kept the prime minister blind to the gravity of the situation as he had witnessed it.[19] The French Army did indeed recover itself. Not only was Spears acquainted with Pétain after 1916, and later with de Gaulle, from 1915 he had been friends with Winston Churchill – a small world of the great and the good indeed.

The French commander, General Philippe Pétain, told the French Cabinet of the situation and confessed that there were only two reliable divisions between Paris and the enemy. If the Germans had known this they could have been in the French capital within a few days. Incredibly, Pétain managed to retrieve the situation and, by the end of 1918, the Allies, including the French, had defeated the Germans and their allies. De Gaulle, languishing in Fort Nine, had no idea of the situation of the French Army in 1917. Field Marshal Douglas Haig, the British commander, was kept, however, fully in the loop as Pétain kept him informed.[20] De Gaulle, by not experiencing the mutinies of 1917, appeared to be immune to the despair felt in France in 1940 when the Germans again invaded the country. In 1940 de Gaulle refused to recognise French fears which enabled him to lead France to victory in 1945. Ignorance was probably best in the case of de Gaulle. It is interesting to observe that the British biographer, Margaret Crosland, noted that the French writer and thinker Jean-Paul Sartre, in his 1945 novel *Le Sursis* (*The Reprieve*), has one of the characters declaim: 'The bourgeoisie don't want war ... . They're frightened of victory, because it will be the victory of the proletariat ... .'[21] And that was very much the point of the 1930s. It was a turbulent decade with the capitalist classes and the establishment fearing that a major war in Europe might well upset the apple cart and give ordinary people a voice and a chance. This was often the very reason why many European elites clung on to the shirt tails of fascism as it was a bulwark against communism or the fear of it. It was something that neither Churchill nor de Gaulle feared. They both rose above such craven attitudes and sought allies who had previously been deadly enemies and imprisoned former colleagues.

The armistice of 11 November 1918 bought de Gaulle liberty. He returned to Paris and from there to his family home. De Gaulle was astute enough to realise that the two and half years spent as a prisoner of war would hamper his military career and so sought a remedy to overcome this perceived handicap. The swiftest way to promotion for a soldier is to find a war and participate in it. De Gaulle swiftly found one in east-central Europe which was seething with discontent owing to the collapse of the east-central European empires between 1917 and 1918 which, after 1918, saw the re-emergence or emergence of new states. As a result, 1919, the first year of European peace since 1914, was far from peaceful east of France. One of the countries to re-emerge was Poland, wiped from the map in 1795 having been triparted for the third time by Russia, Austria and Prussia (later Germany). But, on 11 November 1918, aided and abetted by the US president, Woodrow Wilson, together with the German government, Poland declared independence. The French government, seeking new friends in the east, having lost its traditional ally, Russia, in 1917, began to court Poland and Romania.

It was French influence in Poland which found de Gaulle his war. The French were very interested in being involved in the Poles establishing their own army, which included General Józef Haller going to France to recruit for the newly founded Polish Army. This was a great chance for de Gaulle as Poland and Soviet Russia were at war by the summer of 1919. De Gaulle saw the war between Poland and Russia as a great chance to re-start his military career as action often meant promotion. Furthermore, as a staunch Catholic, the Polish struggle against the heathen and godless Russian Bolsheviks might have appealed to de Gaulle as well. Poland was considered to be one of the great and old Catholic states. Whatever, the motivation, May 1919 saw de Gaulle join the 4th Polish *Chasseurs* and a few months later he was en route for Warsaw, the Polish capital.

The war between Poland and Soviet Russia, despite initial Polish success, which had in May 1920 seen the Polish Army enter Kiev, had gone sour for the Poles. By August 1920 the Red Army commanded by Marshal Tukatchevsky, de Gaulle's former cellmate, was at the very gates of Warsaw. Both the British and French governments made feverish attempts to obtain an armistice with the Soviet government. In addition, both the UK and France sent military missions to Poland. The French military mission was headed by General Maxime Weygand who was to be instrumental in the unlikely Polish victory on 15 August 1920 at Warsaw. Weygand had not only noticed the stand that de Gaulle's division had taken against the Red Army but had also noticed de Gaulle's capabilities as an officer. Weygand wrote of de Gaulle as 'a remarkably intrepid officer with exceptional intellectual and morale'. De Gaulle's Polish gamble had paid off. He had swiftly made up for the years of captivity and returned to France with his fourth Mention in Despatches and with his career intact. Once more his career was on the move.[22]

De Gaulle returned to Paris where he married Yvonne Vendroux on 6 April 1921. In October 1921 de Gaulle was appointed lecturer in military history at St Cyr.[23] It was during this period that de Gaulle, having time to reflect, began to consider the future of warfare as well as the future of the French Army, and its shortcomings. He did this against a background of considering that war in Europe was a real fear. At the end of 1929 de Gaulle was posted to Lebanon for two years. Lebanon was territory which had been part of the former Turkish, or Ottoman, empire which had been defeated by the Allies in 1918. France had been granted the territory, as well as Syria, to govern as part of the terms of the peace treaty with Turkey which concluded fighting in the Middle East after 1918. The two years that de Gaulle spent in the Middle East matured him and made him more amenable towards views held by others as opposed to his previous attitude when he was quite intolerant towards others, especially his military superiors.[24]

In 1933, against a vile background of worldwide economic and social meltdown, already a concern for de Gaulle, Adolf Hitler came to power in Germany. Quickly, de Gaulle saw through Hitler's pretensions towards peace and regarded him as the threat that he really was. De Gaulle considered Hitler and Nazi Germany as not only a peril to France but also to the world as a whole. This was quite clear by a reading of Hitler's work *Mein Kampf* in which Hitler bluntly stated how he wanted to obtain his plans for the world. His views were and remain hideous. However, the British historian, Julius Jackson, puts forward the thesis that de Gaulle, never a fascist, was during the 1930s not overly worried about fascism but was 'first and foremost an adversary of Germany'.[25] This is how de Gaulle should be viewed, even if during wartime some considered that he wanted to establish a dictatorship in France; he never did nor did he want to, and history proved that his democratic credentials remained intact, but he always put France first. This can be seen throughout his life, often in his speeches and writing, an example being the publication of his thesis for a future French army, *L'Armée de Métier* in 1934.[26] The work was not about de Gaulle but about his concern for France and its army.

During this period, in vain, de Gaulle tried to persuade senior French politicians to be more assertive, if not aggressive, towards Germany. De Gaulle also railed against the idea that the Maginot Line would defend France against German aggression. French planners considered that all the French Army had to do was sit in this line of concrete forts and bunkers which defined the frontier between France and Germany and fight off any attack from Germany.[27] The Maginot Line, however, finished at the Belgian frontier and, despite the lessons of 1914, it seemed that few in senior French military and political circles considered that an invading German Army might just cut through Belgium to get to France as had been the case in 1914. It was enough to make one despair.

De Gaulle, drawing on his experience of the Polish-Soviet War, did not agree with the concept of static warfare; the war in Poland had been one of movement, attack and counterattack, using large numbers of horsed cavalry which in a more modern army could be replaced with armoured fighting vehicles, especially tanks. Whilst it is true that tanks were in their infancy, it was clear to any intelligent commander that they should be deployed in large numbers. In a report to the French General Staff, de Gaulle wrote 'tanks should be brought into the field in a body, not separately'.[28] This thought was not exactly original as there were several other officers from different armies who had their own thoughts on the use of massed armoured formations and mobility, but it certainly went against the grain of orthodox French military thought. For the remainder of the 1930s de Gaulle continued to study most of the problems of the French High Command and French military doctrine; it would be de Gaulle who would have to solve the moribund attitude in the future. During this period of thought he made a lot of enemies at High Command, but also a lot of friends.[29] De Gaulle's lobbying of French politicians for the introduction of armoured divisions earned him the nickname of 'Colonel Motors'.[30]

While de Gaulle was studying the problems of the French Army, the army itself was removing itself from society and criticism. This is best described by George A. Kelly in a monograph published in 1961. Kelly wrote that, at the time of de Gaulle study of French military *ipse dixit* or sheer stubbornness, the French military remained 'cut off from the influences of rapidly changing political and social factors. The Army High Command transformed itself into an impregnable citadel and clung to doctrines that had been serviceable in bygone times.' As the French military was banned from 'healthy communication' with other national elements, military commanders dedicated themselves to military science but in isolation from the rest of society and so most of their ideas were, apart from a few like de Gaulle, outmoded as they set them out on paper.[31]

Overall, the French military and French society on the whole were unprepared for war and invasion when, in May 1940, western Europe was invaded by German armed forces and swiftly defeated. De Gaulle's calls for armoured divisions angered most cavalry officers who still saw horsed cavalry as essential and hated the idea of being replaced by tanks, even if Colonel du Vigier, Commandant of Saumur's Cavalry School, agreed with de Gaulle. Money was also another problem as the French equipped themselves with a modern large navy under Admiral Darlan and naval minister Georges Leygues. This was considered to be an 'imperial necessity'. It was considered that land wars would be static as in the First World War – hence the building of the Maginot Line.[32] The name Darlan will be quite visible throughout this narrative since he, as we will see, cut a controversial figure later.

However, it should be realised that war had long been coming, something that both Churchill and de Gaulle had recognised almost as soon as Hitler and the Nazis took power in Germany at the beginning of 1933. By 1938, after the so-called Munich crisis which averted war with Germany that year, French and British interests in east-central Europe began to be more earnest when, after completing his annexation of the Czech lands and reducing Slovakia to a German vassal state, Hitler turned his ire onto Poland. He began his campaign against Poland during March 1939 with the use of verbal attacks followed by obstruction and lawlessness by local Nazis from within German communities in Poland and in Danzig (today Gdańsk), the so-called Free City on the Baltic coast. It was from then on, that the French and British governments took an interest. This led to ill-defined guarantees from the French and British governments to Poland.

The basic guarantee was that, in the event of a German attack on Poland, both powers would defend Poland. Just how this was to be achieved was ignored since the UK was not a land power; its strength was maritime with a large navy while its army was small to be used for home defence and for the defence of India, the most important British overseas possession. The French may have had a large army, which was believed to be very strong, but France lacked a border with Poland. This meant that any French military force going to Poland would have to be transported by sea, or invade and cross the entirety of Germany, or find a southern route into Poland. Basically, the Anglo-Franco guarantees to Poland may have been morally well intended but, practically, were pie in the sky. There was to be further Polish disappointment as when, on 17 September 1939, following up the German invasion of Poland on 1 September 1939, Germany's ally, the Soviet Union, invaded and annexed eastern Poland. It was learned that the Anglo-Franco treaty did not extend to dealing with Soviet aggression against Poland. Furthermore, in the small print it was observed that the British government did not guarantee Polish frontiers but only Polish independence. It was game over for the Second Polish Republic.

After the fall of Poland in October 1939, the west settled down to see what might happen next. And so, during the cold winter of 1939–1940, little, if anything, happened on the western fronts. True, the Soviet Union invaded Finland in November 1939 and wished that it had not as it took until March 1940 before Finland sued for peace and thousands of Soviet troops had been killed or wounded. But little on land happened in the west as the British, French and Germans faced one another until 9 April 1940 when Germany invaded Denmark and Norway. The war in the west had begun and it was not good for the British or French.

By 19 May 1940, the situation for the French Army and the British Expeditionary Force (BEF) which had been sent to defend Europe was desperate. The German Army, supported by the Luftwaffe, was overrunning Europe at will as the Netherlands, Belgium and Luxemburg had been consumed by Germany and France was about to be. The worse aspect of the situation was the perception of the inability of the French Army to do anything to stem the German advance. Sir Alexander Cadogan, permanent undersecretary at the Foreign Office (FO) recorded in his diary, 'News very bad – French won't fight.'[33]

Two days later Cadogan wrote of the French Army, 'There are masses of troops there, trained and with good material, but the command paralysed. If Weygand (French Commander) can get a grip, we may have something.'[34] It should be noted that during June 1940 Weygand did not believe that France could fight on and considered that the UK would be forced to negotiate with Germany within a week. He derided de Gaulle's notion of France fighting on using its empire and considered it to be a childish notion.[35] As Julian Jackson notes, Weygand was an old reactionary who blamed politicians for getting France into a war that could not be won. After a final battle Weygand wanted the politicians to acknowledge responsibility for a French defeat.[36] Quite simply, many high French officials hadn't any faith in a French victory and seemed mesmerised by the German onslaught. And there lay de Gaulle's problem in 1940: the defeatism at French elite level, and he was not the only man to recognise this fault.

The Polish leader in exile, General Władysław Sikorski, also witnessed how the French High Command seemed to be paralysed. He was shocked to learn that the French High Command had arranged for Polish armed forces in France to surrender to the Germans with the French Army. Sikorski, previously a Francophile, refused to surrender his exiled troops and, in a bitter row with French commanders, decried the 'paralysed defeatism at the top of France's military and political commands'.[37] It should be seen that Sikorski and de Gaulle had a lot in common, but only de Gaulle lived to liberate his own country.

General Edmund Ironside, Chief of the Imperial General Staff (CIGS), minuted that indecision reigned in the French High Command in the North (of France) until the arrival of General Weygand and that basically there was nothing wrong with French troops.[38] General Alan Brooke wrote in his diary that he had seen Weygand who told him that the French Army had ceased to offer organised resistance and was disconnected groups.[39] Morale was a problem for the French Army during the 1940 campaign. There was a sense that the German Army was invincible, and that France would fall, no matter what. The fear of another senseless bloody war, as had been the case between 1914 and 1918 in which France and its people had suffered horribly, had been another factor. Many French people did not want to undergo such an ordeal once more, but few suspected what they were about to have to endure until 1944 as a result of the coming German occupation.

It had been noted by the British War Cabinet as early as October 1939 that the French government and people might show signs of weakness if Germany launched a peace offensive against France alone with the aim of detaching her from the UK.[40] This proved to be the case in 1940. It was from this poisoned atmosphere that General de Gaulle arrived in the UK. A French soldier, possibly on the run from his own countrymen, he had nothing to offer the British except the will not to accept defeat and for France to rise once more with its honour intact ready to fight Germany. De Gaulle's escape from France was extremely dramatic as he was saved by General Edward Spears who pulled him into an aircraft bound for the UK and away from his 'certain arrest and probable execution at the hands of the surrender party.'[41] Spears was to be closely involved with de Gaulle, especially in the Middle East, throughout the war. Their relationship was rarely harmonious, but that was the nature of de Gaulle and probably that of all great men – difficult and hard to manage, but in 1940 one could not be choosy about one's allies as the British began to regroup and face the possibility of a German invasion.

The year 1940 was fateful for Europe. It may have been the year of defeats for democracy and decency as Germany was able to overrun Europe, but it should also be seen as a year of recovery. Two examples were the destruction by the Royal Navy of much of the German surface fleet and the defeat of the Luftwaffe during the Battle of Britain in the summer of 1940. These setbacks ensured that Germany was unable to invade and annex the UK. Furthermore, both events should be linked to Winston Churchill.

We left the Churchill story on the outbreak of war in 1914. In the years following, like de Gaulle, Churchill was extremely busy and often quite frustrated with the inability of others to see his point of view and, in the case of the rise of Hitler and the Nazi party, could not see why others failed to see the obvious danger that Germany was posing under Nazi rule. De Gaulle, as we have seen, had a similar problem with his countrymen. Churchill's career since 1914 had been chequered. He had been appointed First Lord of the Admiralty during October 1911, a post he held until 25 November 1915 when he resigned because of the failed Gallipoli campaign for which he shouldered some of the blame since he had backed the entire venture.

In January 1916, Churchill was made lieutenant colonel and commanding officer of 6th Battalion Royal Scots Fusiliers with whom he decided to spend a period of penance or, more likely, reflect on what he would do next. After a period of training, the battalion was sent to a section of the Belgian Front near Ploegsteert where, for the next three months, it was shelled regularly by German artillery, but no German offensive came during the period in which Churchill and his battalion served in the trenches together. During May 1916, following restructuring Churchill lost his command. He did not request a new appointment but asked and received permission to leave active service and return to politics.

Once back in the House of Commons, Churchill spoke on questions to do with the war but was extremely frustrated by his position as a backbencher rather than as a member of the government from where he might be able to influence things. It should be mentioned that during Churchill's period of exile on the backbenches the Dardanelles Committee absolved him of any personal blame for the failure of the expedition. Churchill's luck as ever held as, in October 1916, Prime Minister Herbert Asquith resigned and Asquith's rival, David Lloyd George, succeeded him. During May 1917 Lloyd George sent Churchill to inspect the French war effort; in July 1917 he was appointed Minister of Munitions, a post he held until 1919.

In 1919 Churchill was appointed Secretary of State for War and Air. This post he held until 1921 but he was very busy. During the period Churchill promoted British intervention in Russia as part of a larger international offensive to try to foil the Bolshevik takeover. As we have seen, the French, including de Gaulle, played their part in this operation. Between 1921 and 1922 Churchill served as Secretary of State for the Colonies.

In the November 1922 general election Churchill lost his Dundee parliamentary seat and was out of Parliament for two years. However, on 29 October 1924, having mended fences with the Conservative party, Churchill won the Epping seat and returned to Parliament. Curiously, the new prime minister, Stanley Baldwin, made Churchill, Chancellor of the Exchequer – a position which he was no way qualified to undertake but he held the post until 1929. The 1929 general election saw Churchill retain his seat, but his party lost the election to the Labour party. In October 1931, the Conservatives won a landslide victory but Churchill, having resigned his position in the shadow cabinet, was not offered a ministerial post. This left him with no collective Cabinet responsibility which gave him the freedom to snipe at his own government and party.

Between 1933 and 1936 Churchill, using his newfound freedom, was able to warn about the rise of the Nazis and the fact that Germany was re-arming illegally. This did not sit well with many British politicians who frequently dismissed him as a warmonger. Churchill, however, slipped up through his support of King Edward VIII during the 'abdication crisis' of late 1936. Churchill urged the king to hold fast and marry the American divorcee, Wallis Simpson. At the time, Churchill was unaware that it was possible that Hitler might well have intended to use the British king as a puppet if Germany was able to conquer the UK. Nevertheless, between 1937 and 1939, he continued in his anti-appeasement position and badgered the government headed by Neville Chamberlain. At every turn Churchill denounced the British position of trying to accommodate Hitler and his ambitions in central Europe. Eventually, by spring 1939, even Chamberlain had to concede that Hitler wanted war in Europe and that the British government could no longer deal with Hitler who broke all agreements at will.

War came to Europe in September 1939. Churchill was returned to the government as First Lord of the Admiralty, the very post he had held when the UK had declared war on Germany in 1914. Many were glad to see the return of Churchill to high office. He certainly was. Churchill remained in the post until May 1940 when the UK faced the prospect of invasion by Germany – cometh the hour, cometh the man. Indeed! Churchill was about to lead his country and was also about to accept some very interesting characters from overseas as allies. One of those was the exiled Polish leader, General Sikorski, who, like many Polish officers, was a political soldier and all too frequently put politics above the defence of their own country while another was de Gaulle who in 1940 probably deemed politics as vulgar and in bad taste. But he was about to learn some sharp lessons.

The concept that de Gaulle was a political soldier after 1940 is interesting as the French Army since 1890 had been an apolitical organisation.[42] This meant that de Gaulle, often perceived as an arch-conservative, had to change his way of thinking and accept that, to ensure the survival of France, he needed to reject much of what he believed and embrace politics. Indeed, like those French people who collaborated with the occupying Germans (the French of the unoccupied zone, Vichy France, unoccupied so-long as the line was toed), de Gaulle rejected the French Republic and, for the period 1940–1941, broadcasts of his Free French movement were introduced by the slogan 'honour and *patrie*' and not the better known call of the 1789 revolution 'Liberty, Equality and Fraternity'.[43] From his family de Gaulle took a heritage of respect and feeling for the state as well as a sense of justice and liberty.[44] The French historian René Rémond observed that Pétain's regime was counter-revolutionary and opposed the principles of 1789, which had allowed for the establishment of the modern French state.[45]

However, it could be argued that the French Army had already been involved in political struggle as, during the 1930s, it had seen deep cuts in defence at a time of European re-armament, especially in Germany.[46] Alexander asserts that the French Army had been 'bedevilled' by politics as much as 'military misfortune' since the 1890s; beginning with the infamous Dreyfus Affair, misfortune continued after the Second World War until 1954 with the defeat of the French Army in Indo-China (Vietnam) at Dien Bien-Phu.[47]

De Gaulle, however, was not as conservative as people might have thought: during the 1930s he wrote two military treatises on the question of how the French could adopt a modern professional army. In 1932 he wrote *Le Fil de l'épée* (*The Edge of the Sword*) followed in 1934 with *Vers l'armée de Métier* (*Towards a Professional Army*). De Gaulle argued that successive reductions in the duration of conscript service and excessive concentration in fixed frontier fortifications (the Maginot Line, for example) in the late 1920s and early 1930s, coupled with budget cuts between 1932 and 1934, had reduced the French Army's combat readiness to the extent that it could not defend France in wartime. France's military capacity was further compromised during August 1936 when Germany extended its period of conscription to two years of compulsory service.[48]

A further problem which was to have unintended consequences for French defence spending and later wartime French politics was that of the French Navy. At a time of fiscal restraint, the French Navy was modernised in the pursuit of 'imperial necessity'. This was during the watch of Admiral Darlan and naval minister Georges Leygues.[49] Darlan will become a vital part this narrative and prove to be a controversial figure. Leygues was to die in the year that Hitler came to power in Germany, 1933, and so was spared the humiliation of France in 1940 and the collaboration of Darlan. The money spent on the modernisation of the French Navy was at the expense of its army and air force and, ultimately, led to the undoing of France in May 1940. The newly modernised French Navy was also to figure in the tensions between the British and French as the British feared that the Germans might seize the French vessels and use them against the Allies. As early as July 1940, the Royal Navy put the French fleet moored in Algeria beyond the use of anybody by attacking it at anchor, killing nearly 1,300 French sailors and destroying a number of vessels.

The problem for the French senior army command was that during the 1930s only General Maurice Gamelin, who was trying to devise French defensive planning against a background of cutbacks, understood the military danger that Germany posed. It would seem that only de Gaulle had any sympathy for Gamelin's fears.[50] Even so, in *Vers l'Armée de Métier*, de Gaulle failed to recognise the implication of a joint armoured and aerial offensive or *blitzkrieg*. De Gaulle only called for the use of armour in large numbers, which was revolutionary at the time. Once de Gaulle had read and understood reports of the German Army's success in Poland during September 1939, he recognised the significance of *blitzkrieg*.

In January 1940, the then Colonel de Gaulle submitted a memorandum to his military and political superiors, all eighty of them, recognising the capabilities of armour supported by massed aviation. De Gaulle predicted that the French Army would be defeated unless it concentrated its armoured forces. He was ignored. Later, after manoeuvres, de Gaulle again predicted the defeat of France, declaring, 'Gentlemen, this war is lost. We must therefore prepare another one and win it – by using mechanised power'. British politicians observing those war games also ignored de Gaulle.[51]

Within six months France was defeated, exactly as de Gaulle had predicted. But, as de Gaulle had suggested, all the clues were there and very obviously so. The London based financial weekly *The Economist* reported on 20 January 1940 that German troops were massing on the Dutch and Belgian borders and were an obvious threat: they had been there as early as the end of November 1939.[52] It is not clear why Allied strategists were so unwilling to do anything but perhaps it was just wishful thinking that the neutrality of states in the west would be respected by Hitler, and that the German Army would be happy to establish some form of western front, as had been the case between 1914 and 1918, and wait until somebody gave in.

This didn't happen, as on 18 May 1940 *The Economist* was reporting on 'Total War', beginning with the attack on the west.[53] The Poles might have wanted to beg to differ but had already been ignored by the Allies and, so during May and June 1940, western Europe was desperately trying to save itself as the Germans continued to march towards Paris. The Germans had already invaded and occupied Denmark during April 1940. Invading Norway at the same time, they had been forced to fight there owing to an allied intervention as well as more than expected stubborn defence of their country by the Norwegian Army.

By June 1940 Norway was evacuated by the Allies, even though they had succeeded in their mission to deny the ice-free port of Narvik to the Germans; it became necessary for Norway to be abandoned as it seemed that the UK was on the cusp of being invaded by Germany. The reason for this fear was that the war in the west had been going terribly wrong. The Netherlands and Belgium had been subdued swiftly by German armed forces while France and the French had already seemed to have doomed themselves to defeat and occupation. The BEF headed back to the Channel ports in anticipation of evacuation to the UK. Meanwhile as many men and as much equipment was being taken from Norway ready to defend the British Isles.

Events in France happened swiftly. The Germans invaded on 10 May 1940 and moved rapidly. Between 26 May 1940 and 4 June 1940, around 338,000 Allied troops were evacuated from the beaches at Dunkirk in northern France, and elsewhere and taken to the UK, including my own grandfather, Frank McGilvray, Royal Artillery. The French nation was in shock at the speed of the German advance and perhaps in many ways still traumatised by the horrors of the 1914–1918 war. The veteran American foreign policy adviser, Henry Kissinger, notes in his latest work that, between 1914 and 1918, France suffered two million dead, which translates as 4 per cent of its population, in addition to the devastation of its northern regions.[54] It was no wonder that the French were reluctant to fight another war against Germany, let alone host it once more.

At the beginning of June 1940, *The Economist* claimed that power in France was largely in the hands of three men. The first was Prime Minister Paul Reynaud who was also the French Minister of Defence. Reynaud was no defeatist and refused to agree to any armistice with the Germans. He resigned on 16 June 1940. The French Commander-in-Chief (C-in-C), General Maxime Weygand, however, was quite the defeatist and often suspected of treachery, but cleared in court. His name will occur again in this narrative and it's not altogether flattering. The other individual was the Minister of the Interior, Georges Mandel, who also refused to have any truck with an armistice with the Germans. Many French people considered that it was owing to his Jewish origins that he was unwilling to co-operate in this matter. After 1942 Mandel was detained in two concentration camps and was eventually murdered by members of *la Milice*, a French para-military organisation which collaborated with the occupying Germans in keeping what was seen as order in France. Quite simply, traitors. It seemed that the two civilian politicians had more backbone than their military counterpart and, as the war continued, it would seem that they were the braver and more honourable of the trio.[55]

The agony was piled onto France as, on 10 June, Italy decided to snatch, jackal-like, the French Riviera. As we have seen, Reynaud resigned his offices on 16 June. On that day Marshal Philippe Pétain formed a new French ministry which included General Weygand and another unsavoury character, Admiral François Darlan. This new French ministry allowed for the division of France with northern France and its entire Atlantic coast being occupied by Germany while the remainder was left unoccupied until the end of 1942 with its capital being at the spa town of Vichy, hence Vichy France or the Vichy regime. This regime worked closely with the Germans, especially Pétain who was condemned to death after the war by a French court but reprieved. He spent his dotage in a prison on a lone isle, L'ile-d'Yeu, off the French coast. It was a sad but fitting end for a man who had promised so much earlier. Pétain remains a controversial figure in France. His motivations for collaboration with the Germans are not totally clear. He was an old man in 1940, being 84 by then. He died in 1951, aged 95. He is both hero as he saved France at Verdun in 1915 but is also seen as betraying the same country twenty-five years later. In his defence, perhaps he had not been clear about what the Nazis would really do in France, especially against the Jews but in 1940 except for those in east-central Europe who really understood what the Nazis were capable of doing? De Gaulle declared of Pétain as once being 'a great man who died in 1925'.[56] The contempt is obvious.

By 22 June 1940 Pétain had signed an armistice with the Germans with another being signed with the Italian government two days later. It is often overlooked that there were actually three partitions of France between 1940 and 1945. The first as discussed above; the Italians also took their share. That such an ancient and honourable European state as France should fall so quickly had been unthinkable, even at the beginning of 1940, but now we examine how the French were able to retrieve their honour and status as a great nation once more as we follow the narrative of this work. The short-sightedness of a majority of French and British politicians and planners was the very reason de Gaulle fetched up in the UK in the summer of 1940 and was forced into politics, owing to the failings of those who should have been his political masters, had they done their jobs properly. Now the two mavericks, Churchill and de Gaulle, were to work together and win the war.

Chapter 2

De Gaulle Arrives in the UK

In the summer of 1940 General Charles de Gaulle was a relatively unknown French general. This can be detected by the tone of a message from Churchill to the American president, Franklin D. Roosevelt. Churchill was describing the attitude of the French government just before France was overwhelmed by German armed forces. Churchill wrote that the French prime minister, Paul Reynaud, was set to continue to fight the Germans and that 'he has a young general de Gaulle who believes that much can be done'.[1]

In his commentary on Sir Alexander Cadogan's diaries David Dilks noted that in 1940 de Gaulle was something of a mystery – nothing was known of him at the FO. Indeed Dilks commented that the ever waspish Cadogan, following his first meeting with de Gaulle, reported to his colleagues, 'I can't tell you anything about de Gaulle expect that he's got a head like a pineapple and hips like a woman.'[2] Cadogan, who detested de Gaulle, wrote in his diary that he had had a long talk with General Catroux, an ally yet a rival of de Gaulle, and was quite impressed with him.[3] Churchill, however, after the war, with many, often bitter arguments with de Gaulle behind him, magnanimously wrote of de Gaulle that, when he escaped from France, 'de Gaulle carried with him, in this small aeroplane, the honour of France'.[4]

But in 1940 things were slightly different. Historian Brian Crozier notes that when de Gaulle left France in 1940, he had crossed his personal Rubicon and knew that he could not return, except in victory or defeat.[5] When de Gaulle arrived in the UK, Churchill bitterly complained to Spears, who had been responsible for de Gaulle's escape, that nobody knew anything of de Gaulle and that he must be put 'on the map'. Spears suggested that a public relations exercise might be the answer. De Gaulle initially resisted this move and complained to his entourage that 'they want to promote me like a brand of soap'. He generally fretted about any negative reaction against him in France. Eventually his objections were overcome, but de Gaulle always maintained a reserve towards the press, especially regarding his family, if least because of his handicapped daughter, Anne.[6]

It is unlikely that de Gaulle really knew or even bothered about the efforts that were made on his behalf in getting recognised as the official leader of the

Free French; he received little support from the British government. However, Spears once said of the situation regarding the recognition of de Gaulle:

> day in, day out, I have fought through the trammels of Departments and fiercely torn down the network of prejudice, hesitation and procrastination .... I know that I have impressed my personality on Whitehall by pushing and shoving.

A friend told Spears that he had made sixty enemies a day.

The Royal Navy was the least co-operative as they were strongly supportive of the French admirals because, as Spears complained, 'they were admirals'. The First Sea Lord, Sir Dudley Pound, would believe no evil of Admiral Darlan, the French naval chief, despite him having joined the Vichy government which openly collaborated with Germany.[7]

What Churchill's real feelings towards de Gaulle in June 1940 really were is not clear, but he did seem to understand that de Gaulle was a Frenchman with whom he work with. Nevertheless, this did not prevent Field Marshal Alanbrooke writing after the war of de Gaulle that:

> Whatever good qualities he may have had were marred by his overbearing manner, his megalomania and his lack of co-operative spirit .... In all discussions he assumed that the problem of the liberation was mine, whilst he was concentrating on how he would govern it, as its Dictator, as soon as it was liberated! Added to these disadvantages, his Headquarters were so lacking any sense of security that it became quite impossible to discuss any future plans with them.[8]

Therefore, to underline de Gaulle's position when he arrived in the UK in 1940, he was an unknown French general arriving in a country threatened with invasion at any moment by Germany whose armed forces had just overrun most of Europe, including France. The Germans were on the verge of partitioning France; the northern part was to be occupied by the Germans while an unoccupied zone, south of Paris, was to be governed by a French puppet government known as the Vichy government and led by the veteran soldier, Marshal Philippe Pétain and basically fascist in nature. If de Gaulle was to return to France, he was subject to arrest while a further humiliation was heaped onto France as Italy, after checking which way the wind was blowing, entered the war on Germany's side and seized parts of southern France.

However, what was quite clear about de Gaulle as far as Churchill, at least, was concerned was that he was a different French narrative. De Gaulle was not a defeatist, and he was no fool. De Gaulle understood modern warfare, especially armoured warfare, and he knew how to wage war on the European mainland, which was something that few European senior commanders did, save those in the German Army. Few British or French commanders had any idea of how to wage war against the Germans. The only force to have managed to bring the Germans to anything like a halt was the Norwegian Army in the very north of Norway. The Norwegians had used their native terrain and ghastly winter weather against the Germans during the spring of 1940 when Germany invaded Norway and was caught out by conditions in the Norwegian Arctic. The UK, France and the Free Poles had sent troops to aid the Norwegians but the Allied input during the Norwegian campaign was negligible. The Allies were too few in number, as was the Norwegian Army while the British, under threat of invasion, evacuated Norway, bringing home to the UK troops, ships, aircraft and as much arms as possible ready to defend their homeland. The use of an alien landscape such as that experienced during a Scandinavian winter was also one that almost defeated the Red Army in Finland during the Winter War of 1939–1940. Once more it was lack of numbers which ensured victory to the aggressors as Finland, possessing only a small population, despite causing huge casualties to the Red Army by March 1940 was forced to capitulate to the Soviet Union which, having the larger population by a long way, was able to fill the gaps caused by the Finns and maintain its campaign against Finland until victory. However, it was clear to those who cared to look that, as early as 1940, Germany and her allies, namely the Soviet Union could be defeated with the right tactics, the correct equipment and the necessary numbers. Churchill and de Gaulle were two men who cared to look and understand the lessons of spring 1940. However, the most important necessity was leadership – both Churchill and de Gaulle had this in spades. This meant that, by the summer of 1940, the German goose was already cooked. Hitler was not going to win the war, once faced with resolute opposition from two determined men with vast empires behind them.

After de Gaulle's escape the British War Cabinet debated whether he should make a speech on the BBC urging French soldiers to rally to him and to declare that France was not defeated. There was no objection to this proposal, but it was observed that de Gaulle was *persona non grata* in France which made such a move undesirable regarding the Anglo-French alliance.[9] John Terraine notes the differences between the British and French mentalities regarding de Gaulle in 1940. De Gaulle's moves in 1940 were considered by the French authorities as revolutionary as here was an unknown 'two-star' general on foreign soil defying the constitutional authority of France by proclaiming that

France may have lost a battle but yet might win the war and to this end called on the French people to rally to him personally, '*Moi, Général de Gaulle*'.

This act was one which the British did not grasp as revolutionary as in the eyes of some Frenchmen. To the British it seemed only right and natural that patriotic Frenchmen should keep their country alongside a country which, led by Churchill, never seriously considered surrender and persisted in fighting on. To many French though, especially the French Army, de Gaulle's actions were seen differently whilst, strictly speaking, it was mutiny.[10] Part of de Gaulle's revolutionary zeal is illustrated when he arrived in the UK and was greeted by Charles Corbin, the French Ambassador to the UK, and Jean Monnet, a distinguished French businessman, who informed de Gaulle before he met with Churchill of a plan they had been working on with the FO to unite France and the UK into a single country – a 'Declaration of Union'. The plan called for a single constitution, one government, common citizenship and an absolute commitment to their respective destinies. Churchill was aware of the plan but had not discussed it with the British Cabinet. Corbin and Monnet pressed de Gaulle to raise the question with Churchill.

De Gaulle was enthusiastic about the plan and recognised that, in the short term, it would aid Reynaud in trying to continue the war, but it was an ambitious scheme and might need time to bed down. De Gaulle raised the question in his meeting with Churchill who confirmed that Lord Halifax had already told him of the proposed Anglo-French union; Churchill considered it to be 'an enormous mouthful'. De Gaulle agreed but pointed to the possibilities of the plan of keeping France in the war. Churchill understood and said that he would present it to his Cabinet that very afternoon. De Gaulle accompanied Churchill to 10 Downing Street where he waited in an office adjoining the Cabinet Room for the result of the British War Cabinet's debate.

During this period de Gaulle telephoned Reynaud to tell him what was happening. The French prime minister considered that it was the only thing possible for the future, but action had to be swift. After several clarifications by de Gaulle, two hours later Churchill, very pleased, was able to tell de Gaulle that the Cabinet had agreed to the plan. Immediately, de Gaulle called Reynaud. Churchill took the telephone, confirmed de Gaulle's news and told Reynaud that the French must hold out and that he would see the French leadership the next day in France. Reynaud, of course, was overjoyed at the British acceptance of the plan and said that he would present it to the French cabinet which was due to meet almost immediately.

This ambitious plan was promptly derailed at the French cabinet when it met late on 16 June 1940. Reynaud presented the proposal for an Anglo-French union, but the French rebuffed it. Pétain considered the idea to be 'a marriage with a corpse' while another voice proclaimed that France would be better off as a 'Nazi province' as 'at least we know what that means'. Clearly, he did not. The idea of supporting the proposed Anglo-French union within the French cabinet only had one taker, Georges Mandel, the French Minister of the Interior. The French cabinet, instead of supporting Reynaud, opted for an alternative plan suggested by Camille Chautemps, a former prime minister. Chautemps suggested that Hitler should be asked for surrender terms and that they should be considered. It was then that Reynaud halted the meeting and submitted his resignation to President Albert Lebrun.

Reynaud's government was finished. De Gaulle was on his way back to France in an aeroplane provided by Churchill and learned of Reynaud's defeat when he landed. Worse news was to follow as President Lebrun had appointed Pétain as prime minister. This was a blow to de Gaulle as he was aware that he was no longer in office and the appointment of Pétain meant that France was about to surrender. De Gaulle sought out Reynaud immediately. Like de Gaulle, Reynaud was fully aware of the consequences of Pétain taking power – surrender. Reynaud told de Gaulle that, although he was no longer in office, he wished to remain in France. De Gaulle replied that he intended to return to the UK the next morning to continue the war. Reynaud supported de Gaulle in this venture and gave him 100,000 French francs from secret funds to which he still had access. De Gaulle requested diplomatic passports for his wife and children so that they could join him in the UK. Jean Laurent, who was on Reynaud's staff, gave de Gaulle the keys to an apartment which he had in London and told him he could stay there as long as he wished. Just after 09.00 hours the next morning de Gaulle returned to the UK in the same plane which had borne him to France the previous evening. He had no real idea of what the future might hold for him, but he did not believe that the war was over.[11] On 18 June 1940 he was to become an alternative France – *l'homme du 18e juin*, 'the man of 18 June', after making his famous broadcast via the BBC to France and its people on that day, late in the evening, at 22.00 hours.[12] De Gaulle was the rallying point for all Free French, and he meant it to be so. As did Churchill!

They were uncertain just how this might be done and how their respective countries might stave off the Germans, but they both knew it had to be done in order to prevent a second dark age crossing Europe. De Gaulle in his *Appel* to the French on 18 June 1940 stated clearly, 'Whatever happens, the flame of French resistance must not and shall not go out.'[13] It was what was needed in France as the first phase of the war drew to an end; de Gaulle's words were inspiring and meant to many that there was a way forward.[14] However, it was not clear what lay ahead and how freedom might be eventually realised.

Within a week, events in France reached their regrettable end as, on 22 June, armistice conditions were demanded by the German government of the French government. The Germans got their way. The armistice was the subject of a meeting of the British War Cabinet on the same day. There was a further meeting at 21.30 hours that evening in which the German demands were further discussed, as well as the fact that de Gaulle was to broadcast to France at 22.00 hours the same evening.[15] De Gaulle, in his broadcast, like Churchill who could only offer the British people blood, sweat and tears, had little to offer his countrymen. He told them, 'I have neither funds nor troops. I don't know where my family is. We are starting from scratch ... .'[16]

Events moved even faster the next day, Sunday, when the War Cabinet met again. This meeting on a Sunday underlined the gravity of the situation. On the table was a discussion of the departure from France of the British Ambassador to that country, Sir Ronald Campbell, and the formation of a 'Council of Liberation' (*Comité National Français*) for which de Gaulle asked for British recognition. The War Cabinet agreed in principle to this request.[17] The next day saw three more meetings of the War Cabinet as the disaster in France began to reach its bitter climax.

The first meeting held at noon on 24 June considered a general policy towards the French government. Having virtually accepted de Gaulle as representative of France, a new France that is, the War Cabinet decided that the French government still in France could not be relied on as it had broken a solemn treaty of obligation with the UK and was now completely dominated by Germany. The War Cabinet feared that the 'rot' would spread from the 'top' (government) through all three branches of the French armed forces and to all the French colonies. Furthermore, it was feared that the Germans would put pressure on the French government to work against the UK while the fate of the French fleet remained ambiguous with widespread dread amongst the War Cabinet that the enemy might seize it.

However, Canadian historian Jean Edward Smith notes that the French Navy was treated somewhat better than the French Army under the terms of the armistice of 1940. The French Army was reduced to one of 100,000 men, while the navy was required to collect in French ports with a German undertaking that 'the German government solemnly declares to the French government that it does not intend to use the French war fleet which is in harbours under German control for its purposes in war'.[18] Of course, any undertaking with the Nazis was not worth the paper it was written on – previous deals with Hitler had witnessed that already.

Returning to the meeting being narrated, the Foreign Secretary, Lord Halifax, told the War Cabinet that the French Ambassador and M. Alexis

Léger, General Secretary of the French Foreign Ministry, were concerned about British support for de Gaulle, whom they both loathed. From their point of view, it was only natural that in certain official French circles de Gaulle should be hated and feared. He was to alter the French political situation forever. By the end of 1940 it was found that de Gaulle's fame was rapidly spreading amongst French youth but, it was also noted, 'but is regarded by the traditional French objection to a soldier setting himself in opposition to the *de facto* Government, especially a soldier hitherto unknown to the French people at large … .' The British government was also cautious of the politics of de Gaulle's movement, the Free French movement. It was considered that de Gaulle favoured a return to the status quo before the war, which was considered to have been the prime reason for the French military defeat during the summer of 1940.[19] An earlier report from summer 1940 but only logged at Chancellery on 26 December 1940 considered what action needed to be taken by de Gaulle. The report stated:

> It is clear that the de Gaulle movement in not making any real headway either here or in the French colonies, a number of which seemed inclined at first to rally to his cause but have since fallen away and are now obeying the order of Vichy. It is essential to give the movement some fresh impetus if it is not to risk dying of inanition. It is desirable therefore that General de Gaulle should go off and raise the standard somewhere on French soil. The point contemplated seems well chosen both for strategical reasons (provided the operation were successful) and on general grounds. If General de Gaulle were able to establish himself there, there is a good chance not only that the movement might spread southwards through the French West African Colonies and in French Equatorial Africa but might also affect the position in North Africa for the better.… As to the effect on the Vichy Government, it will of course infuriate them, and they will utilise the incident (as they did after Oran) to generate as much bad blood as possible between the French people and this country. It is very doubtful however whether it would provoke them to declare war. They would have done so before (notably after Oran) if it had been to their interest. Their energies are concentrated on re-establishing as normal conditions as are possible in France at present. To make peace with Germany only to go to war with their late Ally would vitiate all their actions and promote serious trouble among the French people. Nor does it seem likely that it is in the German interest to push them into a declaration of war. But short of that, there is a danger which I mentioned to you yesterday and which, I believe, is very present to the

Admiralty. The Vichy Government, moreover, would have no difficulty in presenting the affair in a light which would not only upset the French people (as would a declaration of war) but would give fresh impetus to the feelings created by Oran. An important factor militating in favour of the operation is that the Germans are already taking an interest in the place in question and may be contemplating using it as a submarine base as soon as they can complete the necessary preliminary arrangements. If that is so, it is very desirable that we can take any action that would prevent this. The problem is, therefore, one of assessing the balance of advantage. It is thus a matter mainly for the General Staff.[20]

The possible operation under review was probably Operation MENACE, the attack on Dakar during September 1940 which ended in embarrassment for the Allies as the Vichy French put up a fight, but it possibly forestalled any attempts by the Germans to establish a submarine base there. While, later in 1942 in an interview with Churchill, de Gaulle asserted that Dakar should have been taken but for the British failure to prevent Vichy warships sailing through the Straits of Gibraltar. Churchill agreed with this statement.[21] The advantage of establishing Free French positions in Africa in 1940 would have been beneficial for the British who were waging war against Italy, the main ally of Germany, in Africa. However, what was obvious was that, after the British attack on the French fleet at the Mers-el-Kebir naval base just off the Algerian port of Oran, French support for the British had 'cooled off considerably'. The failure of de Gaulle to give a real lead in the immediate aftermath of the British assault had also been a factor in the drop in French support which caused the author of these observations regarding French attitudes post-Oran to ask, 'is there any prospect of a more positive lead than more radio talks?'.[22]

There was certainly a need for championing de Gaulle and his movement as some French people were conducting a campaign of misinformation against him as can be seen in a translation of propaganda directed against French volunteer forces attributed to the former French naval attaché in London. It was claimed that Frenchmen had been persuaded to join the Allies with the use of misinformation. It was further stated that de Gaulle was liable to arrest in the UK. It was alleged that war might soon break out between the UK and France and that those who continue to fight for the UK will find themselves fighting 'their own brothers'. Furthermore, there was also a false account of events leading up to the seizure of French ships by the British.[23] The question of supporting de Gaulle needed defining as, even though Churchill had very publicly done so, in a message to the Foreign Secretary, Lord Halifax, Churchill outlined the limitations of his support as he stated: 'It is not our policy to engage large numbers of Frenchmen or other friendly foreigners in our own forces. We do not have enough weapons for ourselves, our Dominions and the large Indian expansions which are in prospect'.[24]

It was probably the case that in the summer of 1940, with the UK facing the real prospect of a German invasion and lacking sufficient arms to defend the British Isles in the case of actual enemy landings, did not want extra foreign troops getting in the way. Therefore, it was made more sense if French volunteers could be retained on French imperial territories rather than making their way to the UK which was in great danger of falling to the Germans and then where would they be?

Churchill in his statement was leaving all of this unsaid but it was uppermost in his mind that summer. However, no matter the urgency of the summer of 1940, de Gaulle and his followers still managed to play politics. They were not alone as the Poles in exile managed to have a coup in central London. Major Douglas noted that de Gaulle wanted *Capitaine de Frégate* Auboyneau to be his representative in the event of de Gaulle leaving the UK rather than be represented by Admiral Muselier.[25] (Auboyneau's rank is equivalent to that of commander in the Royal Navy.)

Muselier was a definite rival to de Gaulle and, as a senior naval officer and a commander of the French Navy which had never surrendered to the enemy or entered any form of armistice, he was a creditable alternative to de Gaulle. But it was an unnecessary distraction during 1940. In 1940 it was far too early to read what de Gaulle was going to do – the UK had staved off an invasion while de Gaulle was trying to retrieve some tattered remnants of honour for France. The larger conflicts and trials were to come.

However, as Spears noted, de Gaulle learned very quickly that the British were easily bullied and so he bullied them. Spears often had to intervene putting it as being 'in a central position between the hammer and the anvil'.[26] De Gaulle's apparent discovery meant that he often pretended that he had strengths to work from but was all too frequently bluffing when he was doing his best to protect France and French interests when dealing with the British. This, Spears claimed, de Gaulle did with 'Hitlerian thoroughness'.[27]

The British government immediately began to consider what could be done with those French armed forces who had arrived in the UK during the summer of 1940. In June there were 21,000 French servicemen in Britain; 9,000 were naval personnel while the remainder were mountain troops of the *Chasseurs Alpins* and two battalions of the French Foreign Legion. The French government, still operating in Bordeaux, had ordered all French armed forces back to France with many of those men asking to be allowed to return home to France. Anthony Eden, the Secretary of State for War, was asked by the War Cabinet to discuss the matter with de Gaulle with the intention of inducing experienced troops such as the French Foreign Legion to remain in the UK while others could be allowed to return to France but without their equipment.[28] It is quite clear by looking at the dates and the French service organisations in the UK in June 1940 that those were members of the French contingent that had served in the Norwegian campaign between April and June 1940. Allied armed forces had been evacuated from Norway during June.

In the summer of 1940, there was not a particular manpower shortage, but there was a definite weapon deficiency to face the threatened German invasion of the UK. This was one of the reasons why the Norwegian campaign had been abandoned; the heavy weapons used by the Allies there, especially anti-aircraft artillery and ships, was needed back home. Churchill wrote to Lord Halifax stating, 'is it not our policy to engage large numbers of Frenchmen or other friendly foreigners in our own forces. We have not enough weapons for ourselves, our Dominions and the large Indians expansions which are in prospect.'[29] The relationship between the wartime British government and its European allies, especially with the French and Poles, was always difficult. The main problem which faced the British government regarding the French in the summer of 1940 was how best to deal with them and with whom. The War Cabinet meeting of 24 June 1940 had already noted that the French government had demanded that de Gaulle should be returned to France to face a court martial. The French were further angered when the British government allowed de Gaulle to broadcast to France and so bypassing the heads of the French government still governing from Bordeaux.[30]

Of course, it was a matter of debate who was determining the attitude of the French government battened in Bordeaux. Was the French government still acting independently, or was it already under German influence? At best, French officials still in France were considering their immediate futures as it was obvious that Germany was just about to absorb France. However, the problem was how to unify the French living outside France in its vast empire, mainly in Africa, where entire military units, if not armies, were stationed and waiting for their futures to be decided. The big question was: would they declare for de Gaulle or for Vichy? And how would the Germans view those troops? Those questions were becoming most immediate as the armistice signed between France and Germany came into effect on 25 June. On that day Pétain addressed the French nation: he did not accept that France had been defeated by military adroitness but by secular democracy as enjoyed in the French Third Republic since the 1870s. The French Catholic church considered that France had received 'divine retribution' for its godless behaviour.[31]

Almost immediately, information relating to the French Empire and the French living there and their feelings towards de Gaulle was received. It was not good as Eden received a message from the British Military Mission to Syria. France had occupied Syria since 1920 following the defeat of the Turkish Empire in 1918; the local Syrians were naturally quite hostile towards French rule. The message to Eden from Syria emphasised that de Gaulle was not strong enough to carry French colonial opinion with him.[32] The attitudes of French armed forces and the French Empire were to be crucial for the future of de Gaulle. It was for the British government to be certain of its policies towards de Gaulle and to those who rallied to him. It had to be quite clear that those French men and women who took their lead from de Gaulle would enjoy the wholehearted support of the British government; especially from Churchill himself, and that British policy should reflect this. This was the clarity which General A.P. Wavell, Commander-in-Chief of the Middle East Theatre sought. Wavell sent a telegram to London regarding the future of French troops serving in the Middle East which was discussed in Cabinet on 26 June. Part of Wavell's telegram read as follows: 'Consider immediate statement should be made by British Government to Algiers, Syria and Djibuti, either new French Government is formed to continue war or authorising French forces to join British, Army and Air Force'.[33]

The War Cabinet agreed with Wavell and an immediate response was drafted which went along the lines of not knowing if a new French government was being formed but would welcome French forces serving with British armed forces. A final statement was to be drafted after consultation between the three British service departments and with the FO. However, a cipher telegram was sent by Eden to Wavell authorising, at Wavell's discretion, all French forces wishing to fight on in 'defence of the common cause' can count on full political and financial support of the British government. It was emphasised that all such forces were welcome 'should they at any time wish to be incorporated in the British Navy, Army or Air Force'.[34] Basically Eden was via Wavell publicising that any members of French forces prepared to fight alongside the British from French imperial territory or even to become part of British armed forces would be welcomed and completed supported by the British government not only politically but also financially. This was quite a development as the future for those French outside of mainland France was confused; an element of certainty was probably welcomed by some French nationals.

A further consideration for both de Gaulle and the British government was the morale and expectations of the French who were then in the UK or living in overseas French colonies. There was a strong sense of defeatism amongst French service personnel, as well as a chance of returning to France and their families as long as the French authorities were negotiating a ceasefire with the Germans. In the French Navy there appeared to be a split between officers and ratings but overall, the feeling was that the war against Germany should continue – the French Navy was united in its contempt for French politicians, it was further reported that feelings would run high if there was any attempt to include French politicians in the French National Committee. Perversely, the British considered that there was very little hope that the French Navy as a whole would continue to fight while things were no different with the French Army. The CIGS minuted that the morale of French troops in the UK was deteriorating with several men from the French Foreign Legion being detained in custody by their divisional commander, charged with being communists. Their commander wanted three of those arrested to be executed by firing squad. The British proposed to send the legionnaires to North Africa with their personal arms but with no heavy equipment if they had any. It was also decided that French troops should be transported to North Africa using ships from French territories rather than French ships in the UK in case the British lost control of those ships.[35]

Over the following days it seemed that Churchill had thought about the situation regarding French troops and was quite determined to make every overture to them to convince them to remain with de Gaulle and, ultimately, with the British in the war against Germany. In Cabinet, Churchill suggested that, before French troops left the UK, de Gaulle should have an opportunity to address them and invite those who wished to fight on to be formed into French units under the command of French officers with the possibility of receiving British rates of pay. The War Cabinet agreed to this measure.[36] The next day the question of transporting French troops to North Africa arose. It was eventually decided that, if there was such a need, it would be better if British ships were used in case French ships were seized by the Vichy authorities in North Africa.[37] The question of equipment was much more important to the British than manpower, of which there was a surplus. Ships were at a premium in 1940. Later, the same day it was proposed that before and after de Gaulle's broadcast to the French that evening he should be recognised by the British government as the leader of all 'Free Frenchmen'.[38]

By the beginning of July, the plan to recruit French volunteers swung into action. De Gaulle addressed various bodies of French troops on 30 June in an appeal for volunteers. From the French Foreign Legion, twenty-one officers and 1,000 men came forward. This was in addition to 400 men of mixed military units and 400 to 500 naval personnel. De Gaulle also wanted French colonial Senegalese troops to remain in the UK; the British War Office for some reason, perhaps racism, had anxieties about this, but the Senegalese troops were allowed to remain in the UK. There were also indications that other French people wanted to fight on, but the reception given to them by ordinary British people was often discouraging.

Following these revelations, Churchill made the following decision and made it clear that it was of the utmost importance to have a French contingent but he had noted that the British authorities appeared hesitant about welcoming French volunteers, mainly on the grounds of the lack of suitable equipment. Churchill decreed that this attitude was unfortunate and must not be allowed to continue. The War Cabinet then instructed the Secretary of State for the Colonies and service ministers to issue instructions to British governors and commanders-in-chiefs overseas to ensure that French volunteers were encouraged and that every effort be made to assist in building up a French contingent.[39]

It was quite clear that Churchill was determined to assist de Gaulle in his war against Germany. By obtaining foreign support from outside the British Empire and Commonwealth, the war would be validated. Furthermore, there should be no question of the UK seeking terms with Hitler but, instead, it was obvious to the Germans that, if they wanted to defeat the British, they would have to invade the British Isles and conquer them. Equally, Churchill, supported by the British, was not only willing to face up to German invasion but by the summer of 1940 considered defeating Germany. The eventual defeat of Germany was something that Hitler had not considered. However, the main problem remained. What was to be done regarding relations with France, given that it was partitioned and in Germany's grip despite the unoccupied Vichy-administered zone south of Paris.

A problem that de Gaulle and the British government faced was that certain French troops who wished to ally themselves with de Gaulle did not want to be considered to have deserted their parent units. De Gaulle himself was considered by the Vichy regime to be a deserter. Indeed, de Gaulle had been sentenced to death by the collaborationist French government, an action which Churchill considered to have only 'glorified' de Gaulle's name amongst those patriotic French and a short-sighted act by Vichy.[40] Smith notes that the charges against de Gaulle for treason were bought about at the insistence of General Weygand. De Gaulle's trial was held in secret (of course he was absent) and he was found guilty on five of six charges. He was stripped of his French Army rank and sentenced to death, and his property was confiscated. In his memoirs de Gaulle made no mention of the trial and, as Smith notes, the conviction was meaningless, but the British swiftly increased their support for de Gaulle.[41]

A letter to Churchill from the exiled Polish prime minister, General Władysław Sikorski, sent at the end of 1940, sheds light on how Pétain saw the situation regarding his country. The Poles had come across this information following an interview by one of their number with Pétain as Poland and Vichy France were not at war, and Poles were at liberty in that area. Pétain, of course, was against de Gaulle who considered that any support for de Gaulle should be considered to be directed against France. He said that it played straight into the hands of those French who called for closer collaboration with the Germans. Pétain spoke of the difficulties of the Vichy government and admitted that he was 'following a dangerous road'. It was learned that the Germans were demanding free passage across Vichy territory for German troops moving to Italy. This was something that the Italians were afraid of. From Sikorski's letter, Churchill learned that Pétain was not going to recall Weygand from Africa and that he was not going to cede French Mediterranean naval bases to the Germans.[42] This information was important to the British as it was not easily garnered, but such a clear interview was gold dust and its origins should be noted and the willingness of a minor ally to share is important.

However, the rapid British support for de Gaulle had consequences as it caused a threat to the supply of French volunteers for the British cause. The situation in Syria illustrated this point when the No. 8 (British) Military Mission, headed by Colonel Salisbury-Jones, was told by the French authorities there to close down their mission and leave Syria. It was reported that formed-up groups of French troops who had been crossing from Syria into British-governed Palestine had ceased to cross over. Furthermore, the French authorities in Syria were anxious that individual French soldiers should be prevented from entering Palestine from Syria and that those already in Palestine should be persuaded to return.

Colonel Salisbury-Jones stated that such action would have a disastrous effect on the remaining pro-British Frenchmen and that propaganda to them should be broadcast from Palestine, suggesting the following passage:

> The British have undertaken not to encourage desertions from the French Army. At the same time, it is false that volunteers whose honour forbids them to obey the dictates of the Bordeaux Government are not welcome, or that they have returned to the French authorities. No volunteers have been or will be turned back.

Churchill replied that 'such a broadcast might lead to a movement within the French Army which would result in the restoration of the situation under a younger leader'. He concluded with the notion that every encouragement should be given to French troops willing to fight. It was further noted that de Gaulle already had three battalions in the UK, as well as 380 pilots plus another 1,000 young men willing to serve plus a company of small tanks. The Admiralty was asked to consider how Allied troops could be brought from Syria, via the Mediterranean, to the UK or elsewhere. Meanwhile the WO was to encourage French troops to cross into Palestine. The Secretary of State for War welcomed any broadcast along the lines proposed by Salisbury-Jones and would arrange such a broadcast. However, General Wavell, commanding British forces in the Middle East, was concerned that the military position regarding Syria might worsen.[43]

A major problem for the British government and de Gaulle was what would happen to French colonies if they were handed over to Germany or taken over by the Germans? If French territories, such as their North Africa possessions as well as Syria and Lebanon, were to fall into German hands, it would leave British territories exposed. This included the Suez Canal. If the Suez Canal was to fall into enemy hands, the short route to India would be denied to the British and the entire Middle East could be endangered with huge consequences as the British would have been unable to supply or reinforce the subcontinent. Therefore, it became quite imperative that the Middle East should be reinforced and protected to defend against further German and, indeed, Italian aggression. The world was very much at war.

Nevertheless, the situation between the French and British governments remained unresolved in July. The relationship was grave indeed, especially in view of the fact that on 3 July, the Royal Navy destroyed the French fleet at anchor in its Algerian base of Mers-el-Kebir, commonly known as Oran. Monsieur Cambon, the French Chargé d'Affaires, asserted that Anglo-French relations were at a low point and that he was not certain how his government would react regarding the British bombardment. Cambon was in quite a state at this time as he was probably aware that the French government was about to break off diplomatic relations with the British. This, no doubt, was the communication that he feared that he might have to make and that, after living in the UK for twenty-five years, he did not want to make.[44]

De Gaulle supported the British action. His support was made quite clear in a speech made to his countrymen and women on 8 July.[45] After the bombardment, which claimed the lives of nearly 1,300 French sailors and sank three ships including the battleship *Bretagne*, de Gaulle was calm and, via the BBC stated, 'No Frenchman worthy of the name can for a moment doubt that a British defeat would seal forever his country's bondage.'[46] This was de Gaulle clearly thinking outside the box and looking towards the long term. After the war de Gaulle said that if he had been in Churchill's position, he would have done exactly the same.[47]

By 7 July the French government had indeed broken off diplomatic relations with the British.[48] This cleared the way for the British government to work with de Gaulle without having to look over its shoulder to check the reaction of the French. However, this also meant the beginning of a more direct and difficult relationship with de Gaulle and his movement, beginning with the demand for the restoration of genuine French independence.

The question of French independence was one that was to vex both the British and the Free French movement. The stumbling block was not that of independence itself but related to that of the territory of France. The British War Cabinet asserted in a proposed agreement with de Gaulle that he had gone too far in undertaking to 'restore the independence and territorial integrity of France and the French Empire'. It was suggested that a new sentence should be substituted expressing 'the determination of his Majesty's government, when victory has been gained, that France should be restored to her former greatness and the independence which has been taken from her.'[49] During August Churchill drafted a letter to de Gaulle which contained the phrase 'full restoration of the independence and greatness of France … had no … precise relationship to territorial frontiers.'[50] And there was the rub: what exactly was the British government willing to do for de Gaulle and the Free French?

Given the very serious threat of invasion which the UK faced during the summer of 1940 it should be seen that any agreement made between de Gaulle and the British government would be of a short-term nature. It was only after 1941, when both the United States (USA and/or US) and the Soviet Union became part of the alliance against Germany and its allies, that any real agreement between de Gaulle and the British government could be made. However, by then both Britain and France were merely 'bit players' compared with their American and Soviet allies. Basically, the British and the French were destined to be hosts to the Allied invasion of western Europe. Therefore, in 1940 any agreement made between the Free French and the British government was of limited relevance and was basically an affirmation that de Gaulle and his followers, and not the Vichy regime, was recognised by the British as representing France and were thereafter British allies in the war against Germany. But there was little, if anything, beyond this regarding post-war France and its empire once Germany was defeated and France liberated. There was no guarantee of the sanctity of French borders or the restoration of the French Empire. These were not questions that could be decided during wartime.

Given the ambiguous stance of the French in 1940 it was not surprising that the British government made no commitment towards guaranteeing the restoration of French frontiers and overseas territories. Quite simply, the UK was in no position to do so while the sinking of the French fleet by the Royal Navy in early July 1940 ensured that many French people found it very difficult to trust the British. The only thing which Churchill and de Gaulle could agree on was that the war against Germany should be prosecuted to its very end. Therefore, it became important to the British government that they could determine exactly the position and attitude of French service personnel. It seemed that, on the whole, the French political system was broken and could not be trusted; the only hope seemed to lie with the French armed forces. Even then, British officials were deeply suspicious of high-ranking French civilian and military officials. Alfred Duff Cooper, the British Minister of Information, submitted a memorandum to the War Cabinet regarding the situation in Algeria and French Morocco which also reflected the situation in France. Duff Cooper's overall position was that the French administration and chief service officers had 'apparently thrown in their lot with the Bordeaux Government'.[51]

This was not promising as the Bordeaux government was basically defeatist and wanted peace at any price, a position that was anathema to both Churchill and de Gaulle. Duff Cooper noted that French senior civil servants were prepared to follow any government as long as their personal positions were not jeopardised while proposed armistice terms between the French government and the Germans appeared not to involve any changes in the administration of Algeria or Morocco. Officials were assured of their future prospects and, therefore, were quite willing to continue to obey the orders of the French government holed up in Bordeaux. The French military were also acting in a manner which did not suit the British government as many French troops stationed in North Africa were being re-deployed to France. This meant that those French soldiers remaining in North Africa were outnumbered by potentially hostile Spanish and Italian troops posted on the borders of French North African territories. Therefore, French generals were reluctant to take any action which might provoke an attack from either the Italians or the Spanish.[52] Indeed, when de Gaulle tried to reach out to French forces throughout the world for support, he received a negative response from many French military commanders in North Africa and the Middle East who considered him to be a tool of the British and so preferred to remain loyal to Vichy.[53]

The problem which many French commanders were ignoring was that Vichy was not loyal to France. However, exceptions began as, in the Pacific region, the New Hebrides, New Caledonia and Tahiti pledged their support for de Gaulle. In late August they were followed by various French possessions in Africa, the

Cameroons, Chad and the French Congo, rallied to de Gaulle, followed a little later by Gabon.[54] What might have been seen as out-of-the-way African colonies belonging to the French and of an uncertain quality were bought sharply into focus to the British public via the columns of *The Economist* at the beginning of September. It was noted that support from French Equatorial Africa gave de Gaulle a solid basis for his authority; regarding it as a change in tide but 'as yet no idea how fast and how far it may sweep in'. The importance of French Equatorial Africa was underlined as it was noted that it bordered Libya, an Italian possession and Italy was at war with the British while the British territories of Egypt and Sudan also bordered French Equatorial Africa, as did the Belgian Congo.[55] It was clear that French Equatorial Africa could be used as a way of taking some of the fight back against the Axis powers if Italy could be attacked in Libya. Once de Gaulle received support from Félix Éboué, France's first high-level colonial administrator of African descent and Governor General of Chad, on 26 August he was able to work on this development. He broadcast that 'France is France. There is in her a secret spring which had always surprised the world, and which had not finished surprising it. France, crushed, humiliated, abandoned, is beginning to climb back from the abyss.'[56] This has shades of what de Gaulle would say when he arrived four years in liberated Paris.

As we shall see, Africa did indeed become the first stage of land-based operations against the Axis powers as Italian-African possessions were attacked at first by the British, with great success, but it was not always easy. Later fighting in Africa, principally North Africa, involved the British and, later, Americans as Hitler was forced to send German forces to shore up his Italian allies. North Africa was the beginning of the fight back into Europe with the battlefields being principally Libya, Tunisia, Algeria and Morocco, all within striking distance of Italy.

It should be remembered that Algeria, the French equivalent to India as far as imperial possessions were concerned, was also part of metropolitan France, despite being separated from the France by the Mediterranean. Algeria was, and is, Arab, annexed by France in 1830 and eventually treated as part of France until independence in 1962. Indeed, Algeria and its French settlers were to pose murderous threats to de Gaulle in the early 1960s, once he chose to grant independence to Algeria to the fury of French colonists resident there for decades. However, the support for de Gaulle in most of French sub-Saharan Africa gave him a base outside the UK and plans were set to take Dakar, the capital of Senegal and a major French military base on the West African Atlantic coast. Meanwhile, the British were involved in trying to strengthen de Gaulle's hand and therefore their own by sending various missions to areas which might bear fruit in the cause of rallying the French to de Gaulle and the Free French.

Duff Cooper's mission should be seen as a failure. He had been sent to Rabat in French Morocco in the hope of contacting those Frenchmen who were known to oppose the armistice and perhaps to influence General Augustine Noguès, C-in-C French Armed Forces in North Africa, to join de Gaulle. Duff Cooper failed to contact anyone in French North Africa. At the same time, General Dillon, Head of the British Military Mission to North Africa, was asked to leave Algiers.[57] Spears noted that, when Duff Cooper and Lord Gort were sent to North Africa on what he considered to be a 'dangerous mission' to contact Georges Mandel and others who had been allowed to sail for North Africa, it was discovered that Mandel and his colleagues had been arrested and held incommunicado by the Vichy authorities. Duff Cooper and Gort were compelled by Vichy officials in Rabat to leave Morocco immediately, unable to complete or even start their mission.[58] However, as Spears noted, the failure of the Duff Cooper mission and the expulsion of Dillon from Algiers, coupled with the lack of support from most Frenchmen, had a positive effect for de Gaulle as at last the British government was finally convinced to throw its weight behind him. Spears was tasked with setting up de Gaulle and his somewhat limited entourage.[59]

The Fall of France caused other fears. The Allies became concerned that Spain might be convinced by Germany into going to war against the UK. This was made clear by the British naval attaché in Madrid who reported:

> Danger spot is Morocco Protectorate. Spain as protector of part would be entitled to more if the Pétain Government collapsed, Germany's only chance of tricking Spanish Army into war against us lies in situation brought about by such a collapse or in a coup d'état in French Morocco in favour of de Gaulle without the Spanish attitude being taken into account.[60]

The concept of Spain joining Germany in the war against the UK was very much a fleeting idea of the summer of 1940. In early summer that year, the enthusiasm for Spain joining the war was largely that of the Spanish government and not of the German government. Prior to the outcome of the Battle of Britain, Spain had considered that Germany would easily defeat the UK but, of course, the reverse happened, and Germany never invaded the British Isles. During this period German economic and military experts were advising the government against allowing Spain to enter the war. After the Battle of Britain, the Spanish fascist dictator, General Franco, was more cautious. Not only was he wary of joining the war following German defeat over the skies of the UK but Spain was also in dire straits, following three years of civil war which had seen Franco emerge victorious from the ruins of his country. A paper drawn up by the Spanish Naval Staff during October 1940 concluded that the economic consequences of going to war against the UK would be disastrous as the Royal Navy would blockade Spain which would in turn damage the Axis war effort since Spain would be unable to supply Germany with valuable resources such as chrome.[61] Franco, wanting to save Spain and, if possible, prevent an Allied victory, kept Spain out of the war as Spain stood to lose the most if it joined the fighting.

The French Navy in North Africa seemed to be a better prospect for the UK and professed great friendship to the British while expressing a determination to never hand over their ships to the Germans. However, Duff Cooper reported that the French admirals were 'so stunned by events that they were incapable of the mental or physical energy necessary to avert the consequences which they professedly deplore'. He noted that the goodwill of the French admirals was 'deteriorating daily'. An interesting dichotomy in the French situation was that young officers, as well as the rank and file, were willing to fight on against Germany. This equally applied to the civilian population, of whom most were unaware of the terms of the proposed armistice.

This immediately indicates that there was a certain level of French officialdom which was self-serving and merely concerned for their own futures. They obviously did not see their fortunes being linked to a free and independent France. Duff Cooper reported further that in the Algerian capital, Algiers, a committee of prominent citizens had been formed to organise resistance, but the civil authorities offered no encouragement. Lord Dillon, who had been in touch with them, passed on an American offer of rifles, ammunition and other equipment. According to the consul general, the local Arabs or, as termed at the time, 'Moors' from the sultan down were unlikely to accept the armistice terms and would continue to fight. Therefore, Duff Cooper was making a case for the need to find an alternative to the Bordeaux government and so the resistance in North Africa needed supporting and rallying. Duff Cooper had swiftly recognised the need for the Allies to take North Africa to prevent the Italians and Spanish from doing the same and therefore called for an expeditionary force in Morocco.[62]

The problem with the French fleet was one that led to some attempted horse-trading with General Dillon, who headed the British Military Mission in Algiers. Dillon informed Churchill that the French in North Africa were unlikely to fight, but it remained most urgent that French warships there should be prevented from reaching their home ports in France, and the

Germans, but there was a chance that the French might surrender their ships to the British.[63] What is interesting is that now it seems that Admiral Darlan had no intention of surrendering 'his' fleet to the Germans or to any of the Axis powers. On 3 July he threatened to end his career with *'un acte de splendide indiscipline'*, an act of gross insubordination in which he threatened to rally his fleet to the UK should the Axis armistice conditions include the surrender of the French fleet. By 16 June, Darlan decided that perhaps it would be possible to have an armistice with the French Army, which was defeated anyway, and the cessation of hostilities, but without the surrender of the French fleet. This was what Hitler had had in mind as he never understood the importance of sea power and, therefore, did not, as the British and Americans feared, have any intention of seizing French warships. Indeed, Hitler would have preferred to have seen the French ships either interned in a neutral port or, best of all, sunk.[64] Churchill had already made requests to Pétain and General Weygand that the French fleet should not be handed over to the Germans but instead should sail for American or British ports, thus 'saving the honour of France'.[65]

A memorandum sent by Lord Halifax, the British Foreign Secretary, which considered the situation in Syria, reported that both Syria and Lebanon were already out of the war and that the wavering attitude of French officials there was typical of French officialdom at the time.[66] The ambiguity of French officials was probably something that irritated the British government as the UK faced up to the threat of invasion. The uncertainty of what the French intended to do regarding their warships forced the hand of the British and led to the seizure of French vessels in Plymouth and Portsmouth, as well as the British attack on the French fleet in Algeria. On the same day as the British naval assault in Algeria, nine French cruisers and a single destroyer sailed from Algiers to an unknown destination.[67] French ships in Alexandria harbour, Egypt, surrendered to the Royal Navy.

Following the British attack on the French fleet in Algiers, Churchill authorised the secretary of state for the colonies to arrange negotiations to be started with the governor general of the French Cameroons.[68] Basically, Churchill was trying to discover the best strategy of using the Free French in the war against Germany. The African continent seemed to offer the best prospect as both the British and French were already established there. Furthermore, so was Italy, the weak ally of Germany, which presented an opportunity to show the world that the British and French had not been defeated and that, by fighting Italy, the war against Germany was far from over. World opinion was important, especially public opinion in the USA.

A further memorandum was submitted by the secretary of state for the colonies which considered the situation in French Equatorial Africa and West

Africa to be satisfactory. In those French territories there was evidence of widespread resentment at Pétain's capitulation and there was a general desire to work with the British against Germany. An example was that those French living in Chad had already been in contact with de Gaulle. The local French authorities in French West Africa were cooler towards the British and seemed inclined to acquiesce with the peace terms accepted by Pétain's government but, overall, the problem was seen as a lack of leadership while French West Africa was strategically important to the UK.[69] And so, to this end, it was necessary for the British government to champion de Gaulle as the only leader of free Frenchmen who could provide leadership in the French colonies, if only to prevent them from going over to the Axis powers.[70]

The fears for the French colonies were also discussed by the British Chiefs of Staff (COS) who reached similar conclusions as those of the War Cabinet. The situation with French warships and the intentions of the French government were just as sinister, since the service chiefs feared that certain French ships had already been ordered by the Bordeaux government to attack merchant ships.[71] There was also some consideration given to the concept that France might even declare war on the UK after the British attack on the French fleet. It was also thought, however, that the French had little, if any, fighting spirit left.[72] It was in this atmosphere of mistrust and fear of what the French might do next that the British government decided that something had to be done to rally the French colonies in West Africa to prevent them falling to Pétain.

The Economist wrote at the time that the fact that French Equatorial Africa backed de Gaulle was important as it provided a solid base for his authority and that the tide had turned in favour of de Gaulle but 'as yet no idea how fast and far it may sweep on'. In addition to French Equatorial Africa going over to de Gaulle, it also appeared that the Cameroons and Gabon were also leaving Vichy whilst there was also the possibility of a coup to remove Vichy authorities in the French Pacific territory of New Caledonia.[73] It should also be noted that French Equatorial Africa bordered onto Libya, then an Italian colony, as well as the Anglo-Egyptian Sudan and the Belgian Congo and was potentially an ideal launch pad for military operations against the Italians. This was the kernel of the thought behind the eventually disastrous attempted invasion at Dakar – Operation MENACE – later that year. The evidence is a meeting which concluded that the entire aim of MENACE was to establish de Gaulle at Dakar.[74]

To add to the fevered atmosphere in the British War Cabinet regarding its concerns of French intentions, letters received from the governors of the British colonies of Nigeria and the Gold Coast (modern Ghana) contained disturbing information. The first point was the appointment of Admiral

Laborde as Supreme Commander in Dakar. Indeed, he was commander of all French air, land and naval forces in French West Africa but, more worrying for the British, was that he was a representative of the strong anti-British feeling in the French Navy which had only hardened following the British assault on the French fleet in North Africa. There was also a rumour, later discounted, that German and Italian officers had arrived in Dakar while anti-British propaganda was being disseminated from Dakar and Abidjan (Lower Ivory Coast). An instruction had been issued to the population that they must remain on French territory and were not to resist German or Italian armed forces should they arrive. To underline French actions, a group of senior French officers arrived in the Cameroons to put pressure on the governor general who was friendly towards the UK. There was also an indication that the Vichy government was attempting to assume control of French African colonies with further evidence that French officials were paving the way for the arrival of German or Italian armed forces in French West and Central African colonies.[75]

Once more there was a call for a 'show of force' with Dakar appearing to be the favourite site for intervention.[76] The question of British intervention in Dakar and the establishment of de Gaulle there was one which concerned the War Cabinet as its members tried to judge what sort of reception de Gaulle and the Free French might receive there as a result of a British attack.[77] It was judged that some might see de Gaulle as a British puppet but it was still considered that an offensive against Dakar was worth the risk since it seemed that there was more support from French Africa, especially French Equatorial Africa, for the UK when compared with French support from North Africa or Syria.[78]

A further aspect of the need for MENACE to be successful was that the British needed continued success against German attacks for propaganda purposes domestically. By mid-September 1940, it was obvious that the Germans had been defeated in the Battle of Britain. A victory in Africa, for the British, would have concluded the year on a high note. It would have also meant that the British would have been in position to exploit the French colonies in North Africa and Syria. However, it was noted that, in Algeria and Tunisia, the French European population were closer in sympathy to the Vichy regime and were likely to resist any Anglo-French landings. It occurred to the British government that some success in Morocco should overcome this attitude.

However, the British did contemplate coups in Syria and Morocco using local pan-Arab organisations.[79] It should also be considered that, before the end of September, it was clear that the Germans were stripping France and

Vichy of all its worthwhile assets.[80] Therefore, there was a clear need for the British and their Allies to take some form of action against Germany and the Vichy French just to remind them that it was not always possible to do just as they liked.

The idea of a coup in Syria was further explored a few days later when the Free French admiral, Émile Muselier, was to visit Syria. However, it was concluded that Muselier was not the man to lead the coup, but the British government wanted to keep him onside and considered that a senior British naval officer should see him regarding his (Muselier's) plans.[81] At the time, Muselier was considered by some in the British establishment to have been rakish and piratical looking. Furthermore, he was considered to have been highly controversial as he was more noted for his hatred of Darlan than his love of the Free French movement.[82] It should be seen that the British government had many plans and schemes for the French colonies, but it was a matter of which one would be best suited for the British war effort.

The failure of MENACE was virtually predestined owing to the ill-discipline of the French and their extremely lax ideas of security. An early report regarding MENACE was an appalling catalogue of compromised security beginning with de Gaulle himself. While he was buying a considerable amount of tropical equipment in Piccadilly, central London, de Gaulle remarked, incredibly, in public, that his destination was West Africa. A further incident recorded was the toast of 'Dakar' given by French officers in a Liverpool restaurant. Furthermore, an intelligence report received by the British Inter-Service Security Board reported that 'Dakar' was common talk amongst French troops.[83] Jackson denies that de Gaulle could have ever been the source of any leaks given his 'obsessive secrecy'.[84]

Those incidents of compromised security in relation to MENACE ensured that, during 1943 and 1944, the Allies decided not to inform de Gaulle of Operation OVERLORD, the Allied invasion of Normandy on 6 June 1944 until just hours before the operation began. This was despite the fact that northern France was the invasion site. Churchill had concluded that 'in the meanwhile the French should be rigorously excluded from any information regarding our plans for OVERLORD.[85] De Gaulle and his people had proved that they could not be trusted with any information. In 1945 Duff Cooper, also asserted, rather mischievously, that de Gaulle could not be trusted with information for more than thirty seconds.[86] To be fair, de Gaulle, despite his *faux pas* in central London was well aware that French security surrounding MENACE had been breached as the following telegram was sent:

Please transmit the following from General de Gaulle to Muselier and Fontaine. Message begins. Owing to unpardonable negligence a telegram has been sent from Douala to Brazzaville at the same time in clear and in cipher. I therefore forbid use of the code 'MENACE' until further orders. All cipher telegrams for me must come through English cipher. Please study most practical amendment to our cipher to re-establish its security.[87]

A confirmation that, by the end of 1940, even de Gaulle could not trust messages to his own cipher and preferred to trust them to the British.

There were other incidences of poor discipline and security within the Free French once de Gaulle arrived in the UK during 1940. A report from MI5 to British diplomat Mr Mack also indicated that not only was there a problem with Vichy and Germany, but it was also feared that de Gaulle's organisation had been penetrated by Soviet agents. MI5 were suspicious of a Professor Henri Labarthe who had been appointed by de Gaulle to be head of the military side of the Free French. Labarthe's secretary was of interest to the British intelligence services as she had been associated with him for eight years, was a Polish national and a Soviet agent. MI5 considered that 'leakage' about the Dakar operation had come through Labarthe. The evidence of this was based on the fact that, once the Dakar expedition was decided, de Gaulle was told to tell as few people as possible. De Gaulle held a meeting with his own staff at which Labarthe was present. MI5 believed that Labarthe told a Frenchman called Koenigswater (also known as de Koenig) who told another French officer between 4 and 10 August 1940, probably 7 August. MI5 considered that Labarthe had some 'very odd friends'. It was observed that de Koenig had been since dismissed by de Gaulle but was trying to ingratiate himself with Admiral Muselier and induce him to take him onto the naval side of the de Gaulle administration. It was further noted that Labarthe had once been associated with Pierre Cot, when Cot was the French minister for air during the 1930s. It was noted that during this time Labarthe had a Czech communist with him there.[88] It should be remembered that in 1940 the Soviet Union and Germany were allies and, in theory, shared intelligence; therefore, having communists within de Gaulle's entourage may well have benefited Germany. It is thought that Cot may well have been a Soviet agent while the British intelligence service also had traitors within; this was not understood in 1940.

In relation to the allegations against Labarthe, it was claimed by some at the FO that he had been a victim of political whispering of 'Anglo-French blimp'. However, the communiqué remained uncertain as the writer ends with the sentence:

If, however, there is something serious, I should be very glad if you would let me know, as I do not want the Ministry (of Information) to be associated with somebody, who may, pending negotiations with him, be shot in the Tower![89]

Quite a dramatic note, but it does lend to the problem that the British had to try to deal with their allies as well as the enemy. The British had little knowledge of the Europeans who were arriving on their shores and the French proved to be no exception. Gaston Palewski, who had arrived in the UK during August 1940, was appointed by de Gaulle as director of political affairs of the Free French movement. He was a close associate with de Gaulle and helped negotiate between de Gaulle and the British government, who distrusted him. However, this did not prevent him from telling O.G. Sargent at the FO of his shock at the disorder at de Gaulle's headquarters at Carlton Gardens. Palewski stated that de Gaulle was not one for administration or organisation. Palewski considered that an efficient French organisation should be created in London and learn to co-operate with the British. Sargent was not wholly in agreement with Palewski but agreed overall that the Free French needed re-organisation.[90]

However, it was not only the failures in military procedures that compromised the French. There were also personal attributes which seemed to confirm British prejudices concerning French slackness and the perception of the womanising Frenchman! An incident relating to this arose from a report concerning an interview with a young Frenchman who had escaped from a German prison camp and made his way to the UK. The young man wished to join de Gaulle's movement but was concerned at the lack of efficiency and discipline at de Gaulle's headquarters. While it was widely agreed that de Gaulle was a fine soldier, equally it was considered that he was not particularly good at organising his staff. Even worse, when de Gaulle had been in Africa, his temporary replacement, Vice Admiral Muselier, had made things worse. The unnamed Frenchman highlighted two problems:

1. The men involved in organising the Free French movement, who were patriotic and devoted to de Gaulle and France, had little, if any, aptitude for higher administrative work.
2. Women! Of which there were too many and could be divided into two subgroups.
    a. French wives for whom jobs had to be found.
    b. 'English lady adherents'.

Point 'b' was a rather roundabout way of saying girlfriends and mistresses.

The report then gave some detail about the French headquarters, stating that there was not enough administrative work for French officers as the French military force was very small. There were also doubts about the intentions of the British government while (Gaston) Palewski (cited erroneously as Palevski), who was to be hugely influential in the Free French diplomatic circles later during the war, was observed as 'hobnobbing' with important British personalities and was yet to commit himself to de Gaulle's movement. Palewski's attitude was no doubt in part typical of the caution displayed by some Frenchmen before they gave themselves wholeheartedly to de Gaulle and the British. For some of the French there was concern that the British government was becoming half-hearted in its support for de Gaulle and might 'even flirt with Vichy'. Overall, it was considered by many Frenchmen that the British government still needed to make a better impression with the French remaining in France and show that they seriously supported those French people who wanted to continue to support the war against Germany and its allies.[91]

Amazingly the reaction to the minute taken by Mr Codrington was quite positive and not at all dismissive. Major Douglas Morton, Churchill's assistant at 10 Downing Street, wrote to R.L. Speaight at the FO. Morton told Speaight that he considered that Codrington understated the problems at the French headquarters and that the fears expressed were fully justified. The difficulties were highlighted by de Gaulle's absence and made any attempts to rectify the problems discussed difficult. At the same time Churchill considered that the Free French movement must be French and that the British should not interfere too much. Therefore, it would be difficult to put forward the idea of the young Frenchman who had highlighted the incompetence at de Gaulle's HQ and had suggested that a British official should act as *Chef de Cabinet* to de Gaulle. It was noted that there were several Frenchmen who could fit this post but who refused to join de Gaulle until he 'puts his house in order'. The result was as Morton wrote 'a vicious circle'.[92]

The concerns regarding women at de Gaulle's headquarters were further highlighted following the interception of a letter sent by the wife of a Free French official regarding the chaos there.[93] The overall problem was not only that conditions at de Gaulle's headquarters were being openly discussed but that the name of the recipient suggested that French security had been breached and totally compromised. As H. Farquhar at the FO wrote to Lieutenant Colonel Todd of the Censorship Department:

> It may of course be pure coincidence, but 'Francoise' was up to a short time ago the *nom de plume* for a prominent supporter of General de Gaulle and

to send such a letter through the ordinary post make the indiscretion all the more serious. We are taking what steps we can to induce General de Gaulle's headquarters here to prevent their adherents and their wives committing such acts of folly.[94]

However, in 1940 it was obvious that de Gaulle was the only Frenchman who could convince his compatriots of the need to continue the war, but under British direction. Simply, de Gaulle was a rallying point for all free French citizens and those who desired to fight on. Therefore, despite the schisms and splits amongst the French of all persuasions, it was reported that French officials in North Africa were beginning to realise that the only way out of 'their predicament' was a British victory. Gascoigne, the British consul general in Tangier and the author of the report which informed William Strang at the FO that he believed that most French officials were 'disgusted' with Laval and his 'pro-German policy', while Pétain remained a 'figure of veneration' to them. This was the very reason why Weygand was 'slow' to do anything that might hurt him.

The idea of getting Weygand onside was one that perplexed the British government and the FO. The British were already plotting what post-war France might look like as revealed in the following passage:

> If Weygand finally plays our game it may not I suppose, be easy to fit de Gaulle into the new scheme of things, although de Gaulle's patriotism should command his co-operation. The Comte de Paris' attitude towards Weygand is not satisfactory, and as a figure-head the former might be useful – looked at from here I believe that the majority of Frenchmen in North Africa who are sick to death of Republican politics might welcome a return to the Monarchy and from what little I have seen of the Comte de Paris I think that he might suit quite well.

Gascoigne had struck a note of reality when he wrote further that he realised that popular feeling in Britain was running high against the French and with good reason but observed that at the end of the war despite 'the disgraceful treatment we have received at her hands' the British and French would have to return to working together once more.[95]

At times it seemed that the British and French governments were at war but the Anglo-Franco situation in 1940 was difficult. However, given the actions of the French government and many in the French High Command during May and June 1940, actions frequently perceived by many in the UK as being treacherous and craven, it was not surprising that the British government and the FO were extremely cautious in their interactions with the French government and were very distrustful of it. The British government also had difficulties in their choice of Free French leader.

It was noted that de Gaulle had a 'splitting effect' in the loyalties of the French – should they fight for Vichy, or would they have to fight against their compatriots if they were conscripted by de Gaulle's forces in Africa and used against Vichy supporters on the same continent. However, it was also true that, if the British tried to contact their other possible choice, Weygand it would lead to trouble. If British staff officers tried to contact the general the Germans would have quickly discovered this and demand that the Vichy government dismiss him.[96]

De Gaulle, however, was having his own problems with his officials, especially regarding their lax attitude towards security. This led to de Gaulle rebuking the French representative in New York who had made statements for the press which had been published in the UK and hinted at possible military operations in Africa. De Gaulle told Sieyes, his man in New York, that 'such announcements may prove indiscreet'. Furthermore, Mr Hurd, an American radio announcer, on the strength of further statements from Sieyes, had expressed views 'dissimilar' from de Gaulle who said, 'in this respect you should be guided by my own pronouncements or instructions which are that nothing must be said for the time being'.[97] In reply to de Gaulle, Sieyes simply denied all and pledged his loyalty to him.[98]

In Africa itself it appeared that the Vichy authorities had accepted Free French authority in Equatorial Africa as a *fait accompli*. De Gaulle mistrusted this stance as a propaganda ploy by the Vichy government while it is interesting to note that the French struggle against Italy was extremely popular, even in Vichy France. On the strength of this, de Gaulle looked to build up his forces in Africa.[99] From here it can be seen that two points are worth considering – the first being that the Vichy regime did not want to be isolated from de Gaulle as it was not certain which way the war might progress, especially in relation to the French Empire, and the second was that de Gaulle had found from where he could rebuild his forces as well as finding a common enemy which united French antipathy – Africa and the Italians.

Chapter 3

Into Africa

Africa was chosen as the most likely place from where de Gaulle and the Free French could return to continue the war to liberate France and Europe from Nazi occupation. Nevertheless, the British War Cabinet had reservations about this decision since it was also considered that some advantage might remain if the British government maintained relations with Vichy. Such a conduit might well have provided intelligence for the Allies if correct relations were observed with France and the Vichy regime. However, the Vichy authorities saw little purpose in this exercise if the British continued to interfere in French overseas possessions.

Sir Samuel Hoare, the British Ambassador in Madrid, informed the War Cabinet that the French authorities in Madrid were anxious to work with the British government. Hoare considered that some kind of relationship with the Pétain government would help the British government with the Spanish government who regarded Pétain as the only hope against a France totally occupied by Germany.[1] At the time the British government feared that Franco and Hitler might form an alliance and attack the British colony, Gibraltar. The position of Gibraltar, between the Spanish southern coast and the coast of North Africa, allowed the British to control the narrow Gibraltar Straits between the two coasts. This meant that the Royal Navy could oversee who left the Mediterranean for the Atlantic Ocean and vice versa. Furthermore, any Spanish declaration in favour of Germany would have endangered the North African coast and British and French territories therein, while any linkup between the Spanish and Italian armies in Africa would have been a total disaster for the Allies. Lord Halifax, the British Foreign Secretary, considered that indirect relations with the Vichy government were a waste of time but gave leave for Hoare to continue discussions with the French Ambassador in Madrid.[2]

A further consideration for the War Cabinet, when considering their French policy, was how to manage de Gaulle vis-à-vis Weygand who was still respected in senior British circles but was yet to choose between de Gaulle and Pétain. Indeed, during early November 1940, the War Cabinet considered that de Gaulle's actions in Africa may well have antagonised Weygand.[3] There were so many French egos that the British had to stroke in 1940. Churchill expressed his preference that de Gaulle should return to the UK and consult with the British government on the general situation in which his position regarding General Weygand should be discussed.

Halifax noted that de Gaulle's supporters in Cairo favoured a visit by de Gaulle but that he should return to the UK as soon as some of the ambiguities of French Africa had been cleared up. Halifax was asked by Churchill to draft a personal letter from him to de Gaulle in which he was urged to return to the UK for consultation.[4] Memoranda from the British Chiefs of Staff Sub-Committee reflected the contemporary thought of the British authorities regarding Weygand, as there was an assumption that he might break away from Vichy and take French North Africa and Syria.[5] However, this was just wishful thinking.

While these things were being considered, it remained imperative that the British took decisive action in Africa which lead to Operation MENACE. The objective of MENACE was always the installation of de Gaulle and the Free French in West Africa at Dakar, capital of the French colony of Senegal. This was to be done by evicting the Vichy French authorities at Dakar and preventing a possible occupation of Senegal by the Germans who may have used it as a submarine base against Allied shipping in the Atlantic. MENACE was undertaken on the assumption that de Gaulle would be welcomed by the majority of local inhabitants and that a formal show of British support would be sufficient to ensure success.

The intention was to capture Dakar with as little bloodshed as possible and to stress the French nature of the expedition. However, preparations were put in place to counter any serious resistance with the use of British armed forces.[6] There were also other factors regarding Dakar which the British Chiefs of Staff had to consider. During August 1940, the Chiefs of Staff discussed a report from the Joint Intelligence Sub-Committee (JIC) concerning the possibility of a German or Italian occupation of Dakar. The COS considered that the object of such an occupation was twofold – the first being to acquire a base from which to carry out offensive action against Allied shipping or against British possessions in West Africa; in particular to deprive the British the use of Freetown located on the coast of Sierra Leone. The loss of Freetown would have complicated the British task of convoying ships via the Cape route. The second enemy objective might have been the acquisition of new materials.

The War Cabinet considered that the above scenario was unlikely so long as Gibraltar remained in British hands. This meant that, if the Axis powers had wanted to capture Dakar, co-operation with Spain would have been necessary since Spain's southern ports would have been needed for such an operation as well as bases in the Canary Islands (Spanish) and/or the Cape Verde Islands, which would have dragged Portugal into the war against the UK. Overall, though, it was considered by the British service chiefs that much would have hinged on the Axis capture of Gibraltar and the inability of the Royal Navy to operate basically any invasion of Dakar by either Germany or Italy, if not both, would have required a seaborne offensive.[7]

The necessity of keeping British sea lanes open to the Cape (South Africa) was one that Churchill realised was of great importance and so the seizure of Dakar was essential. Even if Germany did not capture the port, it was still controlled by the Germans via the Vichy French. Furthermore, the American government had an interest in the Free French capturing Dakar as an Axis- or Vichy-controlled Dakar compromised American security.[8] Reports of German and Italian officers in Dakar appear to have been exaggerated or just plain wrong. If there were any German-speaking officers in the area they were possibly German-speaking Frenchmen from the disputed frontier province, Alsace, located between France and Germany.[9]

However, it seemed that the Dakar offensive was damned from the beginning. This was to have consequences as it damaged de Gaulle and the Free French in the USA with widespread mistrust of them both amongst American elites. Indeed, Dakar and its failure confirmed to President Franklin Roosevelt his prejudice that the Free French were 'chronically indiscreet' and that de Gaulle was 'a somewhat comical mountebank who didn't represent anything'. It was to take two years before Roosevelt changed his opinion and considered that de Gaulle might be useful.[10]

MENACE was always going to be a political gamble as it ran the risk of Vichy declaring war against the UK and for Germany to occupy North Africa. However, it was also a bold move since it took the war indirectly into the enemy camp and so the operation was not devoid of merit.[11] Nevertheless, as we shall see, the Vichy French did retaliate against the British at Gibraltar.

The risks of French retribution were calculated before the attack on Dakar with several points being considered. The first was that the risk of a French retaliatory attack was low since it was thought that French morale was at rock bottom and, even if French loyalty was nominally to Vichy, many French people did not want war with the UK because it was considered that the French continued to regard the British as allies. Nevertheless, if there were to be any French retaliation, four possibilities were considered: air attack on Gibraltar, air attack on Malta, submarine attacks on the British Atlantic trade routes, and active operations by units of the French fleet in Mediterranean ports.[12]

Even before the task force which was to execute MENACE sailed there were various problems, all down to French incompetence and petulance. A major problem was that the French naval crews who were take part in the operation were already in a state of mutiny and armed guards had to be posted on ships before a single vessel left port for Africa. The reason for the mutiny was soon discovered by the Admiralty and it was simple: the French crews had not been paid for three months. The Admiralty settled this debt, but there were further complications which took a comic turn and no doubt infuriated and baffled the British. French crews continued to refuse to sail unless their rations included champagne and *pâté de foie gras* – a British report cynically stated that some adjustment had been made to the French rations. Then it got worse, even farcical, as one of the French captains lost his mistress and declined to sail without her. This was settled by the long suffering and ever patient Admiralty. Even when the French ships were finally under sail, two of them managed to collide in the mouth of the River Mersey as they left Liverpool while one crew threatened to make for a Vichy port at the earliest opportunity. Nevertheless, eventually all the ships reached Freetown.[13]

There were also claims that security had been further breached as, at railway stations involved in the despatch of troops for MENACE, crates broke open revealing leaflets and medals all connected with Dakar.[14] Furthermore, an anonymous letter was sent to Churchill in which the writer claimed that security arrangements at Liverpool docks during MENACE had been lax but the author was more concerned about the 'Liverpool Irish' dockers being privy to the unfolding events rather than the fact that enemy agents might also be aware of the coming operation.[15] An inquiry was held and it concluded that overall the French security was slack while that of the British was more confused rather than compromised. In response, the British tightened up security so that a single body was responsible for security arrangements rather than the previous myriad of bodies, each responsible for their own arm of operations and planning.[16]

There was also criticism of the proposals for MENACE and how difficult it was likely to be. According to the Inter Service Planning Service, Dakar was geographically similar to Gibraltar. This meant that Dakar was basically a small peninsula jutting out of the mainland of Africa and joined to the latter by a low narrow isthmus about 2.5 miles wide and so defence against a landward attack would be very simple. The bay at Dakar was also defended by coast defence guns and that entrance to the harbour had to be made via the strongly defended point at Cap Manuel. The coast defences, according to contemporary reports, consisted of three coast defence batteries of 5-inch guns or 5.8-inch guns of modern design. The overall armaments for the defence of Dakar were five 9.4-inch turret guns, four 4.8-inch guns and eight 5-inch guns while it was understood that 9.4-inch guns turret guns were being installed at two other batteries. It was therefore considered that 'Dakar can thus be said to be very strongly defended against sea attack'.[17] However, a week later a note from the Vice Chief of the Naval Staff, Vice Admiral Cunningham, complained of the lack of intelligence available in relation to Dakar.[18]

De Gaulle added to the confusion regarding intelligence reports concerning Dakar. The French leader, in a memorandum to the British COS, wrote that, according to intelligence reports made available, it seemed that military and naval attachments guarding Dakar were in a 'somewhat disorganised state both materially and morally'. Furthermore, de Gaulle considered that demobilisation was also in progress in the Dakar area while opinion amongst civilians was confused, but de Gaulle claimed that many still disapproved of the armistice and continued to look to the British as allies. De Gaulle also claimed that the civilian authorities and the general population in Dakar were anxious about food supply as they were aware that nothing could come into the area without the co-operation of the British.

According to de Gaulle, the secret for success at Dakar lay in a surprise attack, especially if heavy casualties were to be avoided. Even though the military force involved was a mixture of British and French, de Gaulle wanted it to be overwhelmingly French with the intention of adequate French detachments (the equivalent of a single company) occupying the principal points in Dakar during the initial stages of the operation, who should be reinforced within an hour by further French detachments which were to bring in such equipment as vehicles, tanks, aircraft and tractors. De Gaulle considered that French troops should form part of the detachment occupying batteries, barracks and the harbour. While the town of Dakar and its defences were being occupied, large numbers of aircraft should fly overhead showering the area with large quantities of suitable leaflets explaining the situation.

Furthermore, de Gaulle insisted that all troops, British as well as French, should wear visible *tricolore* emblems, that tricolore flags should be waved continuously and that French detachments should be provided with megaphones or loudspeakers to broadcast in French to the inhabitants of Dakar and declare their intentions. De Gaulle considered that, if the above measures were undertaken, the operation would be a success. He also considered that MENACE should be carried out as soon as possible, allowing for tides, moonlight, swell and other factors to which he was willing to defer to the experience of Vice Admiral Cunningham.

In the case of the plan not going as well as hoped, de Gaulle also devised an alternative plan of seizing St Louis and landing the whole expeditionary force, with all its equipment, there. However, despite this still being a landing in Senegal, it required moving to Dakar which was not so close and would have been dependent on the use of roads and railways which hardly existed in the area. Furthermore, the French expedition would have had to negotiate with local French officials as well as appealing to the local population. De Gaulle also stipulated that French troops must be landed first and that they were to form a mechanised column before moving to their objectives. In principal, British troops were to be used as a reserve force and hold the base at St Louis. The British naval force was to provide cover from the sea.

However, the British were far more sceptical than their French counterparts about the Dakar operation. A memorandum from Major General Irwin sought to query previous directives regarding the capture of Dakar. Much of MENACE depended on surprise and the acceptance by local forces that Free French forces were taking over in West Africa. Irwin was not as confident as de Gaulle regarding the passivity of the French in the area. Irwin considered that if there were any miscalculations serious consequences would ensue. The British general considered that it was impossible not to feel apprehensive of the effect on the population and the garrison after a British naval bombardment. Equally, it was difficult to believe that de Gaulle would receive a friendly welcome with his troops equipped with British guns and bayonets. Irwin also considered that, once Dakar was captured, a long-term decision would be made by the British authorities regarding de Gaulle's force in Dakar – whether it would be possible to leave it in West Africa or would Dakar have to be evacuated, destroying the ports and forts as much as possible before leaving. Irwin cited a directive from Churchill which stated, 'should General de Gaulle be unable to maintain himself … we will take him off after destroying the harbour facilities.'[19]

It should be noted that senior British officers had reservations about MENACE from the very beginning. In the *Official History*, it was noted that

> if Dakar were well defended by a resolute Commander with alert and determined troops, we consider that the chance of success would be very small. In view, however, of the reports of morale we consider that this operation might be carried out by highly trained British forces, based on a carefully prepared plan, with good chance of success, provided tactical surprises can be achieved.[20]

By 18 August 1940 it was recognised that a surprise landing and a peaceful instalment of de Gaulle had receded to 'vanishing point'.[21] Once MENACE had sailed, it quickly became obvious that there was no question of secrecy. Very quickly there were concerns about the activities of a French naval squadron which had escaped the British net around the western Mediterranean and had sailed past Gibraltar and into the Atlantic. The French squadron appeared to be heading towards West Africa, but its final destination was unknown.

From the war diary of HMAS *Australia*, we can glean what was happening at sea as the British and French geared up for the offensive against Dakar. During the night 13/14 September HMAS *Australia* received reports that three French Cruisers of the Gloire-class, *Gloire*, *Montcalm* and *Georges Leygues*, had slipped through the Straits of Gibraltar and, after calling at Casablanca, were proceeding south, possibly to Dakar. This information was followed up by a report from the aircraft carrier HMS *Ark Royal* on 15 September, which stated that the three French cruisers were not in Dakar. However, later that morning, following further reconnaissance it was found that three cruisers of the La Galissonnière-class rather than the Gloire-class were in Dakar. Further aerial reconnaissance at 15.00 hours on 15 September made sure that the three cruisers were actually in Dakar.[22] By this time the War Office (WO) was concerned that operations in West Africa might cause the Vichy government to declare war or order reprisals, using aerial attacks, against Malta or Gibraltar, if not both. There was also a fear that British shipping might be attacked by Vichy forces; this led to the necessary precautions being taken to prevent such eventualities.[23]

The presence of the French naval squadron in the Dakar area caused MENACE to be cancelled on 16 September.[24] Sir Alexander Cadogan, the anti-de Gaulle permanent undersecretary at the FO, could hardly contain his glee at the news of the cancellation of MENACE. In his diary, Cadogan wrote 'the French ships have forestalled us in Dakar, and so 'Menace' is off! I cannot say that I am sorry!'[25] Cadogan's gloating was short lived as Spears made an urgent appeal to Churchill and sent a report in which Spears questioned every aspect of the operation's cancellation. He pointed out that French ships had been engaged by the Royal Navy under unfavourable circumstances on the Friday. However, on the Monday the same French vessels 'now lying helplessly in harbour under awnings' were not to be attacked. Spears was at a loss why: the French ships were now at the mercy of the Royal Navy who were forbidden to attack them.

Spears also observed that it was widely known that de Gaulle was in the area and that it was quite clear that, if he failed to seize the opportunity before him and rally West Africa to his cause and instead 'agree to vegetate at Duala, his power to rally any part of the French Empire is gone forever'. Spears also pointed out that, if the British fleet departed and left de Gaulle to his fate, French opinion would swing totally against the British in both France and Africa. It was quite clear to Spears that, if Dakar was not 'muzzled', any gains in Africa would eventually be lost as it would only encourage the Vichy regime under enemy influence to threaten British African colonies, especially the port at Freetown where over sixty ships lay within one hour's flight from the French airbase at Konakri. Churchill was impressed with the report and of the opinions of those on the ground in Africa and so allowed the Dakar operation to continue.[26] Predictably, Cadogan was less impressed and noted: 'messages show people on the spot want to go on with "MENACE". I warned against possible result of another Oran. But everyone in favour'. The next day the War Cabinet agreed to the resumption of Operation MENACE.[27] Oran was, of course, a reference to the sinking of the French fleet at Mers el Kebir.

Monday, 23 September was chosen as D-Day. H-Hour was given as 05.30 hours. Within fifteen minutes it was obvious that the Vichy French were determined to oppose the Allied landings as, at H-Hour plus fifteen minutes, British aircraft dropping leaflets over Dakar, in addition to carrying out 'unobtrusive reconnaissance' over French defences, were met with anti-aircraft fire and attacks by French aircraft. An hour later (H-Hour plus seventy-five minutes) a Free French emissary in a motorboat reached the harbour boom and tried to speak to local French officials. He was fired on and wounded. Later, at H-Hour plus three hours and thirty minutes, the Free French tried to land but were shelled by shore batteries and took casualties.

The next day, 24 September, HMS *Barham*, HMS *Resolution* and HMAS *Australia* were ordered to bombard Dakar. Later information from aerial reconnaissance reported two French cruisers, at 90°, 3 miles from Goree; three destroyers were patrolling Goree Bay and two sloops were stopped between Goree and Rufisque. At 09.00 hours, FO (M) [Flag Officer, Commanding Force 'M'] allocated targets for the attack to commence at 10.00. Cruisers and destroyers were directed to engage warships north-east of Goree.[28]

A more vivid account of the Dakar operation comes from the point of view of a young Australian midshipman, Mackenzie J. Gregory, serving aboard HMAS *Australia* at Dakar. Recording the events of 23 September, Gregory noted the attempted parley by the Free French with the local Vichy authorities. Following the shooting up of the Free French party, battle flags were hoisted, and HMAS *Australia* went to war. At 10.00 hours ships were reported to be moving out of Dakar harbour and *Australia* was ordered to turn them back and so fired a warning shot. The French ships turned about and returned to harbour. French shore batteries then engaged HMAS *Australia* at close range and so HMAS *Australia* re-joined the main Allied naval force. The joint-Australian-British task force next attacked the forts which defended themselves with 9.4-inch and 5.4-inch guns. There was also a report that French submarines were in the area and a British destroyer, HMS *Foresight*, had been hit, with a shell passing right through its hull, but it remained afloat. HMS *Dragon* managed to hit a submarine that had attacked HMS *Foresight* but was also hit by shore batteries. Two shells from shore batteries fell very close to HMAS *Australia* as the force turned away from Dakar while HMS *Cumberland* was struck by a 9.4-inch shell.

Later, aircraft reported an enemy destroyer in the Baie de Gloree, to the south and eastwards of the inner harbour. HMAS *Australia* with three destroyers went to investigate. At 16.24 hours, the enemy was sighted, and the Australians opened fire two minutes later. Within three minutes the French ship was on fire 'from stern to stem'. HMAS *Australia* ceased fire and an escorting British destroyer went to pick up survivors but was forced to retire as the French forts opened fire on it. The burning French ship, *L'Audacieux*, described as a destroyer but a light cruiser, burned for thirty-six hours and was eventually beached near Rufisque. By 16.40 hours, HMAS *Australia* broke off its engagement and re-joined the main battlefleet.

The next stage of the MENACE offensive was to try to land French troops from French sloops and the ship *President Houduce*, close to Rufisque. By 17.20 hours, the troops were trying to land but heavy fire from well-appointed, and well-defended positions, overlooking the landing beach, caused the Free French to withdraw after five men had been wounded, two of whom died from their wounds. De Gaulle declared that he 'did not want to shed the blood of Frenchmen for Frenchmen'.

At dawn, the next day, 24 September, action began once more. HMAS *Australia* and HMS *Devonshire* joined the battleships of the Allied fleet and closed in again on Dakar. HMAS *Australia* and HMS *Devonshire*, both heavy cruisers and armed with 8-inch guns were sent to engage the Vichy cruisers *Georges Leygues* and *Montcalm* which had escaped from the British ships, HMS *Cumberland* and HMS *Devonshire*, and had made it into Dakar. Midshipman Gregory on HMAS *Australia* noted that visibility was poor (it was a shock for the Allies to find that sea fogs were a hazard off the West African coast). As a result, the two Allied ships could only fire at gun flashes coming from the Vichy ships. The Australians were then attacked by a Vichy Glen Martin bomber (probably a Maryland, the name assigned the aircraft by the Royal Air Force (RAF) which took over the balance of the French order following the collapse of France) which dropped a stick of six bombs close to the starboard of HMAS *Australia*. Gregory noted the irony that the Glen Martin was one of those sold to France by the USA just prior to the French capitulation to Germany.

Georges Leygues and *Montcalm* retired behind merchant ships in Dakar harbour and so HMAS *Australia* withdrew to the south. Allied ships then fired on the forts guarding Dakar and on *Richelieu*, a new French battleship armed with 15-inch guns and recently in port after being damaged in the attack at Mers el Kebir. It was a fast battleship, commissioned on 1 April 1940 as the lead ship of the Richelieu-class. HMAS *Australia* was attacked once more by a Glen Martin bomber which dropped a large bomb that caused the entire ship to shudder – 'shaking herself as a dog does when wet' – but no real damage was done. A French submarine surrendered while a second was sunk in an aerial attack. Sunset saw the suspension of activities. Action recommenced the next day.

The battleplan for 25 September was for HMS *Resolution* to attack *Richelieu* while the battleship HMS *Barham* and the cruiser HMS *Devonshire* were to engage the forts. HMAS *Australia* was to take on both *Georges Leygues* and *Montcalm* who both remained in Dakar harbour. The fall of fire from HMAS *Australia* was spotted from its spotter aircraft, a Walrus biplane fitted with a boat hull and floats. The Walrus reported that fire was falling short when both French ships disappeared behind a smokescreen. At one point HMAS *Australia* came under fire from *Richelieu*, the forts and the Vichy cruisers. Gregory observed that the Vichy fire was colour coded to distinguish the spotting of their shellfire. *Richelieu* used yellow, the forts white and the cruisers green and red. As Gregory remarked, 'we were almost being bracketed by a rainbow'!

Although the distance between the Vichy and the Australians was between 24,000 and 28,000 yards, HMAS *Australia* was hit twice by 6-inch shells, one of which passed through the rear of X-turret as it trained forward and then exploded in the unmanned captain's galley, which was totally wrecked, and left a hole in the deck. Luckily, nobody was hurt. The second shell passed through the ship's port side and entered the engineers' spare gear store where it exploded. Much of the shock of the explosion was absorbed by the spare gear but the armoured belt penetrated into the engine room where the port water distiller was wrecked, but again there were no casualties. Gregory noted that, if X-turret had not been trained forward, the first shell would have probably penetrated the gun house and then exploded with devastating results.

The Walrus spotter plane reported that the firing from HMAS *Australia* was falling either side of the Vichy ships. This meant that the Australians had found their range and had bracketed the enemy ships with their fire and that the next salvo should provide direct hits. Suddenly, the Walrus plunged into the sea. It had been shot down by a Vichy Curtiss fighter which, in turn, was shot down by anti-aircraft fire from one of the Allied ships. All three of the Walrus crew had been killed. After this the Allied cruisers and battleships withdrew while HMS *Resolution* was struck by a torpedo and began listing heavily. Allied destroyers screened the stricken *Resolution* as a Vichy bomber attacked it. This attack was driven off by accurate anti-aircraft fire. Following this incident, the Allies attacking Dakar left the area. HMS *Barham* took HMS *Resolution* under tow, supported by HMAS *Australia*, proceeding south at a slow speed.

Gregory, rather putting himself down, recorded his views of the Dakar operation in his midshipman's journal with 'all the wisdom of an 18 year old'. However, his observations prove to be quite accurate. His first observation was that the force was not adequate and that the Free French did not co-operate with the Anglo-Australian ships as much 'as they might have done'. The planning was indeed poor; so was the intelligence work. De Gaulle really believed that he only had to land with his troops and all resistance would cease. It was a shock to the Free French when they were fired on by their compatriots. De Gaulle did not want to see Frenchmen fighting one another and so gave up and did not try to land at Dakar again.

In Gregory's opinion, despite the insufficient numbers available for the operation, Dakar could have been taken. The problem had been thick fogs, something the Allies had not anticipated. The resulting poor visibility had caused Allied ships to engage the Vichy forts at close range while the impaired visibility meant that the psychology of a large naval presence was lost as the local defences could not see the size of the attacking force. Midshipman Gregory observed that a fort would always have the upper hand against ships as they fired from a fixed position and are smaller while their fire-control instruments are steadier compared with those of a ship bobbing up and down according to tides, weather and so on. Gregory also considered that Dakar was gridded so that the fort gun controllers would know the range and bearing of every square inch on the harbour charts.

Gregory pointed to further shortfalls in the intelligence and planning of MENACE as he wrote that, when the operation was planned, the presence of *Richelieu* had not been considered. The Vichy ship was used as a land battery with her 15-inch guns easily outranging anything that the Allied naval force could muster. Furthermore, the two Gallissonière-class cruisers, which had arrived at Dakar after escaping British cruisers, added to the defences and had not been expected when the operation was planned. Furthermore, the Allied taskforce was expected to operate in both confined and unknown waters – a bombardment in closed waters was much more difficult than a naval action in open water. Gregory also criticised the air cover for MENACE as he noted that enemy bombers gave the ships 'a lot of trouble' while fighters from the aircraft carrier HMS *Ark Royal* were too slow to catch the Glen Martin bombers used by the Vichy air force. Gregory stated that, in his opinion, there should have been extensive use of the bombers from the British naval arm, the Fleet Air Arm, who he considered to have been underused during MENACE.

According to Gregory, Dakar was defended by a greater number of troops than had been expected. When Free French troops declined to fight unless the Allied naval bombardment succeeded, very little was likely to have been achieved. Furthermore, once de Gaulle received the signal 'Success', indicating that all was well and that he would be gratefully received in Dakar, he believed that his operation would succeed but as we have seen it was not to be the case.

Of the politics, Gregory was quite perceptive regarding MENACE. He correctly noted that it was undertaken for political reasons, with Churchill showing support for the 'prickly' de Gaulle. However, as Gregory stated, in late 1940 there were no other Free French figures on the horizon, and it was thought that MENACE might have propped up de Gaulle and provided a rallying point for those wishing to join the Free French. A further consideration was that the American president, Roosevelt, was anxious that Dakar did not fall under German influence.

Midshipman Gregory concluded that MENACE was a complete failure on the Allies' part. He reached his conclusion by citing the casualties: a battleship badly damaged and put out of action for a long time at a time when every vessel was desperately needed to support the naval war against Germany and to help face the very real danger of a German invasion of the UK. Gregory also recorded that three cruisers and a destroyer had been hit by enemy fire while aircraft, including the Walrus spotter plane from HMAS *Australia*, had been shot down. On the credit side, two Vichy destroyers, another ship had been destroyed and a submarine sunk while another surrendered. There were two possible hits on *Richelieu* from Allied 15-inch guns and a possible torpedo hit on a Vichy cruiser. Gregory reflected that the removal of the two Vichy submarines meant that some of the menace to Allied convoys was eased slightly, but the overall objective of capturing Dakar and handing it over to the Free French was not achieved. Regarding the performance of his own ship, Gregory wrote that 'HMAS *AUSTRALIA* and her crew had performed with ability' her ship's company could be proud of their baptism of fire'.[29] Indeed, Midshipman Gregory was quite correct in his assertions regarding the actions of HMAS *Australia* and the crews of other ships involved and, of course, his conclusions regarding the outcome and politics of MENACE were also correct, but what needs investigating is just how these situations were arrived at. The young Midshipman Gregory was in good company in his assessment of the failure of MENACE as the British novelist Evelyn Waugh, serving with the Royal Marines, was present at Dakar and, in his diary, listed the failings of the operation which largely coincided with Gregory's as well as listing the delays in sailing from every port that the taskforce had departed from.[30] Waugh also writes of the Dakar operation in his novel *Men at Arms*.

Norman Sherry, biographer of the British novelist Graham Greene, noted Greene's concerns regarding Dakar. Greene was working for British Intelligence as part of MI6 and had an interest in West Africa before he served in Sierra Leone between April 1942 and February 1943. In 1935 Greene, with his cousin, had travelled through Liberia, including those parts yet to be mapped. Greene noticed that MI6 was somewhat hazy regarding West African geography, making the point that, for example Freetown, Sierra Leone was over 1,000 miles from Dakar. That seemed to escape the understanding of Europeans hurriedly trying to understand Africa and its challenges.

In 1942, Greene reported that the failure of the Dakar offensive had made the British unpopular having failed to capture the port in September 1940. It seemed that the French liked victors and Vichy power in Dakar only lasted until November 1942, which had seen the successful Anglo-American landings in French North Africa. The Vichy governor general at Dakar, Boisson, was not trusted while his deputy was known to be pro-German. Greene reported that, by the end of 1942, de Gaulle and the Free French were not universally welcomed by all but had the potential of being so.[31]

This observation by Greene is reinforced by reports from the FO in 1940 but, overall, it would seem that the British and the Free French were pushing at the open door of French imperial African assets, and it was only the dishonesty of local French officials who were willing to betray their country to further their own personal gain which was holding up Allied progress in French Africa. All of this came to a halt once the Allies gained the upper hand in Africa and the Germans occupied Vichy France. Most of those supporting Vichy were like most traitors: opportunists who did not sincerely believe in what they were doing but just saw a chance to make a better life or sometimes get revenge on those perceived to have harmed them in the past.

One problem, highlighted by the FO, was that, since the British attack on the French fleet at Oran, French sentiment towards the British had 'cooled off considerably' while the failure of de Gaulle to take a real lead was also a factor in this French attitude to the British.[32] Bentinck, corresponding with the FO, enquired of de Gaulle: 'is there any prospect of a more positive lead than mere radio talks?'[33] The disaster at Dakar seems to have been the answer.

Nevertheless, there was also the question of whether de Gaulle might be welcome in Konakri (French Guinea) or anywhere in Africa after the failure of MENACE. The British government was worried about the proximity of Freetown and Gambia, both British possessions, to Vichy territories and, therefore, under possible threat of attack by Axis forces. The British considered that de Gaulle should not be permitted to land at Konakri but instead should be encouraged to set himself up at Douala in French Cameroon. It was considered that Douala would be more favourable to de Gaulle and, once he was installed, he could consolidate his position throughout French Equatorial Africa and exercise a favourable influence on the Belgian Congo. It was also hoped that de Gaulle would be well placed to move north into Chad should any threat appear from that direction.[34] Typically, de Gaulle had other ideas as he sent a telegram in which he stated:

> I have decided to go to Konakri and land my troops there. My intention is to rally French Guinea and march on Bamako with a view to eventually operating against Dakar. Request to be covered by fleet during landing. I suggest Force 'A' goes to Freetown from where they could act in support if needed.[35]

However, the main result of the failure at Dakar was reached by the British chiefs of staff who concluded that,

> in view of the failure of 'Menace' and the impracticality of operations from Konakri, General de Gaulle's movements in the immediate future will be governed more by political than military considerations, except that he may require a naval escort for his forces when they leave Freetown.[36]

This was to be the fate of de Gaulle and the Free French, not only in the short term but, also, in the long term. This loss of status was to be shared by all the exiled European leaders and their various movements. They were only called on by the senior Allies when they were needed. This was exaggerated once the USA and the Soviet Union got the upper hand in the alliance fighting against Germany after 1943. This included the UK, as it also lost its place, while, at the end of 1943, President Roosevelt considered that France would not be a first-class power for at least the next twenty-five years.[37] He wasn't far wrong. William Taubman, the biographer of the Soviet leader Nikita Khruschev, points to de Gaulle in the late 1950s as still trying to restore France to the status of a world power.[38]

The post-mortem on MENACE revealed a tale of confusion but it was all on a learning curve which would eventually lead to successful amphibious landings in North Africa, Italy and Normandy, landings which eventually drove the Germans back to Berlin and defeat. However, in 1940, Allied land operations left a lot to be desired, especially regarding security and co-ordination of planning between the various branches of the armed forces. The most urgent question in September 1940 though was just how did Vichy warships pass through the Straits of Gibraltar without being intercepted by the Royal Navy?

Vice Admiral Somerville, Flag Officer Commanding Force H, told the Admiralty that he was aware that the enemy warships passing through the Straits of Gibraltar were to be intercepted. This should have included Vichy French ships, but this had not been carried out by Somerville as he had assumed that their lordships at the Admiralty were aware of the movements of French ships, and he did not want to provoke an incident. Thus, Somerville accepted responsibility for this lapse.[39] Nevertheless, he was exonerated as it was observed that signals were not sent in time for him to see or to intercept the French ships.[40] Historian Jean Lacouture notes that Somerville was 'a man of little breadth of understanding, unsuited for any enterprise or negotiation'.[41] This rather suggests that Somerville was out of his depth but his later career makes it quite clear that he was not and, as already noted, he was exonerated from neglect in 1940. Somerville was merely being cautious during a time of uncertainty.

A further report revealed the lack of co-operation as Somerville revealed that he did not know that MENACE had started until a BBC news bulletin was received at 21.50 hours, which stated that de Gaulle had been resisted at Dakar. The serious lack of information made it difficult to judge how to act locally.[42] Charitably, at least one historian had blamed the confusion surrounding the French naval squadron suddenly appearing in the middle of MENACE on to mistakes in communications, largely due to a German air raid on London.[43]

Indeed, the confusion regarding the whereabouts of the French naval squadron was spreading widespread anxiety as General Spears signalled to Admiral Cunningham on 13 September at 17.50 hours, requesting confirmation that six French warships had passed Gibraltar. At 18.27 hours Cunningham confirmed that this was the case; three cruisers of the Montcalm-class and three large destroyers of the Fantasque-class had called at Casablanca in French Morocco and were sailing southwards. Later that evening Spears signalled Cunningham with a message that de Gaulle felt that everything possible should be done to prevent the French cruisers from reaching Dakar or any other French West African port. De Gaulle considered that, if the Vichy ships got to Dakar, it was unlikely that the port would surrender to him. He suggested that the British felt that, accompanied by the Free French ship *Savorgnan*, they should intercept the Vichy squadron. The French ship was to carry a letter from de Gaulle ordering them to surrender and place themselves under his orders to commence a withdrawal to Casablanca or take the consequences. Spears reiterated that de Gaulle looked to Cunningham to prevent the Vichy ships from reaching Dakar.[44]

It might be argued that the intention of installing de Gaulle and the Free French force at Dakar 'in order to hoist the Free French Flag in West Africa and rally the French colonies there to his standard' was basically a coup.[45] However, that is to assume that the Vichy authorities present at Dakar represented the legal authority of the French state, one that had just been defeated by Germany. Therefore, the motivation behind the assault at Dakar was symbolic. The hoisting of Free French colours at Dakar and the announcement of de Gaulle as an alternative French leader, but backed by the British government, was all part of the tactical consideration behind a successful capture of Dakar. These considerations were blown out of the water with the failure of the operation. This could have been forestalled if the limited intelligence available had been better interpreted and noted more judicially rather than being motivated by political considerations. De Gaulle was already a political pawn as far as the British government was concerned.

During August it had already been noted that,

> if Dakar was well defended by a resolute commander with alert and determined troops, we consider the chance of success would be very small. In view, however of the reports of morale we consider that this operation might be carried out by highly trained British forces, based on a carefully prepared plan, with good chance of success, provided tactical surprises can be achieved.[46]

As we have seen, none of this was achieved. An entry in the war diary of 20 Military Mission, commonly known as 'The Spears Mission' in tribute to its head, General Spears, makes interesting reading as a Mr Field, chief representative of the Vacuum Oil Company in West Africa, told the mission about Dakar, where he had been present, during and shortly after the operation. Field was quite clear that there had been no Germans or Italians in Dakar while the overwhelming feeling amongst the French was definitely anti-de Gaulle. Furthermore, military and naval damage to the port and military targets was insignificant, but damage to the town and civilian casualties had been considerable. Field considered that de Gaulle must have been definitely misled about the attitude of the French at Dakar.[47]

Certainly, a contemporary report from the mayor of Dakar, a de Gaulle supporter, noted that the colonel in command of the colonial infantry regiment (in Dakar) had said to him,

> Count on us not to move (when Dakar was attacked) forty per cent of the population is Gaullist, forty per cent is neutral, twenty per cent, including [personnel] of the warships and coastal artillery, is hostile to de Gaulle.[48]

This report alone does not really clear up the levels of support or otherwise that de Gaulle and the Free French could have met. Once the attack on Dakar began, its mayor was arrested by the Vichy authorities.[49]

The apparent misleading of de Gaulle regarding the levels of support for him at Dakar explains why one British liaison officer of The Spears Mission stated that the French were 'flabbergasted' at encountering resistance and appeared to have no plan to cope with it despite the fact that, however remote, it had always been considered that the Free French landings at Dakar might be opposed by the Vichy French there. The problem was that de Gaulle was 'firmly fixed in his mind' that Frenchmen should not shed the blood of other Frenchmen.

The British considered that, until this concept was eliminated from the Free French command and from the Free French Navy, it would be almost impossible for Free French forces to succeed in further operations against Vichy-held territories in Africa or elsewhere where the Vichy occupied imperial French possessions. It was noted that General Larminat and Colonel Leclerc, later to be a distinguished commander of French armour and liberator of Paris, did not share this tame view of de Gaulle and were essentially 'men of action'. The Spears Mission considered that de Gaulle, even if he was 'uninspiring' at a first meeting, had control over his men and his ships. This cannot be said of his subordinates, and his chief-of-staff came in for particular criticism and was considered to have been 'ill-serving' de Gaulle. Further divisions were revealed in French fighting units when The Spears Mission reported that, on the first day of the Dakar operation (23 September), Free French naval officers and ratings would not have 'put up a fight against their countrymen' but the Foreign Legion and the *Fusiliers Marin* (Marines) were angry and would have probably fought.[50]

The most obvious problem revealed by the Dakar debacle was that the British, while blaming the French for the disaster, did not have a clue about launching any offensive at any level in 1940. The Free French were revealed to have little support amongst French forces in West Africa and that, in obedience to the Vichy leader Marshal Pétain, many Vichy French officers were prepared to lead their men against the British and de Gaullist Frenchmen 'but *not* the Germans'.[51]

Dakar cast a long shadow over Anglo-Franco relations. After the war, when there was a fear that Vice Admiral Cunningham was going to publish an account of the Dakar operation, it was realised that MENACE remained politically sensitive. John Hingham, Head of Military Branch I, wrote:

there is still a certain misunderstanding in France about the Dakar operation and M (Military) Branch. I would welcome the publication of any account of the operation and the decisions leading up to it, which would serve to allay this residue of ill feeling. It is not however considered that the publication of these despatches or any part of them could do anything but re-open an old wound. It would be essential that the full background of the political and military situation at the time should be given in any account for publication.[52]

A minute published later revealed the real problem with MENACE after the war. The minute read 'that while the political effects of publication are for the Foreign Office to assess, we for our part are inclined to take no action which may now harm the esteem felt in France for her resurgent Navy by accentuating its pro-Vichy feelings in 1940'.[53]

And there was the legacy of MENACE. The French Navy had backed the wrong side in 1940 and in 1946 was trying to live down its ill-advised actions. A reminder from the British of their wartime craven actions was not useful in 1946 as France and Europe tried to rebuild. The FO had the final say in 1946 in a minute to the Admiralty which clearly stated that no publication should be attempted at that time but eventually an official history (sanitised no doubt) might be a suitable platform for Cunningham's despatches on Dakar.[54] The final word on the immediate consequences of MENACE should come from Viscount Rothermere, who, in a telegram to Churchill, stated: 'Dakar incident ridiculously magnified by carping newspapers. Nobody in Canada or United States gives a thought about it. Every Britisher throughout the world knows you are winning the war and that is all that matters'.[55]

Operation MENACE was a failure; indeed, Spears recorded that eventually the British realised that world opinion judged Dakar to have been a major disaster.[56] But was it? Events at Dakar and elsewhere put the enemy and neutrals on notice that the UK under the premiership of Winston Churchill remained undefeated and that the Allies would probe every weakness in the Axis armour and exploit those exposed chinks until victory was achieved.

Chapter 4

1941: What to do with the Free French?

After Dakar, and into 1941, the question for the British government was what to do with de Gaulle and the Free French since both had the potential of being powerful in the Allied struggle against the Axis powers but had thus far failed to really do so. That failure was partially due to the British authorities which, at times, underestimated de Gaulle's abilities and then, perversely, were overconfident in him but then professed disappointment and dismay when he failed to deliver, such as in the case of Dakar. Most of the time, the British refused to understand de Gaulle or his concept for post-war France.

In 1941 it was still unclear how the British government wanted to proceed with de Gaulle. Furthermore, the British were still unsure about their relationship with Vichy France. At times it was considered that Vichy could be used in the war against Germany since there was a perception that certain figures, such as General Weygand, could be persuaded to join the Allies. Concerns remained that the enemy might be able directly to control French overseas possessions, especially those in Africa. As the British had a large African empire it was of great concern if the Germans did intervene in Africa; the Italians were being relatively easily defeated by the British, in North Africa even if they proved to be quite formidable in East Africa. The FO noted that the Free French and de Gaulle were not making any 'real headway' in either the UK or in the French colonies. The few Frenchmen who had joined de Gaulle had 'fallen away' and were now working for the Vichy regime. Therefore, it became necessary for the British government to provide de Gaulle and the Free French movement with 'fresh impetus' or the whole enterprise risked dying out through a lack of interest.[1]

As a result of the confusion in policy by the British government towards de Gaulle and the Free French during 1940, as that year ended further assessments were made on how to proceed further in the war. An encouraging report from the Australian Foreign Ministry, the Department of External Affairs, to the FO, observed the attitude of Frenchmen towards the Free French movement, most particularly in the French Pacific colonies, namely the New Hebrides and New Caledonia. The Australian report read that approximately 90 per cent of Frenchmen in these colonies were anti-German while about 80 per cent admitted that the present Pétain-German situation was intolerable. It was also disclosed in the report that between 75 and 80 per cent of Frenchmen were desirous to aid the UK in its war effort and prayed for its victory. It was observed that 'Free France' was a well-chosen name and very popular and was the party name under which the 'Pétain-German government' was most likely to be overthrown by the French.

Those French concerned in the Australian report wanted change but remained cautious in their approach. There were objections to de Gaulle and his associates. This discontent was linked to the collapse of France during June 1940. Those polled suggested that de Gaulle, as a military leader, should have taken his share of the blame for the failure of the French Army to defend France during May and June. The French military collapse was believed by many French people to have been the results of poor leadership, as well as insufficient and inadequate equipment, while no blame should be placed on the ordinary soldier serving in the French Army.

It was conceded by those polled that de Gaulle was a brilliant general, but petty quarrels had emerged owing to his relative youth (he was 50 years of age) and the lack of a political base: de Gaulle was considered by those questioned to be 'a rebel, upstart and insurgent'. The French Navy, which had not been compromised as the army, did not want to serve under de Gaulle or indeed under anyone associated with the collapse of France. This included Admiral Muselier, who was seen as influential in exiled European political circles, but the colonial French polled held that 'these sentiments apply force to Admiral Muselier whose abilities as a sailor are rated very low by the seagoing personnel, by whom he is regarded as a politician'.[2]

Relations between de Gaulle and Muselier were to hit an all-time low when de Gaulle illegally sentenced the admiral to 'fortress detention' because Muselier had no allegiance to de Gaulle since he had never signed any declaration of loyalty to him.[3] De Gaulle was not the only exiled European leader imprisoning his enemies – the Polish leader, Władysław Sikorski, was quite fond of doing the same. However, back to de Gaulle: at the time of the Muselier/de Gaulle fall-out, the British Admiral Dickens wrote to William Strang at the FO stating:

> there is an inescapable fact that in the welter of misunderstanding, jealousies, irritation and intrigue in the Free French body which throws a great deal of light on the French Navy attitude. It is that: Although we may have signed an agreement with de Gaulle, the French Navy never did and if they had been asked to sign it they would, I am sure, have

insisted on certain modification. Further, the French Navy had already settled down to work with us long before the agreement was signed. Admiral Muselier and a good many others do not look upon de Gaulle as Commander-in-Chief of the Navy, but merely as the more or less titular head of the Movement. Had de Gaulle been wise enough not to interfere in Naval affairs, especially where no interference was necessary, he might have got away with it; but as he had gone out of his way to show at every turn that he is Commander-in-Chief, opposition has become stronger and stronger. I am sure that as soon as we have patched up the affairs on our hands at the moment it would be wise to convene a small Committee to try to get to the roots of the problem and propose new machinery, even if it means a drastic renunciation of the former agreement. But for heaven's sake a *small* Committee![4]

Twice, records Edward Spears, de Gaulle had to be told that the British no longer lived in Tudor times and that one's enemies cannot any longer be sent 'to the Tower' as de Gaulle had twice sent French officers to the Tower of London, for imprisonment without a trial. De Gaulle was informed on the second occasion that 'neither the use of the dungeons nor the services of the executioner were among the amenities we were prepared to place at his disposal'.[5] The gulf between de Gaulle and British officials was quite clear when it came to the law, even if Spears in his narrative treats the two incidents with humour. But clearly, as the preceding note at footnote 4, makes clear, British officials were extremely exasperated with the French.

The frustration of the British at a senior level is quite obvious. Two days later Hoare, in a communication to Mack, reflected more of the British regret with de Gaulle and the Free French. Hoare wrote 'that you had better drown de Gaulle *and* simultaneously remove Catroux to some quiet place!'[6] General Catroux was a prominent de Gaullist but also a keen rival of the French leader.

The above remarks were all very damning and revealed a distaste for French politicians and leaders of the old France now conquered. However, even if British officials sought a new French leadership and men of action who would eventually lead France to victory and to freedom, which they had in de Gaulle, they found him very difficult to work with. So, what did British officials really want?

The reader should wonder at the consideration by conservative Frenchmen that de Gaulle was relatively youthful and, by implication, inexperienced at the age of 50. His combat experience in the First World War and the Polish-Soviet War counted for naught as far as they were concerned. De Gaulle's apparent lack of a political base should not have been seen as a hindrance, given the incompetence of the previous decade by many democratic politicians and their refusal to face up to the threat from Nazi Germany. However, what de Gaulle did have was corporate support from the French Army in exile and, possibly, within France and its empire. In wartime, this is a much sounder base than any political system. Even Churchill during wartime had to govern using a coalition government. His was basically a government of talents, of which the War Cabinet was comprised, and, of course, he worked closely with his Chiefs of Staff even if they fell out several times a day. In wartime all bets of governance are off and what needs to be done is often done. De Gaulle was no different.

However, it was beginning to emerge that the British government sought a possible alternative to de Gaulle. Discussions began about trying to get Weygand onside and so feelers were put out to that end. This was done largely in the capitals of neutral countries or via neutral states. Thus, we have a report from the British Embassy in Lisbon. The British naval attaché had seen Captain Colbert, his French counterpart, on 17 December. In that meeting Colbert declared that he thought that Weygand would be the de Gaulle of the future and that once he declared himself the entire French Empire would rally to him. It was noted that French feeling in North Africa (even if it was ambiguous in relation to Germany) was very anti-Italian. Furthermore, Colbert believed that Marshal Pétain 'is resisting all German threats towards occupied France with the menace of declaring the French Empire in favour of England'. It was considered that if anything happened to Pétain; Weygand would be his successor.[7]

The confusion at the end of 1940 and the beginning of 1941 was not helped by the attitude of the Vichy leaders as reported by *The Economist* which noted that French leaders outside France were unclear what the real situation was in their homeland since it seemed that the Germans were being held at arm's length. Furthermore, de Gaulle in a recent broadcast aimed at French forces in French North Africa had offered to serve once more under 'the old leaders', provided they returned to their duty to fight for the restoration of France. This earned de Gaulle great kudos. Therefore, it was clear that de Gaulle did not have an irresolvable problem with potential French leaders, only with the Vichy regime,[8] even those who might have been considered to have failed in their obvious duty to defend France. It was noted that General Weygand had 400,000 men in French North Africa who could be used against the Germans.[9]

There were further considerations to be made about the nature of the Vichy government. Pétain was still considered not to be the useful ally that Hitler had wished for, owing to his lack of co-operation. There were three factors which apparently concerned the Vichy government: the UK's continued resistance,

1941: What to do with the Free French? 73

the undefeated French colonies and the so-called 'watchful presence there' (in North Africa) of General Weygand.[10] It was quite clear that the Vichy government remained very nervous of how the war was to develop. It was further noted that, in the preceding nine months, there had been eight changes of government in Vichy.[11]

Clearly, Hitler's ability to control Vichy without using naked brutality, which the Nazis were quite capable of doing, was not working well. During April 1941, the German government renewed pressure on Vichy. It wasn't clear to the British authorities, who were out of the loop, what pressure was being applied but it was clear that it certainly was being used. However, the Vichy government had a single bargaining chip – their fleet and their control over it.[12]

The inability to totally dominate Vichy no doubt frustrated Hitler but, at that point of the war, it would seem that he and his followers remained content to use persuasion rather than brute force. If the large French modern fleet, coupled with a large French Army in North Africa went over to the Allies during April 1941 it would be a disaster for future German military and foreign policy since preparations to invade the Soviet Union were entering their final stages. It was noted that both Marshal Pétain and the Spanish dictator, General Franco, were seen to be blocking Germans plans by non-co-operation in fields such as economic help, while Admiral Darlan and the French politician Fernand de Brinon were considered to be traitors to France or, as quoted, 'quislings'.[13]

The term 'quisling' was derived from the arch-Norwegian traitor and prime minister, Vidkun Quisling (1887–1945), who served the occupying German forces and established a puppet Norwegian government. After the war he was tried by his countrymen and executed for his treachery. De Brinon suffered the same fate, executed by a firing squad. However, before May 1942 was out, it was obvious that Vichy indeed was an enemy of the Allies. It was reported that the British had a tendency to 'misread the men of Vichy'. This attitude was reinforced by American policy towards Vichy as well of romantic historical memories of Lafayette and the First World War.[14] Lafayette was Gilbert du Molier, Marquis de L'Fayette, a Frenchman and popular figure in the history of the American War of Independence. The reference to the First World War is more oblique, since the USA was only involved in 1917–1918 and so, perhaps in the popular British mind of the time, had been spared the horrors of 1915 and 1916. The British were very good at jibbing that the Americans only entered a war once the fighting was done.

It quickly became apparent that, in North Africa, Admiral Darlan, rather than Weygand, was the key to the area as he controlled the harbours, which were the lifelines to the region. It was considered that, unless the Germans threatened North Africa, Weygand was unlikely to march and was still not ready to commit himself. It was quite clear that the British had to continue to support de Gaulle whether they liked it or not. Furthermore, the British also needed to take precautions against any active Vichy French participation against them in the war.[15]

De Gaulle, however, came up with a scheme which was to cause embarrassment and trouble later when he suggested that, if the USA joined the war, North Africa might be assigned to them and give them 'the separate jumping off points they would require'. De Gaulle considered that the Americans disliked sharing common harbours with the British and French. Casablanca and Dakar seemed to be natural bases and ports for the Americans to use.[16] The South African prime minister, Field Marshal Jan Smuts, was equally desirous to see the Americans using African ports, especially Dakar and Freetown. He urged that high priority should be given to the Americans at the two ports. Smuts also hoped that the bad relationship between the British and French, coupled with American influence in West Africa, might deeply influence the French and turn the scale of public opinion against the Vichy regime.[17] Two days after Smuts's telegram it was reported that the Vichy government announced its intention to defend Syria and Tunisia 'singlehanded' against any British attack.[18]

By June 1941 the war was spreading rapidly. As already mentioned, the Germans were on the cusp of invading the Soviet Union but first had to deal with a situation in the Balkans while there was fighting in Greece and in its islands, notably Crete, which saw a final Allied withdrawal from the European mainland until 1943. The British withdrawal to the Middle East and into Egypt ensured that Africa, especially North Africa, was fated to become the next battlefield between the Allied powers and the Germans and their Italian allies: ultimately, the springboard for the Allies back into Europe. It seemed that some Vichy officials understood, and some had every intention of defending Vichy territory, no matter where it lay. If Allied armies were to try to take it, Vichy forces were quite willing to try to prevent this. It was a recipe for disaster, especially for Vichy.

The uncertainty continued throughout 1941. Churchill cabled to Franklin Roosevelt, the American president, that it was still unclear what Weygand was likely to do if the Germans made demands for Vichy facilities in French North Africa. A demand like this, in Churchill's opinion, might have forced Weygand into the war against Germany.[19] By 1941 it had been noted that Pétain did not believe that Germany would win the war whilst the French arch-traitor, Darlan, very anti-British, remained convinced that Germany would emerge victorious.[20]

It would seem that, at this relatively early stage of the war, despite de Gaulle's seizure of power whilst in exile his position remained uncertain since there were other viable senior French officers who commanded greater respect than he did. It could be argued that French politics, within and outside France, between 1940 and 1941 was a stage being set for post-war political power in France. It was a matter of waiting to see which French military-political leader emerged in liberated France with the most 'honour'.[21] There was a similar situation across occupied Europe; some of the kingdoms had natural leaders in their monarchs, but republics had hard choices to make, while the east-central European republics were merely annexed by the Soviet Union between 1944 and 1945. There were to be few easy choices in post-war Europe. France was to prove to be relatively lucky in de Gaulle making his stand during the summer of 1940.

The British government continued to probe the world as it tried to discover how the colonial French felt about de Gaulle. The British made inquiries in neutral Japan where it was discovered from Baron Guy Fain, Counsellor to the French Embassy in Tokyo, that there was no hostility towards de Gaulle. He was regarded as a good technician, a good officer, a patriot but not a statesman while some of his activities were considered to be 'stupid'.[22] No doubt this stupidity was a reference to de Gaulle's political activities.

There is further evidence concerning the suitability of de Gaulle as leader of the Free French from a Polish report, dated 11 November 1940 and originating from the Portuguese capital, Lisbon. The report was primarily about Soviet Foreign Minister Molotov, and his visit to Berlin that month. It should be remembered that Germany and the Soviet Union at this point of the war were allies and had jointly invaded and occupied Poland. The writer, possibly the Polish military attaché to neutral Portugal, noted that Molotov's visit to Berlin was one of a series of visits. Hitler had already visited Mussolini, Franco and Pétain on separate occasions. And now Molotov was visiting Hitler. The writer noted that these were the preliminary steps towards a 'New Europe' or, as was discussed, 'European Union', eventually leading to world domination.[23]

The question then should have been who was going to dominate whom as both Soviets and Nazis were committed to world domination. The observations made by 'K', possibly a lieutenant colonel of the Polish army (perhaps Lieutenant Colonel Jan Kowalewski, a brilliant intelligence officer) attracted further notice as the academic Professor Olgierd Gorka, working in exile in London, made significant observations on the meetings between the Nazis and their possible collaborators. Gorka believed that the success of Germany throughout 1940 represented an opportunity for reactionaries across Europe to re-set the clock. He noted the Vatican and Pétain particularly but was not certain how those two would react: he considered that the Vatican would be a distant observer while Pétain was already in two minds regarding the future. Having started out opposing Laval, Pétain was now considering events in Africa and was hovering between Weygand and de Gaulle. As early as November 1940, according to Gorka, Pétain could see that de Gaulle, taking advantage of French possessions in Africa, might well be the eventual winner in French circles.[24] However, as noted by W.H.B. Mack, Head of the French Department at the FO between 1940 and 1942, before a meeting with de Gaulle, there was a strong personal antipathy between de Gaulle and Weygand.[25]

This should not allow the Polish observations to be forgotten – the Poles, more than anybody, were aware of how the Nazis and Soviets operated and knew that it would only be a matter of time before there was war between Germany and the Soviet Union – a horrific war of destruction, mass killings and ideology which removed rational thought and decency. Gorka's observations of Pétain are incredible as it would seem that Pétain did not even believe in himself, or the Vichy regime, or Hitler to whom he was betraying his country. In reality, at this point de Gaulle had achieved very little but already the British had caused Germany a serious setback with the Battle of Britain in 1940. De Gaulle had nailed his colours firmly to those of Churchill and the UK. Pétain could already sense Germany's defeat.

After the meeting between Mack and de Gaulle it was considered by de Gaulle that Weygand was 'too old and too timid and would never initiate or lead any movement'. At the time of the 1940 armistice between France and Germany, Weygand was afraid of communism; later he was afraid that the Pétain government would fall, and that Germany would occupy all of France.[26] The fear of communism spreading into France had been a pre-war pre-occupation amongst the French ruling class and elites, of which the French officer corps must be included. Weygand was clearly yet to see that Germany was the greatest threat to France. Weygand was not alone as many European politicians had feared the spread of communism during the inter-war period but failed to notice the threat from Nazi Germany. Churchill, despite being a veteran anti-communist, was one of the few senior western politicians to recognise quickly the danger from Germany with the rise of Hitler during 1933.

The British authorities, anxious to weaken the Vichy regime, continuously sought to bolster the Free French whilst doing their best to damage Vichy France at every opportunity. At the beginning of December 1940 reliable information was received by the FO that Admiral Delaborde, commander of the Brest Naval Squadron, was due for retirement within a fortnight. It was considered that he could be persuaded to join de Gaulle. Speight minuted the British Foreign Secretary: 'It would be an excellent thing if we *could* get another French admiral instead of Muselier. He is a real handicap. Delaborde might conceivably act as a sort of counterweight to the poisonous Darlan'. A further minute noted that:

> This would be a feather in the cap for the Free French movement. If Admiral Delaborde is a popular figure, might have a favourable reaction in the Vichy navy, where anti-British feeling is particularly strong. It would of course make Admiral Muselier's position difficult at a time when our relations with him are improving, but we should scarcely wish to neglect such an opportunity for the sake of Admiral Muselier's sensitivities.[27]

However, it should be noted that, by late November 1940, de Gaulle was already taking his and France's future into his own hands as on 17 November he had broadcast from Brazzaville his own 'Organic Declaration' in which he assumed authority for the French Empire and established a Council of Imperial Defence. De Gaulle's broadcast impressed Churchill who minuted Lord Halifax stating, 'it shows de Gaulle in a light very different from that of an ordinary military man'.[28] Nevertheless, Sir Alexander Cadogan, permanent undersecretary at the FO, was against de Gaulle's move and declared him to be 'a loser'.[29] It was also considered to have been a virtual declaration of war against Vichy, but de Gaulle's overall aim in his declaration was to bind the Allies to his cause.[30] Even the Vichy French accepted de Gaulle's authority in Equatorial Africa as a *fait accompli*. As it was noted that the war against Italy was very popular in France, on the back of this information de Gaulle sought to build up his military forces in Africa.[31]

While it had been already noted that French officials serving the Vichy regime in North Africa had considered that the only way out of their predicament was a British victory, it was believed that Frenchmen in French North Africa suffered conflicting loyalties. Even though they were disgusted with Pierre Laval (twice Vichy prime minister and executed as a traitor by a French firing squad in 1945) and his pro-German policy, Pétain remained 'a figure of veneration' to them. It was considered that Weygand was 'slow' to do anything that might hurt the Marshal. Gascoigne, the British consul general in Tangiers, wrote to William Strang at the FO:

> if Weygand finally plays our game it may not, I suppose, be easy to fit de Gaulle into the scheme of things, although de Gaulle's patriotism should command his co-operation. The Comte de Paris' attitude towards

> Weygand is now satisfactory, and as a figure-head the former might be useful – looked at from here I believe that the majority of Frenchmen in North Africa who are sick to death of Republican politics might welcome a return to the Monarchy and from what little I have seen of the Comte de Paris I think that he might suit quite well.[32]

It is quite clear from the above narrative that de Gaulle was not the only possibility for the British government to consider as French wartime leader. Furthermore, it is quite clear that some were proposing a radical but unlikely motion that the Comte de Paris might be offered and accepted the French crown as an alternative to the perceived muddle of republican politics. It should also be considered that, by the end of 1940, popular British public opinion was running high against France. However, the FO recognised that, at the end of the war, despite 'the disgraceful treatment we have received at her hands' [France] the British and French will have to return to working together.[33] This is revealing as it was quite clear that the British government and the FO, even in those dark days of 1940, did not consider defeat and saw only victory against Germany. Once that was achieved, the FO knew that international relations in Europe would return as near normal as quickly as possible where the British and French governments were concerned.

However, it was becoming very clear to the British government that de Gaulle was determined to be the sole French leader in post-war France, as was illustrated when he sought to consolidate his position as head of the Free French in Africa with the establishment of the Council of Defence. Even if reports of it being a rival government were proven to be false, the British War Council noted that 'it was perhaps tiresome that he [de Gaulle] should have chosen this moment to set up a Council of Defence without prior consultation with us'.[34] As already discussed, de Gaulle had a 'splitting' effect on the French camp; he had the same effect on the British. Cadogan, who appeared to have taken an instant dislike to de Gaulle, declared of the Brazzaville telegram:

> that ass de Gaulle is contemplating 'summoning Weygand to declare himself'. Just exactly what de Gaulle should not do at this moment. Drafted a reply to that effect and sent it to P.M. (whose faith in de Gaulle – and – Spears – is, at least, I think, shaken).[35]

Cadogan was mistaken in his assumption.

De Gaulle's independent movement in Africa caused anxiety to the War Cabinet which was hoping to court Weygand, and de Gaulle's proposed action might well antagonise Weygand and push him in the opposite direction.

Churchill preferred that de Gaulle return to the UK for consultations on the general situation in Africa, but this was a pretext to get de Gaulle to discuss his position regarding Weygand. Lord Halifax, the Foreign Secretary, observed that de Gaulle's supporters in Cairo favoured a visit by de Gaulle but there was also something to be said for his return to the UK once his position in West Africa was settled. Halifax was invited by Churchill to draft a personal telegram from the prime minister to de Gaulle, urging him to return to London for talks.[36]

By the end of 1940, once the situation in France and the French Empire was reviewed, it was noted that de Gaulle's fame was spreading rapidly amongst French youth 'but is retarded by the traditional French objection to a soldier setting himself up in opposition to the *de facto* Government, especially a soldier hitherto unknown to the French people at large'. It was also observed that the politics of the Free French were somewhat suspect while de Gaulle was considered to favour a return to the pre-war status quo in French politics, which was seen by many to have been the prime reason for the French defeat earlier that year. The French Navy was still considered to be disciplined by the British authorities, but under Darlan very anti-British.[37] The situation between the UK and France was obviously complicated and unsure by the end of 1940 but so much had changed during that year. Events in 1941 were to render the Free French the junior party amongst the Allies but confirm de Gaulle as its leader.

In the months after Dakar the British reluctantly began to see that, from within the Free French camp, de Gaulle was the best option as leader. With the Allies fighting the Italians in Africa and doing well, the only good news regarding land fighting for the Allies, and with Free French participation, the War Cabinet decided that it would be good for French morale if de Gaulle made his long anticipated visit to his forces in North Africa. It suited the British government if the visit could be undertaken during late December.[38] As ever, whatever de Gaulle and the Free French might have wanted was irrelevant to the British government.

The idea of capturing North Africa from the Italians and the Vichy French as well as ensuring the safety of Egypt and the Suez Canal area had been on the table since the Fall of France. Alfred Duff Cooper, the Minister of Information, after a visit to French Morocco and with the approval of the government sought a way to continue the war from North Africa. His overall assessment was that the atmosphere in the area was negative with French flags being flown at half-mast and no sign of welcome being made towards him. French officials made no commitments regarding fighting on in North Africa.

Indeed, those French living in North Africa seemed dazed by the defeat of France and had no idea of what should happen next.[39]

This clearly meant that the British and the Free French should take command of the local situation since clearly in Africa the Italians were the enemy while the Vichy French were certainly a threat but remained unpredictable. Nobody was sure just what the Vichy French were going to do with their North African territories. It seemed that, in the unlikely event of North Africa being handed over to de Gaulle, Germany would intervene militarily. Sir Samuel Hoare, the Ambassador to Spain, reported that the Spanish foreign minister and the Portuguese Ambassador to Spain were convinced that a de Gaulle march into Morocco would be immediately followed by a German march through Spain.[40] A German move such as that would no doubt have removed Vichy and Spanish sovereignty at a stroke.

Therefore, it was in British interests to take control in North Africa as early as possible, especially with the fear that Vichy might negotiate away their strategic bases in North Africa into German hands. It became obvious that the British had to treat the Vichy French as the enemy.[41] There was hope that, if the British could detach Weygand from Vichy, he might bring with him French North Africa and Syria.[42] However, it was noted by General Spears that, unless Germany directly threatened North Africa, it was unlikely that Weygand would march – his ultimate loyalties remained unclear.[43]

During early 1941, whilst discussing propaganda for French North Africa, the British Chiefs of Staff wanted North Africa to be with the UK as soon as possible but propaganda had to be dealt with carefully as the British did not want to set French officers against men of the Vichy army or local Arabs against the French.[44] A further report on the situation in North Africa suggested that the greatest chance of victory would be if French North Africa and the French fleet joined the British in the war against Germany.[45] The situation with the Vichy French had been confused for some time, especially as Sir Hughe Knatchbull-Hugessen, the British Ambassador to Turkey, reported that Pétain was convinced of a British victory and that Pétain was really in sympathy with de Gaulle. The same report also confirmed that the Germans had abandoned the idea of invading the UK and were preparing defensive positions along the Channel coast. It was also asserted that the Germans had handed in invasion barges and other amphibious invasion paraphernalia.[46] This should have also suggested that the Germans had other plans regarding the war and, given Hitler's own words in his diatribe, *Mein Kampf*, it should have been obvious that the Soviet Union was endangered already – a full six months before the German invasion of the country in June 1941. But no one picked up on this and probably did not even consider that the Germans would invade the Soviet

Union at that time. During the spring of 1941 Stalin was warned from various sources that Hitler was planning to invade the Soviet Union but he declined to heed these warnings.

To further muddy the waters between the UK and Vichy French, in early January 1941, Cadogan recorded that telegrams had been received from Tangiers to the effect that Weygand had decided to 're-enter the war' but could do nothing until he received materials: and how were the British to supply him? This question was passed to the Chiefs of Staff to study while further reports indicated that Germany and Italy were going to attack Tunisia. The FO warned both Weygand and Vichy of this intention.[47] This is interesting as, even though Vichy was perceived as an enemy, it was not in the same class as Germany and Italy. It also revealed that Weygand was still seen as a potential ally. Clearly, it remained the case that the British government, despite its alliance with de Gaulle, still deemed it necessary to have back-channels with Vichy and not totally halt relations with the Vichy government.

Nevertheless, Churchill continued to support de Gaulle as leader of the Free French. After actions in both Djibouti and Syria, Churchill stressed the importance of de Gaulle and of upholding his authority, announcing that 'we have signed a solemn undertaking to support him and due weight must be given to his views and advice'.[48] This clear evidence of how Churchill saw de Gaulle and, to a certain extent, how the War Cabinet was expected to see him – a public contradiction of Churchill was unthinkable – and he knew it.

Churchill was probably responding to an earlier communiqué in which Major Douglas Morton, a senior advisor and long-term friend, after seeing de Gaulle, reported that the French leader was unhappy with propaganda being sent to France by the Ministry of Information via the press and radio. De Gaulle considered that he should be further involved in propaganda relating to France. Furthermore, de Gaulle was reported to want to play an active role in the 'military field' and was 'chafing at his impotence'.[49]

De Gaulle's impotence was to increase after June 1941 when France became less important to the alliance, once Germany invaded the Soviet Union. By the end of the year the USA, after being attacked by Japan, was dragged into the war. De Gaulle did little to help himself and the cause of the Free French when, to the surprise and embarrassment of the US government, he offered use of French bases in French West Africa to the Americans. This move seemed to snub the British, but Africa was the key to further operations to win the war since Italy was the weakest link on that continent.

Chapter 5

North Africa: War and Politics

Africa had been the scene of land fighting since 1940. As we have already seen, de Gaulle tried and failed to seize French West Africa at Dakar in September. However, fighting had been taking place in Africa since 10 June 1940 once Italy declared war on the UK. In many ways this was what the British had hoped for. On 14 June 1940, the 11th Hussars with 1st King's Royal Rifle Corps crossed into Italian-held Libya and captured Fort Capuzzo. The Italians counter-attacked, moving into Egypt on 9 September and, with that, the Commonwealth forces of the UK, Australia, New Zealand and South Africa with Indian troops, redoubled their efforts against Italian armed forces in Africa. Eventually huge elements of the Italian Tenth Army were destroyed. The Italian defeat led to German intervention which saw the arrival of what was to be widely known as the *Afrikakorps* but properly titled *Deutsches Afrikakorps* (DAK), commanded by the recently promoted Lieutenant General Erwin Rommel. The Germans were sent to North Africa to prop up the Italians. The reinforcement, code-named SONNENBLUME, was designed to prevent a total Axis rout in North Africa.

The fighting in North Africa was to decide the fate of Europe. If the Axis powers had prevailed, it would have been impossible for the Allies to have opened a second front as demanded by the Soviet dictator, Stalin, as the Soviet Union was fighting a brutal war against the invading Germans on Soviet territory. The Middle East and North Africa in 1941 were to be key for the successes enjoyed later by the Allies and this included the French territories in the Middle East. However, this meant that de Gaulle had to be brought to heel. The British government, concerned that de Gaulle had too much free rein, planned to put an end to this, even if de Gaulle had to be replaced.

It was considered by many in the British establishment that the Free French programme of the BBC or independent movements such as *France Libre* were good examples of best practice and assets in the British media war effort while de Gaulle was seen by some as a liability. The British were concerned that de Gaulle was more interested in settling scores with Vichy and not with fighting the Germans. Furthermore, he was liable to glorify himself while he was quite anti-British, anti-democratic and vain, in the view of senior British military and political actors. In his relationship with Churchill some considered de Gaulle to be personally disloyal to the British prime minister since, after an interview with Churchill, de Gaulle openly boasted to his own people that he had 'gained the day' and had put Churchill on the defensive.

As a leader it was generally agreed amongst the British authorities that de Gaulle was a failure, as illustrated by the insignificant numbers of 'white Frenchmen' who had rallied to him. It was further considered that de Gaulle's military and civil personnel were 'puppets', dependent on him. It was decided that these staff were useless except for the naval staff under Admiral Muselier working from Westminster House where the atmosphere was wholesome compared with the poison found at de Gaulle's headquarters at Carlton Gardens. It was noted that Muselier's poor health was an obvious problem but, nevertheless, he worked well with the Admiralty while his chief of staff, Moret, whom de Gaulle detested, was said to be the most efficient staff officer in the Free French forces. Many Free French personnel would have preferred to have served in British units while it was also noted that a number of Free Frenchmen in the UK and outside de Gaulle's ranks were quite anti-de Gaulle. This also applied to many French people in the USA and other parts of the world. Simply, de Gaulle was not universally loved.

In France, most of the population was believed to have been primarily pro-British and, to a lesser degree, pro-Free French and, to a considerably lesser degree, pro-de Gaulle. However, de Gaulle rose in popularity when his name was invoked in France as symbolic of French hostility towards Germany. Most people in France looked to the UK for liberation. The British considered that many living in occupied France thought that de Gaulle, living with his family in the UK, was lucky not to be living in occupied France. Therefore, many considered that this meant that a French leader in post-war France should not come from the ranks of those who had lived in exile but from those who had endured the German occupation. This was a theme not restricted to French circles after 1945.

It was agreed that the agreement between the British government and the Free French of August 1940 was out of date and proving to be unsatisfactory. It had forced the Free French to serve a man imposed on them by the British government, who had proved to be a failure as far as the British was concerned. The National Committee at the time was subservient to de Gaulle, some through self-interest, some because they were dominated by de Gaulle's personality, while a few actually believed in him. It was considered that, unless the relationship between the UK government and the Free French movement improved, there was a danger that the Free French might break up as a unified body. Experience had shown that without complete British control the movement was liable to hamper rather than assist the British war effort.

In 1940 there had been an underlying belief that de Gaulle would fight alongside the British as the military leader of those Frenchmen who had rallied to him but 'instead of leading French troops into battle, he dwells on alien soil as the mimic head of a non-existent state'. Therefore, it was considered that there might be a reversion to the principle of military leadership. The idea of a 'Foreign Legion' had long appealed to many non-de Gaullists and so it was considered that the Free French military force could be translated into a 'French Legion' under de Gaulle's command. In turn, de Gaulle would be under the command of the British commander-in-chief. This meant that de Gaulle's representations would have to go through normal British military channels and so to the War Office.[1] At a stroke, de Gaulle would be under British control.

It was also considered that the problem of French forces in North Africa, nominally under Vichy control, could be resolved if they decided to enter the war on the side of the Allies. Furthermore, it was considered that French naval forces from North Africa should come under the command of Admiral Muselier who would continue to co-ordinate its activities with the Admiralty. The question of the French Air Force was much simpler since it was attached to the RAF, while the administration of Free French colonies was to be conducted by General Catroux. The Free French relationship with the UK government was to be conducted in Africa by a mission of experts under a diplomat to deal with the daily problems of the various departments and, when practical, represent the views of French leaders in the area. Then, after some consideration, de Gaulle could be dropped but caution was added as it would mean that the symbolic nature of de Gaulle's name would also be lost and that might aid enemy propaganda as the Germans probed for weaknesses amongst the Free French. It was made quite clear that, despite problems with de Gaulle, it would be very difficult to replace him. Nevertheless, it was considered that Catroux might fill de Gaulle's position.[2] Churchill largely agreed with Morton's note.[3]

However, the years 1940 and 1941 were to colour the relationship between de Gaulle and Churchill as the war twisted and turned in various unexpected ways. Part of the narrative has to do with the French mandates of Lebanon and Syria, the Levant as it was termed frequently at the time, and seemed to entwine two quite separate peoples into one whilst the opposite was the reality. The knock-on effect of the French mandate is still being realised even today in the Middle East with Syria frequently accused of interfering in the affairs of Lebanon, often with deadly consequences. We pick up the story for the purposes of this narrative with a cable sent from Cairo by General Spears to de Gaulle informing him that there was no need for Free French forces to remain in Syria. Furthermore, even though Spears claimed that he was happy to see de Gaulle, there was no need for him to be in Cairo then or any time in the near future. Spears' attitude was not isolated, and he was clearly working on the behalf of Churchill who had already cabled President Roosevelt with his concerns about Syria. Churchill was worried that Admiral Darlan might allow the Axis powers to invest Syria if possible. There were already signs that Vichy was willing to co-operate with Germany in the Middle East. Churchill also feared that Germany might try to seize the Azores and Cape Verde Islands if they were to attack Spain or try to convince the Spanish to join the war.[4]

During May 1941 German aircraft had already begun to land in Syria but the British, using Free French forces under British command, moved from Transjordan into Syria, aided by British logistical, military and air support to counter this. The British Defence Committee considered the opportunity to be 'too good to miss and the advance must be regarded as a political coup in which time is all important rather than a military operation'. After this the committee began to seek a French declaration of independence for both Syria and Lebanon.[5] By this move, the British had managed to forestall a German advance into the Middle East, from which the Germans would have endangered the British position in the area. Furthermore, if the Germans had been successful in their occupation of Syria, a month later it would have been very difficult to have defended the Soviet Union when the Germans invaded in June 1941. Not surprisingly, de Gaulle was furious and replied to Spears, saying that he had no intention of returning to Cairo in view of the British unilateral action in Syria and Djibouti.[6]

Events in Syria occupied the minds of the British, the French and, to a certain extent, the Germans. Perhaps even the Soviet government might have considered the consequences of Syria falling into German hands but given the narrow understanding of the world by so many Soviet leading political and military actors, this cannot be certain. Syria was, however, of great importance to the war. Had it fallen to the Germans, it may well have provided a gateway to the Middle East, to the heart of the Soviet Union, via the Caucasus mountains, and, if one follows the thought of General Claude Auchinleck, the supply line from India to Egypt was also threatened by any German occupation of Syria.[7] The question before the British government was one of trying to read the intentions of the Vichy French in relation to Syria and other territories in the Middle East and East Africa held by the Vichy regime. A telegram from Sir Miles Lampson to Churchill on 1 April 1941 laid out some of the problems between the British, the Free French and Vichy. Lampson stated:

> In the light of [the] delicate situation in Syria and the presence in Cairo of General de Gaulle who arrived today, it would be of special help to me to learn of repercussions and our relationships with Vichy Government after recent attack by [the] French on British warships in [the] Western Mediterranean. May I be kept informed?
>
> May I also learn whether we have any recent indications of General Weygand's attitude?[8]

There were many areas of anxiety for the Allies at this time. De Gaulle was not understood; there was still a chance to retrieve something out of the Vichy regime and the UK government was continuously looking for a French leader who might possibly replace de Gaulle. This was to misunderstand totally the attraction of de Gaulle to many French people, especially those living under German occupation, while, regarding Vichy activity, there was a deal of worry about how the Vichy, especially Darlan, were going to dispose of large modern warships remaining at their disposal in North Africa.

Lampson telegraphed Churchill once more in relation to the situation in the Middle East. De Gaulle's visit to the region was reported with Lampson commenting on its progress as the French leader visited Egypt and Palestine and was able to meet General Georges Catroux, commander-in-chief of the Free French forces in the Levant. Lampson noted that de Gaulle was given every courtesy in his meeting with Catroux and was seen for over an hour. He was aware that this meeting had been arranged via Churchill. During the meeting, the situation in Djibouti was discussed. This was another area of interest to the British. Of Syria, Lampson stated that Syria was very perplexing but a valuable prize if gained. If Syria rallied to the Free French, Lampson wrote 'at a stroke establish a land connection with Turkey, obtain control of a breeding ground of Axis intrigue in the Arab world and give impetus to the Free French who would obtain some troops and materials'.

However, the question was how to proceed in Syria as Lampson observed that the solution was not to occupy Syria and trying to appease the Vichy authorities there would not go far. Vichy authorities were all for a 'stable Syria' while the Germans were trying to destabilise the country. Regarding Weygand, Lampson claimed that he was seen as a 'broken reed' with neither de Gaulle nor Catroux having any hope in him. An indication of how difficult Syria was is seen by the fact that in 1941 both de Gaulle and Catroux declared to be 'at an opportune moment in favour of Syrian independence after the war on some such lines as Egypt or Iraq treaties'. Both Lampson and General Wavell, the Commander-in-Chief of the Middle East Theatre, were in favour of this pronouncement but questions remained with many from the Free French not in favour of the notion of Syrian independence, even if it was very unclear when and how that might happen. Lampson concluded that de Gaulle was on his way to Palestine and, on his return, Lampson was to discuss with him the question of Syria and the need for 'a more active policy' there from the Free French.[9]

The question of Syria was to run from the spring into the summer of 1941, as can be seen from telegrams from General Wavell to Churchill and vice versa. Part of the problem was that, by May 1941, the British and their allies were desperately fighting to prevent being ejected from the Mediterranean area with desperate fighting on the Greek island of Crete. On 21 May Churchill reported the decision by the Defence Committee that nothing in Syria must distract the battle of Crete. The Defence Committee did allow for British troops to 'mingle' with Free French troops who were to enter Syria but declared that Wavell was wrong to suppose that the policy over Syria came from representations from Free French leaders or by Spears to de Gaulle.[10]

Wavell was unimpressed with Churchill regarding the Free French and Syria and said so. In a return telegram Wavell observed the impracticality of the plans of the Free French. He noted that the Germans had already established their air force in Syria and expressed his fears that Turkey was complicit in the German entry into Syria. Wavell referred to the importance of holding Crete, as well as the difficulty on holding Egypt against enemy bases established in Greece. He considered that the Free French and their plans were unrealistic. Wavell had also seen a telegram sent by de Gaulle from Brazzaville to Spears in which de Gaulle had enquired angrily why Free French troops were not on their way to the Syrian capital, Damascus. De Gaulle was implying that Wavell was preventing Free French troops from taking advantage of the opportunity (the fighting in Crete) to occupy Syria. Laying out his case, Wavell stated:

> I felt that Free French views were perhaps given undue weight and that I was very committed to unsound military action on unverified information at a time when Crete, Iraq and the Western Desert required all resources and attention.

Wavell conceded that the situation was different to that viewed by the Free French but, overall, considered that the situation in Syria was 'disquieting'. He pointed out that the German Air Force established there were closer to the Suez Canal and the Suez area than they would be at Mersa Matruh, on the Egyptian Mediterranean coast. In Wavell's opinion, the local French were 'wholly committed to the Germans'. Therefore, Wavell was moving reinforcements to Palestine after full discussion with his fellow local service chiefs, Tedder, Cunningham and Blamey, in which it was decided 'we feel we must be prepared for action against Syria and weak action is useless'. Wavell considered the implications of a German occupation of Syria; this included the loss of Cyprus since the island could not be reinforced as there were not enough troops in the area. Overall, the entire position in the Middle East in Wavell's opinion was governed by air power and airbases.[11]

And that was the thing the Germans had established an airbase in Syria but were yet to use it. The Allies had to ensure that that did not happen and certainly could not allow the Germans to begin to land ground forces, either by sea or air, and eventually establish a naval port. The loss of Cyprus, of course, would have been a disaster for the British as from there they could monitor the eastern Mediterranean and deny the Axis powers use of the Suez Canal. The loss of Cyprus would have meant the loss of the canal, Egypt and, probably, India once the Japanese joined the Axis powers at the end of 1941. The Free French had to help to prevent this and thus the retention of Syria was to be fundamental to this. However, as Churchill pointed out, that, although he supported Wavell over de Gaulle, Wavell was told that 'you had better have de Gaulle close to you'.[12] Churchill at least still recognised the value of de Gaulle.

The question of Syria continued to rumble on during May while the fighting in Crete raged. Spears sent a telegram to de Gaulle, but the true recipient was Churchill. In this message Spears wrote of some of the problem of transporting Free French troops to Syria:

> Absolutely essential question as far as the Free French are concerned is one of transport. It was suggested that Free French should be ferried which would mean less transport. De Gaulle would not accept this as it would mean arriving piecemeal before possibly stronger positions and giving the impression of weakness to professional Syrian troops. It would therefore limit or nullify any possibility of manoeuvring.[13]

Wavell was left with the logistics of advancing into Syria with Churchill asking what ground and air forces were being used for Operation EXPORTER, the codename for the Allied and Free French advance. He was also asked what he was doing about Polish troops in the area while, at all times, air power was the watchword and key to success in the region.[14] Wavell's reply was slightly delayed, but he gave a full answer to Churchill and listed all the ground forces and air forces being used for EXPORTER and BRUISER, the follow-up to the advance into Syria. The Free French Brigade Group consisted of three battalions of infantry, one battery of artillery with some trucks, one squadron of armoured cars and some anti-aircraft artillery. Wavell said of the Poles that they were, he thought, in the Western Desert at Matruh. He also complained of the BBC's coverage of de Gaulle's 'secret trip' to Palestine.[15]

Clearly, the BBC were not as sensitive to the nature of de Gaulle's visit but surely the security services should have insisted that such a report did not go out. It is also clear that the Free French did not have much in the way of men or equipment while the question of the Poles is interesting. The Poles, prior to the establishment of the Anders' Army after June 1941, were limited in number and, like the Free French, refugees from their own country who had elected to fight on. Most had made their way to France between September 1939 and June 1940 from whence a vastly reduced number made their way to the UK after the Fall of France. The British, as with the Free French, had accepted them as Allies to fight off a German invasion of the UK if necessary but, once that threat receded, were at a loss to know what to do with them. The Poles in the Middle East, the Kopański Brigade, so named after their commander, General Stefan Kopański, had left Poland for French territory but, after France had signed the 1940 Armistice with the Germans, the Kopański Brigade, fearing at least internment by the Vichy regime, left Syria and marched to Palestine, a British mandate. Once in Palestine, the Poles offered their service to the British. Kopański's men were later to distinguish themselves at Tobruk.

Syria was not only proving to be a tough nut to crack militarily but French military-politics began to raise its ugly head. Wavell informed Churchill that General Catroux had assumed the title of 'High Commissioner of Syria'. This had caused objections from those living in Syria while Wavell observed that Spears had failed to persuade de Gaulle to change Catroux's title.[16] Churchill asked de Gaulle to intervene in the question of Catroux's title of high commissioner.[17] The question of Allied intervention in Syria continued as Spears telegraphed to de Gaulle; the message also went to Churchill that the Free French were undermining the British position regarding future Syrian independence. De Gaulle riposted, somewhat rudely, 'you are going into Syria because I consent that you do so.'[18]

Most of the time, de Gaulle was abrupt in his dealings with his allies. He thought, or gave the sense, that he knew better, that all things French were sacrosanct and that the British should keep their distance. But this would be unfair. Even if Spears grew to hate de Gaulle, in 1941 he was still willing to defend him and observe some of the problems which he faced and how they felt. Spears still considered de Gaulle 'a man of his word [who] will not go back on it'. He also wrote that 'De Gaulle confided in me the agony he was going through because of his shame at the way that his compatriots are behaving. He put this forward as an excuse for his difficult moods'.[19] Anyone in a close and difficult relationship will understand this as a loved one's bad behaviour is defended in public but in private perhaps the matter is treated differently.

Churchill also kept faith with de Gaulle and, on 6 June, wished him success in the joint venture in Syria. He also promised not to exploit the tragic position of France and further pledged support for the Free French grant of independence to Syria and Lebanon.[20] De Gaulle responded in the same way and agreed to restyle General Catroux's title to that of *'Delegue et Plenipotentiare'* in Syria. He also vowed to respect the neutrality of both Syria and Lebanon in return for a guarantee of the special interests of France in order to maintain French morale. De Gaulle told Churchill, 'The harder you strike at Vichy, the more necessary is it to safeguard the interests and feelings of France. Despair is a bad counsellor.' De Gaulle also agreed that, in his proclamation to French troops, General Catroux should only be designated as commander-in-chief.[21] However, one should remember that Catroux was a rival to de Gaulle.

The question of Syria was not one that fixated the British and the French or, to a lesser extent, Germany, but one should also remember the extended British commitment to the Middle East. One of the countries, via imperial ties, in alliance with the UK was Australia. Australian troops were deployed in the Middle East and, therefore, the Syrian operation was of interest to the Australian government. In a series of telegrams known as 'Winch', which were complete, confidential and personal, between Churchill and Robert Menzies, the Australian prime minister, Churchill kept Menzies abreast of the war. Syria is an example of this. Churchill told Menzies that the outcome in Syria was dependent on 'which way the two French cats jump',[22] the cats being the Free French and Vichy. Menzies was informed that the Allies were moving into Syria the next morning, 8 June. Despite moving in in 'considerable force', Churchill could not guarantee the outcome of the operation since much depended on how the French reacted.[23]

Equally, Churchill kept the American president in the loop regarding the war. Churchill had courted Roosevelt since 1940 while Roosevelt was playing a dangerous game politically since many Americans wanted nothing to do with the war. Roosevelt was determined to aid the UK as far as he dare. This was, of course, to change in December following the Japanese attack on the USA and the German and Italian declarations of war on the USA. However, Syria was in early June, only a few weeks before Germany invaded the Soviet Union. Roosevelt was still waging his secret war against Germany and her allies.

On 7 June, Churchill telegraphed Roosevelt giving his notice of the Allied move into Syria the following day. He also told Roosevelt of the Free French assurances of independence for the Levant and thanked Roosevelt for Averell Harriman's mission to the Middle East.[24] Harriman was Roosevelt's special

General de Gaulle lands in France at Courseulles in the Juno Beach Sector, 14 June 1944.
(*NAM 2006-12-98-9*)

General de Gaulle at Juno Beach saluting from the passenger seat of a Jeep.
(*NAM 2006-12-98-32*)

Second Lieutenant Winston Churchill, 4th Queen's Own Hussars, 1895. (*NAM 1992-10-143-1547*)

Winston Churchill in South Africa, *c.*1900. (*NAM 1980-02-72-8*)

Photograph of war correspondents returning on the RMS *Donottar Castle* from the Boer War, 1900. Churchill can be seen in the middle row, second from the left. (*NAM 1965-08-63-1*)

Photograph of Lord Gort and General Gamelin, North-West Europe, 1939–40. (*NAM 1985-04-49-49*)

From the shores of wartime Britain coastal guns look out, ready to repel any threat of invasion. (*NAM 2006-12-102-11*)

General Bernard Montgomery, *c*.1942. (*NAM 2008-12-200-72*)

Photograph of Alan Deere's crashed Spitfire, 1940. (*NAM 2001-03-39-12*)

A French officer holding a flag of truce while being driven around the town of Majunga (Mahajanga), Madagascar, 10 September 1942. (*NAM 2002-06-6-24*)

A King's African Rifleman covering a road with his rifle, Madagascar. (*NAM 1963-01-55-81*)

A mine explodes close to a British artillery tractor as it advances through enemy minefields at El Alamein, 1942. (*NAM 2005-05-25-2*)

Three British destroyers return to Algiers harbour to refuel after hunting down enemy convoys in the Mediterranean, 1942. (*NAM 2002-2-06-67*)

Landing Ship Infantry, en route from Newhaven to Gold Beach, June 1944. (*NAM 2001-02-351-8*)

British troops entering Caen, 9 July 1944. (*NAM 1986-11-15-9*)

The road to Chambois cleared by the 53rd (Welsh) Division, 21–25 August 1944. (*NAM 1979-12-74-7*)

advisor for Europe. Churchill explained the Syrian campaign and told Roosevelt that it was necessary to invade Syria to prevent further German penetration. The outcome of the operation was uncertain since much depended on local French troops and if they chose to oppose the attacking Allies. Churchill was aware that de Gaulle and the Free French were not universally popular throughout the French Empire. Perhaps he feared another Dakar. De Gaulle, in a proclamation to the Arabs, had offered in 'the name of France' complete independence and an opportunity to decide for themselves just how they wished to see their futures – a number of states or one large free Arab state. Churchill also had concerns about how the Vichy government might retaliate and feared attacks on Gibraltar or Freetown and, therefore, requested that Roosevelt keep American pressure on the Vichy government. He concluded by stressing that the UK had no interests in Syria beyond denying the Germans an asset.[25]

Churchill was quite right in how he approached Roosevelt as he needed to keep Roosevelt on side. The USA, still neutral, continued to recognise the Vichy government, but it was rather a one-sided affair with the Americans being able to bully the Vichy French, often in favour of the UK. Roosevelt, as we shall see, had a personal dislike for the French, especially de Gaulle, so Churchill had to tread carefully when he evoked the Free French leader's name in discussions with him. Furthermore, Roosevelt, as with many Americans at that time, was very anti-imperialism, despite the USA actually acquiring their own overseas territories. Thus, he viewed an incursion into other lands with suspicion and was always alive to the British and French trying to acquire further colonies, the very reason Churchill assured Roosevelt that the UK had no interest in Syria, beyond winning the war.

Churchill, however, still had to deal with de Gaulle and keep him and the Free French happy. In a telegram from de Gaulle to Churchill, it is clear that the British prime minister had previously sent de Gaulle a message of support regarding Syria. De Gaulle thanked Churchill for his message and was quite desirous to ensure Churchill of the Free French resolve to fight and conquer 'at your side'.[26] Spears was also anxious that the Allies secure Syria as he informed Churchill that de Gaulle considered that any Vichy concession to the US government might be a method of buying time to ensure that the German government was able to fulfil its plans for Syria. Those plans appeared to be wanting Syria as a base and a threat to the Middle East. De Gaulle was very uncertain of Weygand with whom the British had hoped to work and stated that he thought:

it is possible that Weygand, whose resolution not to fight applies even to the British, may have been *frightened* of the consequences of Darlan's calling to Vichy, his creature Abrial, Boisson and Esteva to counteract Weygand's plainly timid attitude.[27]

Once operations began in Syria, co-operation and messages continued. Churchill assured Menzies that the capture of the Syrian airfields was essential for the defence of Cyprus.[28] De Gaulle was also kept happy as, once more, he thanked Churchill for his messages and speeches of support. He also took the opportunity to brief Churchill on the situation in Syria from the French perspective. De Gaulle considered that the situation in both Syria and Lebanon was developing favourably and urged that any request for an armistice from General Fernand Dentz, the Vichy French High Commissioner in Syria, should be refused. De Gaulle stated, 'I think that he will ask to re-embark his troops and send them back to France. In my view this should not be accepted at any price. All troops must remain.' However, de Gaulle said that no officer or man would be forced to join the Free French and that all war materials should be 'handed over intact'.[29]

However, in a telegram to Roosevelt, Churchill revealed that he had hoped for a more rapid progress in Syria but, equally, was grateful that Vichy had not retaliated outside Syria.[30] The Syrian campaign ended in an armistice which led to de Gaulle being furious once again when he learned that the armistice proposals had been sent to Washington DC without his permission. Indeed, Spears wrote that de Gaulle was 'cut to the quick' and went further when he reported a conversation that he'd had with de Gaulle. The Free French leader had noted that Free French troops had been involved in the operation and, therefore,

> the whole of France is involved, he told me. Yet he was not consulted on the vital question of the armistice terms. He is very depressed and wonders whether he can ever hope to collaborate successfully with the British.[31]

De Gaulle was certainly down in the dumps as he often felt that his honour and that of France was ignored by the British when it came to operations involving the Free French and that their needs were ignored since the British pressed ahead with their own agenda. He was not wrong, but the British had a war to win; the French had lost theirs in 1940.

However, the terms of the armistice were generous: Allied forces were to occupy both Syria and Lebanon, but Vichy French forces were allowed to retain their personal weapons although surrendering all other war materials to the Allies; those were either destroyed or re-deployed by the British. All Allied prisoners were to be released while French prisoners were to be freed once the occupation of the Levant was completed. All public services, as well as airfields, aircraft and fuel stocks, were to be handed over to the Allies. Every French soldier and civilian was given the choice of joining de Gaulle or being repatriated to France.[32] Those were very good terms, but de Gaulle had not been consulted and had his own ideas of how events in Syria should unfold.

De Gaulle tried making his case to Churchill for future policy in Syria. He merely wanted the establishment of a British liaison mission, in which General Catroux was to define British involvement in Syria.

De Gaulle made his case:

> The manner in which British policy develops towards Syria will be a criterion of very great importance. It is the first time that British forces united to those of the Free French are penetrating into a territory submitted to French authority. It is further the case that tendencies of British policy in Syria have rarely coincided with tendencies of the French policy. For this double reason French opinion and International opinion are watching carefully the attitude which Great Britain will take towards the position of France in this region.
>
> If, to the satisfaction of Vichy, Berlin and Rome, our common action in Syria and Lebanon seems to result in the diminution of the position of France and introduction there of tendencies and action which are purely British, I am convinced that the effect on the opinion in my country will be disastrous. I must add that my own effort, which consists in maintaining, morally and materially, French resistance at the side of England against our enemies would be gravely compromised.[33]

De Gaulle may have been morally and even legally correct in his arguments over Syria but realistically he had little to offer except territory. The Free French were equipped, armed and transported by the British while many French people living in occupied France, as we have seen, looked to the UK and not de Gaulle for liberation. Early in the Syrian campaign Churchill had, unknown to de Gaulle, questioned the French commitment to the operation when he asked Wavell about rumours published in British newspapers to the effect that the Syrian operation was going slow to avoid shedding French blood. Churchill needed an answer to this question since the affair was likely to have been debated in the next session of Parliament. Churchill, in his telegram, stated, 'I hope that I may receive your assurances that military considerations alone rule.'[34] In the absence of Wavell, his deputy, General Blamey, assured

Churchill that there was no truth in the rumour and that Allied forces in Syria could not go any faster as Vichy forces were resisting strongly.[35]

De Gaulle informed Churchill that it was important to organise relations between Catroux, who exercised power in the name of France in the Middle East, and the British authorities who were interested in Syria temporarily and only by reason of the circumstances of the war.[36] This was something which Churchill could work with; he knew that realistically he had the upper-hand but also wanted to avoid unnecessary antagonism with the Free French as well as Vichy. It was also best if Syria could be taken avoiding German intervention. To this end, Churchill concurred with de Gaulle and stated that, in the light of the declaration by General Catroux on allied entry into Syria, a satisfactory solution should be reached over that country.[37]

The negotiations over Syria had been difficult. On 12 July, General Dentz, the local Vichy commander, agreed to suspend hostilities but did not want to negotiate with the Free French. This offer was refused and so Dentz had to have a rethink. A further discussion included the Free French commander, General Catroux. The British General Sir Henry Wilson initialled this on 13 July and, on 14 July, General Wilson and Vichy representatives signed an agreement for the cessation of hostilities in Syria. This meant that the British minister of state for the Middle East, Oliver Lyttelton, was able to inform Churchill that the treaty had been negotiated with the above personalities and de Gaulle.[38] Churchill was alive to the situation in Syria and sent a telegram to Lyttelton which he suggested might be sent to de Gaulle but at Lyttelton's discretion. Churchill had noted that much of the problem at the Syrian conference lay with the mutual antagonism between Vichy and Free French. There was a further layer of trouble as Syrian people disliked all the French, whether Vichy or Free French, which Churchill considered to be 'strongly marked' while the gallantry of the Free French went unnoticed.[39] It should not be surprising that local Syrians hated the French; the Syrians wanted their country back.

However, all was not going well regarding the Syrian armistice, as Lyttelton reported to Churchill. In a meeting between de Gaulle, General Larminat, governor general of French Equatorial Africa, and General Spears, heading the British Military Mission in Syria and Lebanon, the Free French rejected the Syrian armistice, and further threatened to break their alliance with the UK. Eventually, renegotiations ended in agreement. After this slight hiccup with the Free French, Lyttelton wrote of the problem with de Gaulle:

> He had worked himself into a state of bitter hostility to everything English, he had the appearance of not having slept; and it was impossible to make him see any reason on any points. In the course of

these discussions General de Gaulle stated that he considered himself perfectly free to negotiate if it suited Free French interests, with Vichy representatives in Syria and to move his troops without any reference to the British wherever and whenever he chose.

Lyttelton wrote that careful negotiations made de Gaulle see sense, but only after a particularly stormy scene when Lyttelton pointed out that de Gaulle was more or less breaking off relations with the British government. He thought that de Gaulle was neither thinking nor bluffing at that point. De Gaulle was rude to Lyttelton while de Larminat was thoroughly frightened by the events unfolding before him. Lyttelton admitted that it seemed that everyone was 'over-tired' which had led to such tense negotiations.[40] Churchill agreed with Lyttleton's rough dealing of de Gaulle and told him so, writing 'Do not therefore allow him to upset or impede our policy in Syria. On this basis you should do your utmost to keep him in a good mood, making full allowance for the difficulties of his position.'[41] Clearly, Churchill had great sympathy and his difficult position since basically de Gaulle was waging a civil war as Frenchmen fought Frenchmen, albeit on someone else's territory marked as French mandate, as in the case of Syria.

De Gaulle, however, was quite willing to offer Churchill advice as he suggested that Dentz's army should not be repatriated since Vichy troops were following German orders and would turn up at Tunis, Fort Lamy, Dakar or at Beirut.[42] Those were all places within the French Empire and it might have meant that Vichy troops leaving Syria would return as opposing troops in other regions of interest to the Free French and the British and, of course, would need dislodging. Therefore, it seemed foolish to meekly allow them to leave Syria to oppose the Allies elsewhere. Lyttelton, in a message to Churchill, also touched on the matter of Vichy troops in Syria since he considered that Vichy troops were being bullied not to join the Free French by their officers and were being pressed to swear oaths to that effect.[43]

Churchill took the position that de Gaulle was the problem why Vichy French did not want to join his force. In Churchill's view, some Vichy French just not want to join de Gaulle and he told Lyttelton not to allow this to endanger the safety of Syria. He also sent a personal message for de Gaulle which included an invitation to return to the UK.[44] Whenever de Gaulle was creating problems overseas, Churchill always seemed to recall him for talks or a visit, but the reality was that, on such occasions, Churchill wanted de Gaulle back where he could be controlled and reduce the risk of him causing trouble overseas.

Lyttelton had further bad news to report to Churchill regarding the situation in Syria. It was learned that de Gaulle was planning to re-appoint Vichy officers in Syria in order to control the land. This, Lyttelton feared, would lead to an Arab revolt since it was considered that those Arabs who had supported the Allies in the recent Syrian campaign would be punished by the returning Vichy officials. Basically, Lyttelton considered that the former corrupt order was being re-established in Syria. He advised:

> So far as the rest of Syria is concerned, I propose warning de Gaulle of the inherent dangers but not raise objections until specific instances of bad administration, of corruption or anti-British incidences have been obtained.[45]

Quite simply, de Gaulle was given a free hand in Syria unless he threatened British interests since corruption and malpractice might cause an Arab revolt which would undoubtedly disrupt British war planning in the area.

Syria continued to affect the relationship between the British government and the Free French. It should be observed that there was a sense of agreement over the situation, but that the devil was in the detail. Lyttelton was convinced that de Gaulle was 'quite sincere about his desire to clean up the administration and to reduce the number of officials'. This was a reference to the spectre of the return of Vichy officials as outlined earlier. Lyttelton also informed Churchill that 'I also have little to complain of in de Gaulle's and Catroux's attitude over the military terms' of the Syrian armistice.[46]

Nevertheless, an air of mistrust remained, mostly from the Free French of the British. Lyttelton enlarged on the matter when he informed Churchill that much of de Gaulle's mistrust of the British related to Syria and the negotiations relating to a Free French Navy. However, as Lyttelton observed, de Gaulle was more or less isolated in their matter as Catroux, de Larminat, Lepissier, Valin, Chevigne and others around him, were trying with some success to get him to take a more reasonable line towards Syria. At the time of Lyttleton's message it seemed that de Gaulle was almost persuaded that the British government 'intends to play straight with the Free French in Syria'. But, as ever, there was a hitch to the relationship between the British and de Gaulle as he continued to distrust the attitude of certain British political figures dealing with Arab matters, especially Glubb, (Lieutenant General John Glubb, commander of the Arab Legion, which later became the Jordanian Royal Army). There were other British senior officers distrusted by de Gaulle, especially General Wilson, C-in-C of British forces in the Middle East, whom de Gaulle considered to have a poor attitude towards the Free French. However, there were some

British officers whom de Gaulle did like, such as Generals Platt, Lavarack and Evetts. One suspects that de Gaulle had hostility towards those who had sympathy for the Arab cause.

Nevertheless, Lyttleton hoped to improve the relationship between Wilson and de Gaulle. De Gaulle, however, demanded that Spears be removed as head of the British Military Mission in Syria. The hostility towards Spears arose out of de Gaulle's claim that Spears had twice misled him. He asserted that Spears had, first, whilst in Brazzaville, sent him 'a reassuring telegram about the armistice terms'. This of course relates to the Syrian armistice. The second time that de Gaulle felt that Spears had deceived him was when de Gaulle was informed that Vichy troops in Syria would be made to sign a document stating that they would not take up arms again against the Allies; de Gaulle claimed that this was not done.

Lyttelton made the case for the defence of Spears, stating that Spears was not responsible for the terms of the armistice and, regarding the second accusation, Spears had told de Gaulle in good faith. Lyttelton informed Churchill that there was never any intention of retaining Spears as head of the mission in Syria once it was up and running. He also pointed out that he never hesitated to stand up to de Gaulle and his soldiers whenever the situation demanded such an action. He concluded his communication to Churchill with the information that de Gaulle was anxious to create a 'strong and separate Free French air force'.[47]

It was obviously quite natural that de Gaulle wanted to establish independent branches of Free French armed forces as a marker that there were two separate versions of France fighting the war. However, de Gaulle was always in a difficult position since he depended on the British for just about everything for the Free French prosecution of the war. At the same time, he clearly did not trust the British to work for France and not just work with France whenever necessary. Later that same year, Spears was nominated for a KBE in the New Year honours' list for 1942. This meant that The Spears Mission to de Gaulle was to be replaced. Churchill stated that the 'original conditions under which the Mission have entirely changed.'[48] This was probably an understatement, but it certainly resolved the situation to everyone's satisfaction.

Before leaving Syria, there is an incident which needs recalling. On 15 July Churchill had agreed with de Gaulle that there should not be any difficulty in agreeing a satisfactory solution to the Syrian problem with General Catroux smoothing over any possible difficulties relating to the Allied entry into Syria.[49] However, Lyttelton had bad news to convey at the time to Churchill. On 19 July General Dentz had agreed to an armistice as negotiated with de Gaulle, Catroux and Wilson. Wilson had also agreed to a confidential protocol which regulated the conditions under which Vichy troops might be approached to join the Allies. This protocol suggested that there should be no personal contact between Vichy and Allied individuals to prevent Vichy service personnel being influenced in what they wanted to do in the immediate future – join the Allies or remain with Vichy.

Wilson's protocol had been introduced without any reference to Catroux and appeared to have been a result of a moment of weakness and weariness which the Vichy took advantage of to prevent losing troops to the Allies. Spears had been sent to try to sort out the problem as de Gaulle was seething and had sent an 'acidulated' message to Catroux and to his representatives in Egypt. Lyttelton anticipated further trouble from de Gaulle.[50] This episode illustrated how the British considered the Free French – i.e., not that important as they were quite willing to allow Vichy French troops to be repatriated to France. It would have been nice to recruit further Frenchmen to the Free French, but it was not going to be a sticking point for the seizure of Syria, which was the objective of Allied intervention and not further recruitment for the Free French.

De Gaulle as anticipated was furious. He expressed his fury in a telegram to Churchill. He wrote:

> On arriving in Cairo, I learnt details of the armistice terms for Syria, which British command has concluded with Vichy. I am obliged to tell you that I myself and all Free French consider this convention is basically opposed to military and political interests of Free France, that is to say, of France, and in its form extremely painful to our dignity. I communicated to Captain Lyttelton the concrete measures that I and Conseil de Défense de l'Empire Français considered ourselves obliged to take on the spot in consequence. But I hope that you personally may feel that such a British attitude in an affair vital to us is considerably aggravating my difficulties and would have consequences which I deem deplorable from the point of view I have undertaken.[51]

It is quite clear that de Gaulle did not really understand the British, especially Churchill, who was all out to win the war, and at all costs. The problem with the Free French was one that he was willing to discuss but not give in to without retaining Syria for operational purposes. De Gaulle began to settle down and, in a message to Churchill, stated that 'I believe if we are to wage war we must do so totally'.[52] This must have been music to Churchill's ears as that was how he waged the war against Germany. Churchill was ruthless, he had ordered the attack on the French fleet in Algeria a year previously and in the summer of 1941 had allied the UK with the Soviet Union, a state which, twenty years earlier, he had wished strangled at birth and one led by the most ruthless dictator, Stalin, who had permitted the Soviet Union to form an alliance with Germany shortly before the invasion of Poland. Both Germany and the Soviet Union had invaded Poland during September 1939, on 1 September and 17 September respectively. Churchill was later to understand that there was little between Hitler and Stalin but, as long as the Soviet Union stayed in the war against Germany, Churchill kept faith with Stalin. Therefore, de Gaulle suggesting that the war should be prosecuted 'totally' pressed the right buttons for Churchill who, as we have seen, advised Lyttelton to make allowances for de Gaulle's irregular behaviour since he was under a great deal of pressure.

Lyttelton also admitted to Churchill that mistakes had been made by the British and that the bitterness of the Free French was not without justification. He gave two examples: the first was of a British wing commander who refused to see Free French officials in his office as he had Vichy officials there whom he feared might be offended at the presence of the Free French members. The second incident occurred when the chairman of the Armistice Commission refused to lunch with de Gaulle on the grounds that he was neutral and must not be suspected of bias.[53] The chairman was certainly not neutral since he was a citizen of a country, the UK, that was fighting Germany, an ally of Vichy, whose soldiers had just fought against the Allies in Syria but, as Lyttelton wrote, relations were just not going right and all seemed to be against the Free French. Churchill was informed that:

> The Vichy French were treated throughout with the greatest professional tenderness. We saw the incongruous spectacle of de Verdilliac inspecting, on the quay, an Australian guard of honour mounted to speed up the departure of the first shiploads of Vichy French amidst the strains of the *Marseillaise* within an hour or two of the arrest of General Dentz and thirty-five officers for gross breaches of the armistice. I am convinced that de Gaulle is quite sincere about his desire to clear up the administration and to reduce the number of officials. I also had little to complain of de Gaulle and Catroux's attitude over the military terms.[54]

It is quite clear that Lyttelton was no neutral and came down on the side of de Gaulle and the Free French whom he obviously saw as allies in spite of the difficult nature of de Gaulle. He also throws out a sop in the form that General Claude Auchinleck might be seeking de Gaulle's advice. As Lyttelton wrote, 'he [Auchinleck] will do so [ask de Gaulle's advice] and I can think of no better key to the difficult door of de Gaulle's confidence'.[55]

The question of Auchinleck seeking advice from de Gaulle is interesting since Auchinleck had just been appointed C-in-C of the Middle East Theatre in August. This, no doubt, would have flattered de Gaulle's ego. A senior British commander, a veteran of the First World War, the North-West Frontier in India and the 1940 Narvik expedition, requesting advice from him may well have smoothed over any difficulties of trust between the British and the Free French in the Middle East at least. Earlier, during April and May, while holding a different appointment, Auchinleck also had to face a problem in the Middle East as, like Syria and Lebanon, Iraq was in danger of falling into German hands. As Syria and Iraq shared a common border, this was a concern to the British as Auchinleck considered that British lines of communication or supply lines ran from India to Syria via Iraq. Auchinleck considered the Middle East to be part of Asia, which it really is, and that the defence of Asia, i.e. India, began by ensuring that countries such as Turkey, Syria, the British possession and Iraq were held or sympathetic to the Allies. A local coup in Iraq led to a small war between the British and rebel Iraqis sympathetic to Germany. The British had a toehold in Iraq, an RAF base which was roughly halfway between Basra and Palestine and about 20 miles from the Iraqi capital, Baghdad. There was a further fear regarding the Middle East as the Germans had intervened in North Africa and had advanced towards Egypt as far as Benghazi. At the same time, the Allies were also losing the Greek campaign. If Syria and Iraq had fallen, the Middle East was wide open. Auchinleck ordered British forces into Iraq, an action supported by Churchill. British troops began to land in Iraq at Basra and, by the end of May 1941, the British were firmly in control of Iraq and disaster was averted.[56]

Therefore, an experienced senior officer such as Auchinleck looking to de Gaulle for advice was certainly flattering for the, at times, quite vain French leader. De Gaulle may not have totally agreed with Auchinleck's views regarding the defence of Asia, but he knew the importance of not letting Vichy or the Germans retain or capturing Syria, and possibly Lebanon, while it must be remembered that the French also had a Far East empire in today's Vietnam, Laos and Cambodia.

By 1941 it was clear that the Japanese were not content with gains in China but wanted to expand across Asia. Both the French and British empires in the Far East were at risk and, as it transpired, so were Dutch and American territories in the area. It was quite clear that the French and the British had more in common than perhaps either side was comfortable to recognise and that there was still a long way to go before the tide would turn against

Germany. There were to be further losses during 1941, but the way back to Europe and victory was from North Africa, French North Africa during 1942, but this was to require a great deal of co-operation between the Allies who, after December 1941 included the USA and the Soviet Union. The Soviets fought their own horrific war from Moscow to Berlin while the British and Americans worked closely to ensure the defeat of Germany and Nazism. The land offensives began in North Africa with many dramas behind the scenes as the Free French had to be courted or roughed up when necessary to ensure their co-operation to ensure, firstly, the defeat of the Germans and Vichy in Africa and then to use French imperial territories to land once more in Europe. And to this we must now turn.

Chapter 6

1942

A Wedding or Marriage of Convenience?

The Americans entered the war in December 1941 following the Japanese attack on the naval base at Pearl Harbor on 7 December. That was followed by German and Italian declarations of war against the USA. This made the situation easier for Churchill and Roosevelt as they no longer had to pretend that the USA was not aiding the Allies. Indeed, Roosevelt had had to conceal this from his countrymen since many Americans were opposed to the war. Nevertheless, like many Americans, Roosevelt was equally opposed to imperialism, while failing to see America's own empire, but was suspicious of British and French actions in the Middle East and, therefore, constantly vigilant of what might be further empire building by the two European powers. Most of all, though, Roosevelt did not like France or de Gaulle, which made for a difficult relationship; it took a lot of persuading by Churchill to keep Roosevelt civil towards de Gaulle.

The American entry into the war alongside the British and their allies was just what was needed by 1942. De Gaulle certainly saw victory with the American entry into the war. Although no fan of the USA, he said, 'The war is over. Of course, there are years of fighting ahead, but the Germans are beaten.' He later wrote, 'The attack upon Pearl Harbor hurled the Americans into the war.... The colossal war effort [then] mustered ... rendered victory a certainty.'[1]

De Gaulle was, of course, correct in his assertion. The USA was able to commit millions of men and equip not only the Allies in the west but also supply the Soviet Union with vehicles such as trucks and jeeps. The Soviets were eventually able to push the Germans all the way back to Berlin while the western Allies, after losing their territories in the Far East, could only return via North Africa.

As already mentioned, Roosevelt did not have much time for the French and even less for de Gaulle. To this end, Roosevelt sought a replacement for de Gaulle and his eye lighted on General Henri Giraud, but there was a problem; Giraud had been captured twice by the Germans, once in the First World War and then in the current war. Even though he had managed to escape German captivity in the Second World War, de Gaulle, who had only been captured once, baited Giraud with this. In his private wartime diary, however, Sir Alan Lascelles, King George VI's counsellor, illustrated just how resourceful Giraud was at the time of his escape. Using a rope made from the string fibres from parcels he received in prison, he abseiled from his cell window to a car which had already been arranged for him and was soon on a train bound for neutral Switzerland. The Germans naturally began a manhunt for the French general: any man over 6-feet tall was to be stopped and questioned. While his train was searched, Giraud, a fluent German speaker, began a deep conversation with a German general sharing his compartment and the police, on coming to the pair, dared not interrupt the discussion, thus leaving Giraud undetected. Lascelles noted that Giraud remained a 'mystery man'.[2]

Nevertheless, the American support for Giraud caused difficulties for de Gaulle as he began to think about post-war France and how it might be governed. It was assumed by many that de Gaulle would be at least a provisional leader until elections could be held. The US government often felt that de Gaulle was trying to set himself up as dictator of France. Six months later Lascelles recorded that, in Algiers during a grand parade on the French celebration of Austerlitz Day, a celebration from the Napoleonic Wars, Giraud, 'a king of a man', received the best reception.[3]

De Gaulle did little to endear himself with Roosevelt when, in January 1942, the Free French took back two small islands off the Canadian coast, Saint Pierre and Miquelon. The retrieval of the islands was symbolic. Churchill observed to Roosevelt that the action had been the subject of the overthrow by an overwhelming popular vote of *'Vichy-ites'* on 'two tiny islands'. The prime minister also told Roosevelt that 'coercion of de Gaulle would have been very unpopular'.[4] Roosevelt was probably alarmed by the independent action of the Free French so close to US territory which did nothing to calm his fears of European empire building, notwithstanding that the two islands in question had been part of the French Empire since the eighteenth century. Amazingly, Churchill was the voice of reason; he had tried to reason with de Gaulle over Saint Pierre and Miquelon, stating that Free French action there risked alienating Roosevelt.[5] He wasn't wrong but it still didn't prevent him from saying of de Gaulle and the Free French in the Canadian parliament that

> they have been condemned to death by the men of Vichy, but their names will be held and are being held in ever increasing respect by nine Frenchmen out of every ten throughout the once happy, smiling land of France.

He had no good words to say of the Vichy regime which the US continued to recognise.[6]

It should be noted that the US media, headed by the *New York Times*, along with the British and Canadian governments, applauded de Gaulle's unilateral action against Saint Pierre and Miquelon even if the US foreign ministry, headed by Cordell Hull, spent Christmas 1941 trying to bully the Canadian prime minister, Mackenzie King, into throwing the Free French off the islands using military force. The American media attacked Hull and made the observation that it would be treason to hand back territory now in Allied hands to a German vassal state.[7] It was quite clear that the Roosevelt administration was on the wrong side of history at that point and was even working against its own people and, more importantly, against its own allies. This was without doubt due to Roosevelt's personal antipathy towards de Gaulle. It was to take nearly three years before Roosevelt saw de Gaulle in the same sympathetic way as Churchill had since 1940.

At the end of January 1942, the US government still had diplomatic relations with Vichy France which would become more difficult once the Allies invaded what was technically French territory still being administered by the Vichy regime. Evidence of this relationship is contained in a telegram from Roosevelt to Churchill. Roosevelt shared a copy of US policy towards France with Churchill. The original had been sent to Pétain on 20 January. Enclosed in the same telegram was a message from the American Ambassador to Vichy, Admiral William Leahy, which contained Pétain's response and Leahy's conclusions regarding the proposed American policy. The overall American message was that France, and the French people, should realise that Roosevelt was their best friend. In Roosevelt's head, France included the French Empire. American policy also insisted that any French attack on the USA was a declaration of war and the US would not take this lying down. The Vichy response was that the (Vichy) French government would resist any invasion whether by de Gaullists (Free French), Germans, British or Americans. The Americans considered that, overall, the tone of the Vichy reply changed nothing.[8]

What the Vichy French had not considered was that Anglo-American landings were going to happen in French North Africa with or without their consent and that, in the long term, there was little that they could do about it. The Germans may have intervened, but it was unlikely; Hitler had little interest in Africa. Only the Allies and the Italians had any real stake there. Nevertheless, it would still be easier if the Allies could land with no opposition from the Vichy and negotiations were explored. The war in the Soviet Union was one that attracted Pétain who had told Leahy on 27 June 1941 that

Hitler was correct in attacking the Soviet Union and that he was confident of a German victory. Even by the end of November, when it was clear that a German victory was not certain, Pétain remained confident of a German victory.[9] This, of course, dismayed the British who by then were pragmatically anchored alongside the Soviets since the Soviet Union was taking the German heat away from the UK which, as long as the Soviets endured, no longer faced invasion. Of course, once the USA entered the war, any consideration of a German invasion of the UK was redundant.

However, events were afoot in Vichy circles, good and bad. There was disquieting news that, in possible new negotiations between Vichy and Germany, the Germans were to receive the ports of Cette in France and Oran, Bizerta and Algiers in Africa. Admiral Darlan was rumoured to have been in favour of this but Pétain had refused and had bought Weygand to Vichy to support him in this matter. This naturally alarmed the British government. On 18 August, Anthony Eden, the foreign secretary, suggested to John Winant, the US Ambassador to the UK, that the State Department might warn Vichy that the proposed direction of a new treaty between Germany and Vichy would be dangerous. Already, on 2 August, the Americans had warned the Vichy government after the Vichy authorities had accepted Japanese demands in Indo-China (Vietnam). The State Department had stated that US policy towards the Vichy government would be determined on how France defended its territories against Axis aggression. Eden's suggestion was probably not sent since it was likely that the Americans considered their warning to have been sufficient.

The question of the French retaining sovereignty in North Africa was something which vexed Roosevelt and the US administration. Roosevelt sent another message to Pétain during September. Pétain's reply was not clear. He said that he did not plan to cede bases to the Germans but, as France was a conquered country, the Germans might just take the bases anyway. In a discussion between Sir R.I. Campbell and Welles in Washington DC, it was considered that there was little point in sending any further messages to Pétain and that a complete break between the USA and Vichy would not serve the UK well. If the Americans withdrew diplomatic recognition of Vichy, Leahy would be required to leave France and he was doing a great deal to prevent the French giving into the Germans.

However, things were on the move as, on 18 November, Pétain announced the dismissal of Weygand. Pétain told Leahy that he had been compelled by the Germans to dismiss him. If he failed to do so, the Germans threatened to occupy Vichy France. Pétain had already recalled Weygand to Vichy. However, this was all becoming irrelevant since the British had already opened their offensive in the Libyan province of Cyrenaica. At that point the American government still had leverage with Vichy as the USA was still supplying their territories with oil, for example. The Americans made it quite clear that, if the Vichy regime did anything to endanger the relationship between the USA and themselves, such supplies would cease. It was events on the other side of the world which made things clearer. Following the Japanese attack at Pearl Harbor and the German declaration of war against the USA, on 11 December Leahy informed Pétain that, as the USA was at war with Germany, something which both men lamented, Franco-American relations had naturally altered and that any French help to Germany would be harmful to the USA.

Pétain replied that the German government had not requested that the Vichy government alter their relationship with the USA, but, if it did, he would have to comply since the Germans would threaten to starve France into compliance. Later the Vichy government gave four memoranda to Leahy which stated that:

The French fleet would not be used against the British unless the British attacked first.

The recall of Weygand was not a change in the status of French territories in French North Africa.

The French would not allow Germany to use French territories as bases for hostilities and, finally,

France would remain neutral in the war between the USA and Germany and Italy.

The Vichy government hoped that the assurances would be enough for the US to maintain its programme of supplies for French North Africa.

The Vichy declarations were not enough for the British. The Foreign Office considered that the Vichy intention was to maintain a policy of benevolent neutrality towards Germany. The British did not trust Vichy which had been trying to build up a case to use their fleet for convoy purposes which would have meant that the French fleet and the Royal Navy would eventually clash at sea. The removal of Weygand from North Africa meant that there was no longer a French figure of sufficient gravitas for other French people to rally around and provide resistance to Germany in French territories. Before setting out to meet Roosevelt, Churchill, had considered several possibilities of how Vichy might provide evidence that they were not secretly working against the Allies. He considered that they should scuttle their fleet or hand it over to the Americans. Another proof of Vichy pro-Allied intention might be to start a revolt in North Africa. Churchill just wanted proof of French goodwill. If this was not forthcoming, the British and American governments would refuse to recognise Vichy as the legitimate government of France. The reality was that the British government did not recognise Vichy anyway. However, Churchill considered that war would not be declared against Vichy, but that the British and American governments would feel free to dispose of Vichy in a manner that suited them.

The FO thought it unlikely that Pétain would take such drastic action and would not make any firm move until he could see who was winning the war. The FO suggested that it might be best if Leahy was retained at Vichy, and to press Pétain to resist German demands while arranging a barter system which would continue to supply North Africa and prevent American supplies reaching the Germans. At the end of December, Vichy sent a message through the French naval attaché in Madrid that there was no truth in the report of French naval bases being handed over to German control. It was alleged that Pétain would never give way to the Germans over the ports and that Darlan fully supported him. This meant that 1941 ended as it had begun regarding Vichy: nobody was really certain of how the Vichy government might act. They seemed indifferent to their compatriots of the Free French and did their best to wriggle away from German constraints while trying to keep relations with the Americans. It all seemed rather improbable. The oddest thing was that the Vichy government directed most of its anger at de Gaulle and the Free French for refusing to accept that France, as they saw it, had been defeated in 1940.

Indeed, during 1941 de Gaulle upped the ante in France as, against a background of 'universal but uncanalised revolt' in France, de Gaulle decided to establish a de facto government in the form of the Free French National Committee. This was seconded by a National Advisory Council. It was part of a logical progression of the Free French movement and was building on the resources which had begun in French Equatorial Africa.[10]

Therefore, by the beginning of 1942, it was clear that de Gaulle was having no truck with Vichy or its collaboration with the enemy and would brook no arguments or excuses as to why they were working with the Germans. He supported the overall hatred of the enemy and demanded their removal from French territory. Once the war was over accounts regarding Vichy treachery would also be settled. It wasn't going to be pretty in France at war's end.

It was while Churchill was in the USA that de Gaulle took unilateral action off the Canadian coast in the seizure of Saint Pierre and Miquelon. The islands were under the jurisdiction of an ardent Vichy supporter, Admiral Robert. De Gaulle did not seize the islands on a whim, even though that might have seemed the case. Saint Pierre actually posed a danger to Allied shipping since a powerful wireless station was positioned there and could be used to guide

German submarines. The British government considered that the best course would be to allow the Free French to take and control the islands. The US government refused this as they were still of a mind not to offend the Vichy government. This was partly due to a pledge to Latin-American governments that the US refused to allow any transfer of sovereignty or control of possession or control of territory in the western hemisphere. However, the Americans were willing to allow the Canadians to secure the wireless station. Owing to the American objections to the Free French seizing the islands, Churchill agreed that the Free French should not make such a move. De Gaulle understood the position but ignored it and ordered Admiral Muselier to land, arrest the governor and rally the islanders to the Free French.

Muselier, not happy, nevertheless carried out de Gaulle's orders on 24 December. The British government immediately distanced itself from de Gaulle's actions, but realised that they needed to defend de Gaulle from the consequences of his independent action. The American government was furious and tried not to recognise that it was not really the Free French that had landed. The British government, especially Churchill, was having none of the American bluster and queried just how much one needed to consider the feelings of the Vichy government. One should consider that this was a regime which had been hostile towards the British since summer 1940 and the wireless station on Saint Pierre was not there for weather forecasts – it was there to harm Allied shipping – something that seemed to escape the notice of Roosevelt and his administration in their haste to be anti-de Gaulle and anti-French Empire. At times, Roosevelt's loathing of de Gaulle was dangerous to the USA, especially those Americans fighting later in Europe and North Africa or on the seas and in the air. The Americans even went so far as to threaten to remove the Free French from the islands by force. The FO realised that this was something that British public opinion would not tolerate.

Churchill, in discussions with Roosevelt, in Washington DC, suggested that the French islands, in agreement with the UK, US and Canadian governments, might be declared demilitarised and therefore out of the war. All armed forces, including Free French, should be withdrawn. The Vichy administrator should be withdrawn, and the islands placed under a consultative council. The US and Canadian governments should continue economic assistance to the islands and send observers to supervise the use of the wireless station. However, the British War Cabinet considered that the US State Department had overrated the reaction of the Vichy government and that, after the behaviour of Vichy at both Dakar and in Syria, considered that the British public would not understand why de Gaulle was not allowed to occupy the two French islands. Therefore, the War Cabinet recommended that there should be an attempt to persuade de Gaulle to accept the terms as suggested by Churchill but there was to be no suggestion that he should be compelled to agree.

Predictably, de Gaulle refused to accept the proposal of removing the islands from the war. From de Gaulle's point of view, his reasoning was sound. For de Gaulle it was essential that French territory should be brought back into the war. If he was to make an exception for Saint Pierre and Miquelon, what might happen in the future? De Gaulle feared that, when other difficult French territories were liberated by the Free French, perhaps they might also be withdrawn from the war. Nevertheless, Anthony Eden was able to smooth things over and de Gaulle agreed to a compromise along the lines of Churchill's suggestion. However, de Gaulle asked for a secret understanding that the Free French administrator should remain as a member of the consultative council; that the Council should be under the orders of the Free French National Committee and that, although all French ships should be withdrawn, a detachment of French marines should remain on the islands. Churchill agreed with Roosevelt that he would try to get de Gaulle to drop his reservations once they meet in London.

De Gaulle was seen by Churchill on 22 January 1942 when Churchill made it quite clear that the US government would not accept his suggestions – publicly at least. The State Department, observed Churchill, might agree to an informal approach however, along the same lines as already discussed. De Gaulle, after a great deal of wrangling, agreed to recommend that the French National Committee drop the demand for a formal secret agreement. Nevertheless, not everyone had been kept in the loop since Hull, having apparently not seen the agreement between Roosevelt and Churchill, objected to the compromise on the grounds that it would not be acceptable to the Vichy government. Hull considered that if the Vichy government was offended it would make it less possible for the US to put pressure on Vichy to refuse concessions to Germany. Hull said that Admiral Darlan had already hinted that, unless the question of the islands was settled in a way which satisfied Vichy, American consuls in France and observers in North Africa might be asked to leave and an arrangement might be made with the Japanese to occupy French islands in the central Pacific.

The British War Council considered that Hull was being too easily influenced by Vichy representatives. Lord Halifax, the British Ambassador to the USA, was instructed by London to point out that Hull was not taking sufficient account of the ability of the US to put pressure on Vichy. It was observed that the US in its turn could seize and occupy French possessions in the Caribbean, cut off French trade with the USA and seize all French gold. However, the US government had accepted the proposed compromise and the question of the islands basically receded into obscurity. There were bigger questions to be settled in the coming months.[11]

The previous narrative illustrated the nature of relations in wartime especially with the exiled powers and the major allies. De Gaulle stood on his honour. He had to retrieve French honour and French territory on the way to liberating his country and its people. The islands, except for wireless station, were of no real importance, but standards were being set and the ability to compromise was being proven. Roosevelt detested de Gaulle. One gets the impression that he was not fond of much that was not American but, for the sake of the alliance with the UK or more likely with Churchill, was willing to co-operate and seek answers – as was de Gaulle in the end. What linked the three men – all quite different from the other – was a common hatred of Nazism; that kept them together against all the odds.

Another area which vexed Roosevelt as the war progressed and it became obvious that France would be liberated in the long term was the question of the French National Committee, touched on in this narrative concerning the islands off the Canadian coast. It was obvious that once France was liberated it would need governing. The Free French, and indeed the French people, were unlikely to accept an Allied military government of occupation – why should they?

Therefore, it was widely assumed that de Gaulle and the Free French as the French National Committee would be an interim government until free and fair elections could be held in France and a democratic government elected. Roosevelt detested this situation and sought all ways to thwart de Gaulle becoming at least a temporary French leader since he did not trust him and certainly did not trust soldiers in politics. Ironically, General Eisenhower, would be elected as US president, serving two terms in the 1950s. De Gaulle was not the only political soldier in the western fold.

With the entry of the USA into the war with relations still intact with Vichy, the British government had to re-assess their attitude. As already seen, action between the two European governments had been hostile and had descended into fighting between their forces. To rack up the tension, the British government had recognised de Gaulle and the Free French as the legitimate symbol of a free and democratic France. De Gaulle was anathema to the Vichy government who had also sentenced him to death for his actions against what Vichy perceived as being the legitimate French government. The FO refused to see anything positive in Vichy and hoped to manoeuvre it towards neutrality but in the character of Darlan who hated the UK there was little, if anything, that the British could trust in Vichy. In its turn, the German government distrusted Vichy and made it quite clear that it reserved the right to intervene if Vichy took an independent line and did not follow through with German demands. This led the FO to conclude that there was nothing to be gained in treating Vichy with consideration. Furthermore, from autumn 1941, French public opinion was becoming more critical of French collaboration.[12]

The British had no official relations with the Vichy government and so could only act via the Americans who still afforded Vichy diplomatic recognition. Nevertheless, the British remained wary of Vichy reaction as the Allies began to plan operations in French North Africa which were to call for amphibious landings or invasion. The term used depended very much on one's allegiance. What had been determined was that, during 1942, the Allies, especially the Americans, were going to land in North Africa whether the Vichy authorities liked it or not. The way back to Europe, including what is termed Metropolitan France (mainland France but also Algeria) was to be via North Africa and would include, later, an invasion of Italy, the weakest of the major Axis powers and the closest to North Africa.

The American government may have spoken in a gentler voice to the Vichy government, but it was always made clear that it expected Vichy to fall in line with the demands of the Allies or face the consequences. As the Germans continuously threatened Vichy with an occupation of southern France, Vichy had to decide just which was the worse to deal with, and from where. The Vichy area of France was continuously in danger as the Germans only had to move their forces over a line and down a road into unoccupied France. There was nothing that Vichy could do about that.

The Germans only had limited resources in Africa with everything having to be ferried across the Mediterranean which meant running the gauntlet of the forces of the Royal Navy and the RAF. Therefore, it was clear that Vichy forces in French North Africa could take a more independent role in the face of Allied intervention there. Nevertheless, the British suspected that Vichy was supplying the Germans with war materials from over the Tunisian border, as well as aiding Axis forces on every front. Furthermore, it was learned that Pétain had gone to see Franco in Spain.[13] The reason why was not clear, but it would seem that he had frequent contact with the Spanish dictator.[14] It is highly probable that the two met to discuss relations with Germany and mutual difficulties in this relationship.

By the end of January 1942, the American government began to lay down the line with Vichy. On 29 January Roosevelt telegraphed Churchill, telling him that, on the 20 January, he had sent Admiral Leahy notes to be used in a conversation with Pétain. The American president wanted to remind Pétain and his government that he was the best friend that France had. By this, Roosevelt meant not only all of France but also its empire. However, he reminded Pétain that, if Vichy gave the Germans or Italians 'aid and comfort', this would endanger the correct relationship between the USA and Vichy. Roosevelt made it quite clear that any such act would be regarded by the US government as hostile and would not be taken 'lying down'. Any act of support by Vichy in a German or Italian attack on unoccupied France or French colonies would be 'playing the German game' while French resistance would seem to be 'normal and natural' and would attract 'all possible American military and naval support.'[15]

At that point of the war, even though it was not clear just how powerful the USA was in military terms, it was becoming obvious that, materially, it was about to become the quartermaster of the Allies with the USA, using its methods of mass production, able to supply war materials for the entire alliance against the Axis powers whilst its manufacturing bases were beyond the reach of enemy bombers. The problem was getting materials across the Atlantic owing to enemy submarines, or U-boats. Nevertheless, it would seem that, once the USA was involved openly in the war the tide began to turn against Germany.

Without doubt, Churchill was delighted once the USA went to war against Germany. He was assured by Roosevelt that, even though the Japanese attack on the USA was the reason why war came to his country, the German declaration of war being foolish and unnecessary, he was going to adopt a policy of Germany first. Germany, or rather the Nazis, were to be enemy number one and would be treated as such. Undoubtedly, Vichy officials were very aware of the potential power of the USA. Perhaps it meant little in occupied Europe in 1942 as the Allies were yet to land there but in French colonial Africa it was clear that the Americans could indeed make a considerable difference and it might be profitable in the long term to work with the Allies rather than against them.

Leahy spoke to Pétain, in the presence of Darlan and Charles-Antoine Rochat, Secretary General of the Ministry of Foreign Affairs and International Development, along the lines laid out by Roosevelt. Pétain said that Vichy would resist invasion by anyone – de Gaullist, German, British or American. It was also said that there was no question of the Vichy fleet being used against the US or of Germany being allowed to use French North African bases. What Leahy gleaned from Pétain was that Vichy would refuse to co-operate with the US if the Germans attempted to move into French North Africa.

Nevertheless, it was clear that French ships, from Metropolitan France, were supplying Axis forces in Libya. Roosevelt informed Churchill on 10 February 1942 that, via Leahy, he had told Pétain that he was aware that the French were helping the Germans supply their forces in Libya. Roosevelt said that he knew that the armistice between Germany and France was obviously loaded in favour of Germany and left the Vichy government with little room for manoeuvre but, nevertheless, if Vichy continued to supply Axis forces in Libya, Vichy would be placing itself 'in the category of governments directly assisting the declared enemies of the United States'. Therefore, the Vichy government was required by Roosevelt to give a formal assurance that no aid would be given to Germany, Italy or Japan and no French ships would aid the above countries in acts of aggression. If no assurances were forthcoming, the US government would withdraw their ambassador for consultation regarding future American policy towards France.

On the night 14/15 February, the British Ambassador to the USA, Lord Halifax, reported that the State Department was concerned that there had been as yet no reply from Pétain to the American ultimatum with several points. The Americans were nervous that, once confronted, the Vichy government would decide to openly ally with Germany and were making arrangements to place their fleet in German hands. The staider FO considered that the Vichy government was merely taking its time to answer.

Soon, the answer came and Halifax sent the highlights to the FO on the night of 19/20 February. On 16 February Pétain said that he was surprised at receiving the message after what he had considered to have been a frank exchange of views and information supplied by himself and Darlan in the meeting with Leahy on 9 February. The French had told Leahy that, in January, French ships had supplied 1,029 tons of food and fifty-six Italian lorries to Libya. Leahy had been assured at the time that no oil or war material had been sent. Pétain considered that this information should have been sufficient to demonstrate that shipments were of modest amounts and to put an end to a propaganda campaign launched in London, on what he considered a false basis, of making the Vichy government a scapegoat for the lack of British success in Libya. The American government was reminded that the Vichy government was bound to alleviate, where possible, hardships imposed on France owing to the terms of the armistice and that, at times, they were obliged to accept certain adjustments to gain advantages for their people. Nevertheless, France would continue its policy of neutrality and it would be useful if the US government tried to understand the predicament in which France and its people found itself.

Leahy, while sending the text of the French note to Washington DC, added his own thoughts which were that, basically, Pétain and the French in general wanted to remain on good terms with the Americans. However, the note did not contain any of the assurances from Pétain which had been sought by Roosevelt. The FO was also displeased and detected the hand of Darlan, as the French reply was 'impertinent and evasive'. Halifax reported that such was the American dissatisfaction that there was a proposal in the air to recall Leahy and to make it quite clear to the Vichy government that, should they not make good the assurance demanded by the US government, American policy regarding Vichy would be revised before he left Vichy.

American pressure continued to mount on the Vichy government. On 21 February Halifax told Anthony Eden that, two days previously, Roosevelt had instructed Leahy to deliver an oral message to Pétain. In the message it was stated that Roosevelt understood the position of France and its people, and sympathised and had noted its maintenance of its neutral position. Nevertheless, Roosevelt had wanted official assurances that France would give no further military aid to the Axis powers and Pétain had failed to give such assurances. Roosevelt observed that, at present (February 1942), the USA was involved in a war in which thirty-seven nations had sided against the Axis powers. The United Nations would win this war with a 'final and complete victory'. Roosevelt hoped that there would be no reason to alter US policy towards France, but there would be if the Vichy regime was to follow a policy of open assistance to the Axis beyond the terms of the armistice. As a consequence of the French inaction, Leahy was returning to the USA for consultation; a *chargé d'affaires* was to be left at Vichy. Roosevelt looked for the assurances requested in his note of 10 February before Leahy left France.

Meanwhile, the British were making their intentions quite clear to the Vichy government. On 16 February, the War Cabinet approved a draft notification to Vichy to the effect that six named French ships, which were known to be carrying military supplies from French ports for Axis forces already engaged in fighting and other French ships doing the same, would be attacked without warning by British air and naval forces anywhere in the Mediterranean. Furthermore, all shipping in waters off Tunisia was also under suspicion and any French ships met there by British forces that could not prove their legitimacy would also be attacked. The blame would not lie with the British government if such ships were innocent of providing aid to Axis forces.

This draft was approved by the War Cabinet subject to approval of the US State Department. Halifax then discussed it with his American counterparts but the Americans, still awaiting a response from Pétain following their own approach, delayed answering. However, the FO received reports that enemy submarines were being refuelled off Martinique, a French Caribbean island. The US authorities were informed by the UK government who suggested that the US begin to take a tougher line with Vichy. The Americans still managed to dither and take Vichy assurances at face value. Indeed, Pétain felt emboldened enough to start to make demands of the US government and wanted the resumption of maritime traffic, supplies to North Africa and a decent settlement of the Saint Pierre-Miquelon incident. Vichy also wanted an end to the 'violent and tendentious' press and radio campaign against its government. The British government was informed that the US government was willing to take most of the French assurances at face value but insisted that Vichy supplies to the Axis powers was to cease. Overall, the FO considered that American pressure had paid off and that there was a need perhaps for some give and take and so stayed its hand regarding the draft message regarding future relations with Vichy.[16]

Nevertheless, the American attitude towards Vichy was to vex the British government throughout 1942 until the eventual Allied landings in French North Africa at the end of the year. However, regarding de Gaulle, it is quite clear that he was correct in not trusting his countrymen. The radio station on Saint Pierre was one case of the potential of Vichy aiding Germany and its submarine campaign with the refuelling of a U-boat off Martinique yet another example of the treachery of the Vichy regime. However, perhaps it was useful for the Allies to have a backchannel via Vichy, which could be controlled, and get messages to Berlin in a roundabout way. Such messages would have made it quite clear to the German government that they were not going to win the war and that the fight was to the death and the destruction of the Nazi regime.

Lord Halifax continued to make strong representations against Vichy to the State Department on behalf of the British government. The British government still had much to say but held off. Halifax observed that the question of American re-supplying of French North Africa had not been addressed adequately but the Vichy ambassador in Washington had been told that, until his government had supplied decent answers on the shipments of supplies to Axis forces in Libya, the proposed removal of the French battlecruiser *Dunkerque* from Oran to an undisclosed destination and the refuelling of the German submarine at Martinique, there could be no question of any renewal of American supplies to North Africa. Throughout March the Vichy government tried all sorts of stratagem to avoid giving the Americans any clear assurances of the relationship between Vichy and the Axis powers.

However, Roosevelt, in a personal telegram to Churchill, suggested that perhaps it might be a good idea to resume American supplies to French North Africa as well as Red Cross aid to children in France. The American president considered that the successful bombing by the RAF of Renault factories in the suburbs of Paris on the night of 3/4 March must have demonstrated that France was still at war and that the Vichy regime was weakening the French case, owing to its collaboration with the Germans. Roosevelt was also being pragmatic since he was very aware that the Allies were preparing to take the war to the enemy via North Africa. He feared that, if Vichy openly went over to the Axis, the Iberian Peninsula would be lost. Furthermore, American observers in North Africa and the American mission in Vichy were obtaining important military and strategic information. So, Roosevelt suggested that, instead of being openly hostile towards Vichy, limited economic aid would serve the purpose and, at the same time, German interference could be limited or avoided.

Churchill was swayed by Roosevelt's words and agreed to a limited American re-supply of French North Africa if it meant that importance intelligence work could be continued by the Americans. However, Churchill was clear that British operations on the island of Madagascar, a French territory off the coast of East Africa, should not be impeded by the Americans. He also insisted that the State Department should not accept Vichy assurances which would later allow them to complain of a breach of faith. Without doubt, this would refer to any Allied attacks on Vichy-held territories anywhere. Churchill considered that the time was right to ask Roosevelt to allow the British, when they landed in Madagascar, to drop leaflets explaining that the landing was a joint Anglo-American expedition and not solely British.

On 27 March Churchill sent a message to Roosevelt in which he stated that the British government did not mind:

> your sending very limited quantities of supplies to French North Africa provided the American observers can penetrate the country freely, especially if you can get the compensatory advantages in securing the control of strategic materials now going to Germany. We value your contacts with Vichy and it is well worth paying a price for them but please nothing must interfere with Operation IRONCLAD [i.e., Madagascar] to which we are committed and no assurances by the French [Vichy] about defending their Empire like they did Indo-China should be accepted by the United States in such a way as to enable them to complain of a breach of faith.[17]

Clearly Churchill was doing his best to accommodate American wishes but wanted to remain independent of the US government and be left with a free hand to take certain action against Vichy as and when he saw fit, if that meant bringing the Axis powers closer to defeat. As it was, Roosevelt refused to allow Operation IRONCLAD to be considered an Anglo-American operation. Roosevelt wrote:

we are the only nation that can intervene diplomatically with any hope of success with Vichy and it seems to me extremely important that we are able to do this without the complications which might arise by the dropping of leaflets or other informal methods in connection with your operation.

Churchill agreed to Roosevelt's reasoning on 4 April.[18] However, one can already detect that the American government was beginning to interfere with British war policy. The FO remained unimpressed with Vichy assurances to the US but was learning to accept that the Americans must be placated while intelligence gleaned from American observers in French North Africa might well be useful. By April the FO was becoming vexed with events between the Germans and Vichy and what that might mean for future British operations. The government and the FO remained concerned with the supply of American oil to French North Africa. They were also troubled by a report from Halifax in which he stated that Leahy had informed the State Department that Pétain was trying to resist German pressure on him to restore Laval.

There were further and more serious concerns for the British. On 2 April the FO telegraphed to Halifax a report which had reached them to the effect that the French battleship *Richelieu* and three cruisers, *Georges Leygues*, *Gloire* and *Montcalm*, were to leave Dakar for France on 3 April. As the US government had not insisted on an assurance regarding moving *Dunkerque*, the FO assumed that the Vichy government had presumed that they were at liberty to move *Richelieu* as and when they saw fit. Halifax was instructed by the FO to inform the State Department that the British government was extremely dissatisfied with the latest proposed naval moves and that any attempt to move *Richelieu* or *Jean Bart* into the Mediterranean would not be acceptable. The FO asked the State Department to obtain assurances from Vichy that the ship would not be moved and that two Vichy cargo ships then tied up in American ports would not be allowed to leave until such assurances had been received.

As British demands grew stronger concerning American policy towards Vichy it should be noted that US foreign policy in relation to the regime was one of distancing itself and beginning to embrace de Gaulle and the Free French. However, it should be recognised that this was done with the greatest reluctance – Vichy was useful for intelligence purposes while Roosevelt detested de Gaulle. However, the US was beginning to recognise that it needed to maintain the alliance with the UK which meant that Vichy had to go and de Gaulle be embraced.

Throughout the war the Americans always treated de Gaulle as some kind of leper – Roosevelt loathed the man, and it was really only Churchill's support and the necessity of winning the war from French territory which kept de Gaulle in the American sphere. What the State Department was always loath to admit was that Churchill had backed the right horse and they had not. American support or, at least, recognition of Vichy was always going to be correct as long as both were considered as neutral in the war. It was obvious that Vichy was never neutral and was notorious in its collaboration with Germany but, as we have seen, the position of the Vichy regime was one which the US government could take advantage of by sending supplies to French North Africa while American intelligence work was carried out virtually unhindered.

However, once Germany declared war on the USA this relationship was untenable. With the USA being a declared enemy of Germany, it became difficult for the Americans to supply Vichy without a negative response from the Allies, especially the British who were already fighting the Germans and Italians in Africa. Equally, as time passed it was clear that North Africa was the site for major operations, as it had been since 1940; the Germans wanted more co-operation from Vichy especially its Mediterranean ports and its fleet in the Mediterranean.

Of course, it was also becoming obvious that the Germans were on the point of swallowing Vichy anyway as they feared that the Allies would invade French North Africa and become that much closer to mainland France if such an invasion was successful. The FO considered that the State Department was determined to maintain their relationship with Vichy, but this was unlikely as events were sweeping US concerns away from Vichy and closer to London.

The FO had already observed that the Americans were moving away from Vichy, whom they knew could not really be trusted, as an American consul general had been appointed at Brazzaville. That was Free French territory in what is today the capital city of the Republic of the Congo. This new American policy was pursued from February 1942 in relation to French islands in the Pacific. The State Department was dealing with the Free French National Committee in matters affecting the defence of territories under the control of the Free French and of strategic importance to the USA.

The limited American acceptance of the status of Free French territories was not what de Gaulle craved – complete recognition of the Free French and its territories – but was enough to provoke Vichy to protest against it. The State Department replied to the Vichy ambassador in Washington DC with a 'stiff note' informing him that France could only be restored with the complete defeat of Germany. This was underlined by some quite undiplomatic language from the Americans, stating that this was a fact that must be known even by those who had 'sordidly and abjectly, under the guise of "collaboration" attempted to prostitute their country to the regime in Germany which is bent upon nothing less than the permanent enslavement of France'.[19]

Vichy had been put on notice by the US government that the relationship between them was limited. Clearly, the Americans knew what their long term plan was – the defeat of Germany, no matter what. If Vichy got in the way it would be trampled underfoot. As the Free French were fighting on the side 'of the forces of freedom', the American government could hardly ignore them.[20] But the bottom line was that time was running out for Vichy. It was becoming less important to the USA while the US government could scarcely be seen tolerating Vichy for much longer. As we shall see, the question of continued recognition of Vichy was about to become irrelevant since, by the end of 1942, the Germans had occupied the remainder of France.

The event which caused the Germans to occupy France in total was Operation TORCH, the Anglo-American landings in French North Africa in November 1942. No matter what the Vichy government said, the British and Americans were going to land there anyway but it was the Vichy response to Allied troops landing which did matter: would Vichy forces resist, assist or do nothing? That was something which obviously interested the Allies and it was in their interests to line up Vichy officials in the area who would be sympathetic towards the Allies. This is why the Allies were horrified to see Pierre Laval returned to power within the Vichy regime. Laval was no friend of the Allies and wished to see a German victory since he considered that, if this was not to be the case, the Soviet Union or 'Bolshevism' would rule the world. Despite this, he professed that he would help to defend France and its empire against anyone. Equally, he was deluded enough to believe that he would be able to work with the Nazis to defend French interests as defined by Vichy.

The idea that Vichy had any influence with the Germans was quickly disproved when Hitler, after ordering the complete occupation of France in December 1942, also abolished the 100,000-strong French army maintained by Vichy. This was replaced by Laval in January 1943 with the establishment of a French militia, *la Milice*, a police force of volunteers which was to maintain order.[21] This formation, which the Vichy authorities were to provide for France, was probably the most squalid formation outside the SS. It became responsible for rounding up many French Jews and, ultimately, for their victims' deaths as they were deported by the thousand to concentration and extermination camps outside France. Perhaps the most positive action taken in Vichy France following the German entry there was the scuttling of the French fleet at Toulon. It may have broken the hearts of the French crews, but it denied the Germans the ships.[22]

Nevertheless, Churchill, despite loathing the regime, noted in a memorandum dated 5 June 1942 and circulated to the War Cabinet that the Vichy government was the only French government able to deliver from France certain things that the British government desired – the Toulon fleet and entry into French North Africa. The chances of getting those two objectives through was remote but not impossible. However, it was also known that the Vichy government, no matter who led it, always had to please the Germans. The alternative was German occupation.

Churchill was accommodating towards the Vichy government as he observed that Vichy had done no more than the bare necessities to prevent German occupation of its portion of France. Churchill noted that the Vichy government had endured Oran, Dakar, Syria and Madagascar, the British blockade and British air raids with little in the way of retaliation. Churchill felt that the French, whether living in occupied or unoccupied France, on the whole considered that they must not sever the future of France from the USA. However, the main challenge for the Vichy government according to the FO was 'who will win the war?'[23]

In 1940 it seemed that Germany would, but that was to overlook the lessons of that year. The Germans had lost at sea and in the air to the British and their allies. Once Germany invaded the Soviet Union and had been halted just short of Moscow in the winter, finding out the hard way just how frigid the Russian winter was and how stubborn the Red Army fought, things were no longer clear. In 1942 the German offensive in the Soviet Union had resumed, but it was only a matter of time before winter bit once again and defeated the Germans.

With the USA in the war and supplying the Soviet Union, it was clear that Germany was to be defeated in the east while Churchill had never had any doubt of an Allied victory against Germany and its allies. Once the USA entered the war, it was obvious that Churchill was vindicated in his stubborn attitude against Germany, including his support for de Gaulle and the Free French even if, at times, de Gaulle exasperated him. Overall, however, Churchill wanted to see all of France united in the war against Germany.

Anthony Eden, the Foreign Secretary, noting Churchill's views of the situation with Vichy, sent him a draft memorandum on 11 June, documenting the previous behaviour of the Vichy government. According to Eden, Pétain had tried to keep Vichy within the terms of the Franco-German armistice, believing that France was defeated and that enough French blood had been shed. He regarded that the complete military defeat of France in 1940 justified the desertion by France of the United Kingdom. However, as Eden pointed out, this was not quite true since Pétain and his fellow collaborators had also expected the British to be defeated during the summer of 1940. Therefore, Pétain had concluded that, if France negotiated a treaty with Germany, France would get better terms. Eden told Churchill that, since the French defeat, Pétain had been completely defeatist and there was no reason to see any alteration in his attitude. His prestige in unoccupied France was low and in occupied France non-existent.

If Pétain was more pragmatic, even if his approach was craven in the presence of the German occupier, Laval was quite different and did nothing to hide his antagonism towards the Allies. He told the American Ambassador to Vichy, Admiral William Leahy, that a German victory or a possible negotiated peace was better than a British or Soviet victory. Laval was not only working his passage with the Germans but, as Eden put it, 'had staked his life on a German victory'. Darlan's views were well known. His statement about British actions at Madagascar were more violent that those from other Vichy leaders. Darlan had tried to arrange French supplies for the Axis in Libya and Japanese help against the British in Madagascar which had included hideouts along the Madagascan shoreline for Japanese submarines that sank British shipping going to Egypt. Of course, this was an impossible situation and the Allies had to take steps to halt it.[24]

Eden made the quite valid point that those French people fighting against the Axis powers could only be contemptuous of their countrymen who had allowed the contested French province of Alsace-Lorraine to be incorporated into Germany. Eden concluded that it was unlikely that Vichy could be returned to fighting the Germans under the present regime. Eden, probably looking towards a post-war France, considered that not even Pétain's age would save him in the end. It looked as if Eden obviously considered that France would be liberated, those who had collaborated with Germany would be called to account and would probably pay the price for their treachery with their heads. Eden's assessment was very close to what was to happen in the years leading up to the liberation of France and the immediate post-war period in France.

At times Churchill was conflicted in his relationship with France. He told Eden that he had been a 'friend of France for thirty-five years' and that it was too easy to set out a case against Vichy, but it should be remembered that Vichy was living under 'unnatural conditions prevailing in a defeated country with a government living under the sufferance of the enemy'. Churchill did not want to wage war against the French and wanted the Vichy government to come out of the cold but was also very aware that the Germans would occupy the Vichy controlled area of mainland France at the drop of a hat. He still hoped that the French fleet might sail for Africa: it was Vichy alone which could 'offer those good gifts'. Churchill observed to Eden that one day it might reach the point, when the Vichy leadership records were called to judgement, that certain actions might save them. Little about Vichy was clear. Overall, Churchill considered that there was unity between himself and the FO in the case of Vichy with the difference being 'emphasis'. Churchill allowed Eden's draft to be circulated through the War Cabinet in preparation for discussion in anticipation of trying to convince de Gaulle to remain in the UK where he could be controlled rather than be left to say as he wished in Brazzaville.[25]

Eden replied to Churchill on 29 June, telling him that there was sufficient agreement between the prime minister and himself and proposed to modify his draft which was circulated to the War Cabinet on 8 July. In the amended memorandum discussed information received from various quarters in France. Much was about the confusion in attitude of the French, both in France and in French North Africa. About 90 per cent of those living in occupied France and around 60 per cent of those living in unoccupied France wanted an Allied victory. However, there was no consensus regarding how post-war France might be governed and led. Therefore, it was too early to try to make a guess in this matter.

Nevertheless, by June, *The Economist* reported that, as opposition against the Germans and the Vichy regime gathered apace, the symbolic effect of 'Gaullism' was becoming apparent as the symbol of total resistance. However, some considered that French resistance was too focused on the figure of de Gaulle and that perhaps the basis of any movement leading to French freedom should have a wider basis. It was noted that de Gaulle and the Fighting French belonged to no particular political party but included men from every party and opinion who were united in the single cause: the liberation of France.[26] Simply, that was all that de Gaulle wanted – his country liberated and able to settle its own future; he was also willing to fight the Axis powers, the Vichy regime and, if necessary, the Allies and his own men to achieve that aim. Overall, he was not interested in personal power, just the liberty of his country and his compatriots. It was that simple: small wonder that de Gaulle got frustrated with the attitudes of the Allies, especially, the Americans, as they sought to circumvent some of his policies due to personal prejudice against de Gaulle and his country. As with all prejudice, it was seated in ignorance.

As we have seen, British policy had been to encourage and co-operate with those Frenchmen and women who resisted the Germans and wanted to work with the British to this end. The FO stated that it had always been the British intention that, at war's end and the liberation of France, the French would decide their own fate without any interference from the British. It was noted that many French people had taken this to mean that de Gaulle would not be forced on them as a post-war leader. De Gaulle had been recognised as the figurehead of French resistance. De Gaulle had disliked the description of *La France Libre* (Free French) and so the British government, at his wish, adopted the motto *La France Combattante* (Fighting French). This alteration was to emphasise the 'symbolic value' of de Gaulle in occupied France as the leader of French resistance. De Gaulle was the only French resistance leader to emerge since 1940 but was a long way from being able to substantiate any claim to being regarded as France or as the head of the French government. Indeed, there was no French authority which could be regarded as being generally representative of the French people.

By 1942 the difficulties of the British relationship with de Gaulle were well known but not always understood. De Gaulle could be impetuous, which was dangerous, while he was also prone to deep suspicion, often of those who were trying to help him and his country. Like many of his countrymen he suffered deeply from the humiliation of the defeat and occupation of his country. He was not along in this attitude as the Polish leader, General Władysław Sikorski, felt the same. The British were not the only people to struggle with de Gaulle; his own supporters often did. Nevertheless, since 1940 de Gaulle had kept the French flag flying and French honour intact.

The British government realised that they also had a responsibility to de Gaulle as, since 1940, they had built him up and could not drop him in 1942. If they did it was quite likely that most of his leading supporters would have followed him. The British recognised that they were unlikely to find anybody to replace de Gaulle whose disappearance would have a bad effect on the resistance in France. Eden noted that the British had tried, and failed, to establish direct relations with Vichy following the withdrawal of the French embassy in London. Twice in the ensuing six months, the FO tried to contact the Vichy regime, but the Germans forbade any contact, no matter how modest, including a British financial representative in Vichy. This was probably best in any case as Laval had announced the hope of a German victory over the UK. It would have been difficult to have maintained a workable relationship with such an attitude. With resistance activity gaining strength in France, any British support for the Vichy regime would have weakened this work which was to be so important once the Allies landed in mainland France in June 1944. Pétain, probably the weakest link in the Vichy government, had only one real ambition: to maintain unity in France, and so he collaborated with the enemy so was forced to declare publicly his full confidence in Laval.

Eden and the FO tried to give the Vichy regime some credit; it had not surrendered the French fleet or French North Africa to the Germans. It had also tried to keep the Germans to the terms of the armistice. However, it was also noted that French public opinion also put a brake on more open collaboration with the Germans. Nevertheless, the FO could not find any evidence which suggested that Vichy was prepared to bring France into the war on the side of the Allies. It was considered that it might do so at a time when such action would be of no benefit, no doubt based on Vichy vulture-like sitting around waiting to see who might win. The Year 1942 was certainly a gamechanger. For the first time General Giraud entered the frame as it was considered that he might become more popular than de Gaulle but, in the view of the FO, this was unlikely. Giraud, as we will see, would be blown up by the Americans, notably Roosevelt himself, and pitted against de Gaulle. That exercise was to serve no purpose but underlined Roosevelt's distaste for de Gaulle and was to end in humiliation for the Americans as they tried to impose their ill-informed views on Europeans who had been fighting the war since 1939 and not 1941.

In terms of loyalties within the Vichy regime, Pétain had kept the support of most of his generals, including Weygand, as well as those who were known to be anti-German and preferred the Allies. However, there appeared to be no movement, even amongst those men, of breaking away from Vichy. Finally, by the middle of 1942, the FO had decided against such a background of confusion that its French policy was to continue to make the best efforts to get France and as much of its empire enter the war against the Axis powers, support all forces of French resistance and continue to support de Gaulle and strengthen his forces by encouraging the enlistment of all suitable Frenchmen as could be persuaded to join him.[27]

As the war proceeded and was heading towards the British and American invasion of French North Africa, French morale was considered. At the beginning of October, the FO drew up a memorandum on the subject. It was considered that, overall, the French were anti-Axis but not unified in support of the British. Friendliness towards the UK had been undermined by the shock of defeat and unrelenting anti-British propaganda. British attacks on Vichy targets caused resentment, especially the sinking of the French fleet at Oran in July 1940 with the loss of nearly 1,300 French lives. At this point there was no input regarding the popularity of the USA but, at a superficial level, the USA seemed to be more popular than the UK with the French. Nevertheless, the French looked for liberation from both the British and the Americans. Until Laval's return to power, morale in occupied France was much higher than in the unoccupied zone; in both territories the people were anti-German but in the unoccupied zone they were quite apathetic. Reports, however, had since indicated a rise of morale in the latter zone.

In the occupied zone, anti-German feeling was manifested in acts of violence, often carried out without thought of personal risk. These acts were often revenge and against the feeling of helplessness and despair. At a certain level it was worrying that the only organised resistance in France was the communist resistance. Collaboration in the occupied zone seemed to be from a small number, who included industrialists who had had long-term relations with Germany or hoped to gain from German dominance in the 'New Europe'. There was also evidence of financiers or so-called 'middlemen' who saw an opportunity with the Germans, as well as self-seeking politicians and admirers of the Nazi system who hoped to lead a 'Nazi France'. Overall, the French had reacted well to British air raids and other attacks against the enemy in France but, when there were local casualties, the positive response was muted.

The return of Laval to power, followed by his public statement that he hoped for a German victory in the war, altered the attitude of the French living in the unoccupied zone. This had been especially noticed amongst the middle classes who, prior to Laval's return, had only been passively anti-German and were concerned mainly with food and employment. Laval's pro-German announcement of 22 June, accompanied by the campaign to send French workers to Germany, the deportation of Jews, the compulsory labour decree and increasing evidence of Gestapo activity, had led to a rise of resentment. Labour in industrial areas began actively to resist the Germans. Nevertheless, active resistance to the Germans was not uniform since peasant landowners, who were better fed and less discontented, were also anti-communist and probably feared a Soviet victory.

The French Army was beginning to alter the stance it had maintained since the defeat in 1940. At the outset of the regime, it had been influenced by blind obedience to Pétain. By 1942, the FO considered that the French Army was willing to rally to a non-political general with a nationwide appeal, even if he was not backed by Pétain. However, problems remained as the French Army would not follow de Gaulle and had a poor opinion of the military capabilities of the British Army. It was certainly not pro-British and often xenophobic. The plus side of the French Army was that it was definitely anti-German and, in Metropolitan France, unlikely to fight against a powerful Allied army. In Vichy colonies it was likely that French troops would put up a token resistance against a superior invading force. The French Navy was anti-British but also anti-German and totally hated the Italians. The reaction of individual units was unknown. The results of decent treatment after the armistice and the fact that the French Navy remained undefeated had helped maintain its morale. The morale of the air force was impaired by long inactivity but was favourable to the Allies. Anti-British feeling was largely confined to senior officers while anti-German feeling was widespread in the air force.

It was noted that support for de Gaulle came from within the civilian population. He was considered to be the symbol of resistance, but it was likely that, at first, there may have been a search for such a figure within France. However, since this had turned up the likes of Pétain and Weygand, who had lost much of their prestige, it meant that de Gaulle was turned to since there was simply nobody else suited to the job. The FO noted that, even though de Gaulle's supporters were relatively few, French morale would be crushed if the British abandoned him. It was observed that, after the collapse of France in 1940, the French Communist Party had remained largely intact. The communist resistance was willing to work with other genuine resistance groups but were fearful of betrayal if they co-operated with British or de Gaullist agents.

This was justified given the long arm of Stalin, the Soviet dictator, who could bide his time to deal with traitors, imagined or otherwise. The other consideration regarding working with communists was the fear of many French people that, ultimately, the Soviets might well win the war and occupy France in place of the Germans. Russian armies had been in Paris in 1814. It was quite clear that the British had to continue to support de Gaulle, no matter what Roosevelt said: after nearly three years of war, it was quite clear that de Gaulle was the only chance that the French had in 1942.

Nevertheless, the situation between the Allies and Vichy remained very much controlled by the US State Department which was considered to be weak by the FO. It might have been more beneficial if the Americans had taken a firmer line with Vichy but there was much at stake regarding the coming North African landings. However, the Americans took a tough stance in the Caribbean and closely monitored Vichy movements in the French West Indies, even if a German submarine managed to call in at Martinique and take off a wounded German officer.[28]

However, the British had been dealing with the hostile Vichy attitude since 1940 and largely had been able to contain it, but the obstinacy of Vichy officials and senior officers was extremely vexing. It was made all the more difficult as by 1942 it was quite obvious that Germany was going to lose the war and so it remained curious as to why Vichy officials remained loyal to Germany. The truth was that in their deluded heads they were loyal to France and considered de Gaulle the traitor. They could not have been more wrong, as several were to find out after 1945 when they stood trial at French courts martial and later faced French firing squads. Overall, the UK government did not wish to have a state of war between the UK and Vichy but co-operation and a clear cut-off from Germany. This, of course, would have led to the annexation of Vichy, as happened once the Allies landed in North Africa, but the French colonies could have co-operated more keenly. A further problem was that the French Navy had not been defeated and did not see itself as needing to work with the British. As the Royal Navy had destroyed a French fleet at Oran, the relationship with the French Navy was always going to be difficult. The case of the French senior naval officer, Admiral Godfroy, is a prime example.

As with all problems with Vichy and the UK, 1940 and the Fall of France was the origin of problems with Admiral Godfroy. In June 1940 Godfroy had been in command of a squadron consisting of one battleship, four cruisers, two destroyers and a submarine based in Alexandria, Egypt under the overall command of Admiral Sir Andrew Cunningham, Royal Navy. After the armistice, Godfroy with most of his officers and men, maintained allegiance to Vichy and refused to join de Gaulle or to fight in the war alongside the British. On 4 July Godfroy agreed to discharge all the fuel from his ships and place them out of harm's way and unable to fight. However, in 1942 things began to change as Cunningham gave up his command since he had been appointed to command naval forces for the North Africa landings and was leaving Alexandria on 1 April 1942.

However, it was considered that the best plan was to continue as before. The agreement had rendered the French ships virtually harmless; parts of all the main armament had been removed and torpedo warheads been taken ashore. Later, it was observed that the secondary armament and anti-aircraft guns remained in working order and that some parts for the main armament could be improvised to allow the firing of a limited number of rounds. The crews had been reduced to a third of their normal complement and the ships had been in harbour for two years. Once a week, a ration of oil was issued to work the auxiliary engines. Godfroy had kept all his undertakings and the squadron had caused no real problem. Even during the Syrian campaign Godfroy had kept his squadron in harbour. The British paid the officers and men and kept them supplied.

At the time of the Syrian operation, the British had considered seizing Godfroy's squadron and, later, had considered doing so to replace ships lost in operations. Cunningham had always opposed this move, not only since he believed it to be a breach of faith but also for practical reasons as it was believed that the French had already prepared scuttling charges which could be fired easily. Cunningham also pointed out that, if taken intact, the ships were not immediately seaworthy and would need extensive refitting with special arrangements made for production of ammunition for their guns. The political repercussions at Vichy and Toulon needed no explanation if the squadron was seized. Cunningham was more seriously concerned about trouble with the main French fleet than the squadron at Alexandria.

On 31 March, the War Cabinet considered Cunningham's opinions and agreed that the agreement with Godfroy needed to be improved in favour of the British. An example was to repatriate the crews save those who wanted to join de Gaulle, as well as producing propaganda to secure better terms and, ultimately, British control of the French ships. Therefore, it was decided to renew the existing agreement temporarily and to allow Cunningham's successor, Admiral Harwood, who was leaving in early May to take over the command in Alexandria, to begin new negotiations. The Admiralty wanted little change to any agreements over the French squadron but Godfroy had other ideas as he wanted reliefs for existing personnel with long service abroad. Initially, the British were willing to agree with Godfroy's request and Harwood made the necessary arrangements.

However, the situation changed after the British defeat in Libya when Alexandria came under threat by Axis forces. Harwood discussed the situation with Godfroy who informed Harwood that he had instructions not to let his ships fall into any foreign hands. He also refused to scuttle his ships before the Germans reached Alexandria as there remained a chance that the squadron might be allowed to return to France. Harwood said that the Admiralty might allow the French ships to go to Bizerta if Godfroy agreed to certain conditions designed to ensure that they did not fall into enemy hands.

The War Cabinet considered the affair on 29 June. It was considered that, should Godfroy refuse to sail his ships out of Alexandria if and when the British were compelled to evacuate the port, he would be committing a hostile act and so breaking the agreement. Godfroy was not to be allowed the luxury of delaying action until the last moment; refusal to leave Alexandria would be a hostile act. Furthermore, in the spirit of the agreement, French ships would go to another port under British control. It was decided that if Godfroy refused to leave harbour, the British would destroy the French vessels. The War Cabinet told Harwood that he should hint to Godfroy that this was the action that might be taken unless he complied to British wishes.

On 26 June, the Vichy government weighed in and ordered Godfroy to try to reach a French port in the event of a British evacuation of Alexandria. Godfroy shared these instructions with Harwood, who, on 2 July, reported that Godfroy had asked him to assure the British government that he would never allow his ships to fall to the Germans. On the following day, Harwood was instructed not to take action until the fall of Alexandria was certain: the most drastic action to be taken was to ensure that none of the ships went back to French ports. On 9 July it was learned from Roosevelt that the Vichy government was insisting that the French ships must go to a French port and not, as the US government had suggested, to a neutral port via the Suez Canal.

Roosevelt was proposing to suggest to Laval and Godfroy that the squadron be promised safe passage, via the canal, to Martinique where the ships would be immobilised for the duration of the war on the same basis as other ships there. A similar suggestion had come from Mr R.G. Casey, the UK Minister Resident in the Middle East. The War Cabinet, after determining its refusal to allow the squadron to sail for Bizerta, agreed to Roosevelt's suggestion, irrespective of the military situation in Alexandria.

Once the immediate threat against Alexandria was lifted, the question regarding the French squadron ceased to be a matter of urgency but the question of Godfroy's attitude remained. The FO certainly did not trust him and questioned whether his attitude during the period of urgency was actually in line with his commitment to the terms of his ships lying at the port in Alexandria. There was particular discomfort with the question of Godfroy being in wireless communication with France. However, there was no evidence of his using this facility against British interests. The War Cabinet asked Eden and the First Lord of the Admiralty to examine the entire question. It was concluded that Godfroy had so far carried out his side of the agreement and was unlikely to break it, even if the Vichy government demanded he do so, unless the fall of Alexandria was imminent. All the time, the British remained fully in control of the port it was considered that, out of sheer pragmatism, Godfroy would remain true to the British, but the British had to consider that an officer junior to Godfroy might try to take over the French ships. Godfroy's main aim was to preserve his ships for France and he would resist force from any quarter. There was enough armament remaining in his ships to ensure that any major operation could ensure the destruction of their wireless, let alone the seizure or destruction of the ships. The French wireless facilities seemed to haunt the British and it was concluded that Godfroy was unlikely to allow the British to deprive him of them. In any case he could have rigged up a wireless set for emergencies.

This placed the British in a dilemma. Should they allow the existing agreement to remain and hope that Godfroy would agree to keep to it before the Germans arrived at Alexandria rather than see his ships destroyed? Or should they contend that his recent refusal to agree to sail his ships to another port under Allied control in the event of an emergency made the original agreement invalid? It was decided that there was a need to apply pressure on Godfroy to ensure that he agreed that his ships would sail somewhere chosen by the British if required to do so. Options were discussed, such as cutting off the water supply and supplies as well as stopping all shore leave until Godfroy agreed, but it was considered that the French could distil their own water and had ample supplies. There was a constant fear that he might scuttle his ships as a last resort. The Admiralty and Eden favoured leaving the agreement as it was but on the understanding that Admiral Harwood had clear instructions to destroy the French squadron if the need arose. This view was accepted by the War Cabinet on 13 August but by this time it was irrelevant. The agreement therefore remained in place, but its question arose once more when the military situation on land changed. On 30 November, the War Cabinet learned that some of Godfroy's officers wished to resume fighting on the Allied side while others thought that this would break their oath to the head of state. Godfroy requested permission to be allowed to contact Pétain or Admiral Abrial on this matter but his request was denied by the War Cabinet and he was told to wait a fortnight to see how matters developed.

Nevertheless, Godfroy persisted in his stubborn attitude as, on 2 October, about a month before the Allied landings in French North Africa, he told the British consul general that he approved of the Armistice between his country and Germany since it had also saved the UK. Godfroy asserted that French policy in the interests of France had to be complete passivity and that the Vichy government had no moral right to endanger France by attempts at resistance and that no French soldier or sailor could honourably fight against the Axis. He also claimed that it was impossible to tell who might win the war, but it seemed unlikely that Germany would be defeated. Churchill had hoped that the Allied landings in North Africa might have changed Godfroy's mind but, in mid-December, Godfroy still had not changed his mind. He told Harwood that he would not give away his squadron without the consent of the legitimate government of France (Vichy). Godfroy was willing to accept the orders of a stable government in North Africa which represented all French people outside France but would not accept Darlan as head of such a government. Godfroy also considered that, unless the Allies captured and held Tunisia, they could not justify their claim to be able to liberate France. However, Godfroy stated that he would not prevent any officers or men who wished to do so joining the Allies. It should be considered that a message received by the FO from Paris dated 14 November told of rumours that Giraud, Darlan, Flandin, Bergeret and Pucheu were all in North Africa to form a government with American approval.[29]

It was not surprising that both the British government and de Gaulle were cautious, if not exasperated, when it came to dealing with characters such as Giraud and the US government. Giraud's loyalty was perhaps questionable while the American attitude towards Vichy was vexing to the British, especially Churchill. Indeed, historian Conrad Black asserts that Roosevelt's pro-Vichy stance was deeply unpopular in both the USA and the UK, but considered that he might be able to make it acceptable to both audiences since

Eisenhower, who was popular in both London and Washington, had a plan to for bringing both Darlan and Giraud on to the Allied side.[30] But, as we shall see, circumstances and Eisenhower's more intelligent reading of the situation with France undid Roosevelt's thinking which, as this narrative makes clear, was based on prejudice rather than realism.

However, this is not to leave de Gaulle blameless. The FO had plenty to criticise him for. It was considered that for two years de Gaulle had bluffed the Allies in many matters, which had favoured him, but it was time that he was made to work more honestly. It was to be made quite clear that co-operation was to be the best policy. As already noted, Spears wrote that de Gaulle found that he could easily bully the British and did so. In 1942, de Gaulle still considered that the British government was pursuing a long-term anti-French policy in Syria, which he believed was inherited from pre-1939. It was urged that de Gaulle be corrected in this notion and that the government should state once more its respect for French interests. A major problem remaining was that de Gaulle doubted British sincerity in support for his movement.[31] Six months earlier, senior officials at the FO were extremely frustrated at French behaviour with R.H. Hoare of the Political Intelligence Department remarking to Mack, 'I see no reason to recede from the opinion in my letter to Strang, on receipt of the first two records, that you had better drown de Gaulle *and* simultaneously remove Catroux to some quiet place!'[32] Incredible words from normally quite staid British civil servants.

As the war progressed, so did the problems between de Gaulle and the British. Much of this had to do with the French Navy. In a message to Strang, Admiral Dickens touched on the subject of the French Navy and its possible relationship with the British. Dickens stated:

> There is an inescapable fact in the welter of misunderstandings, jealousies, irritation and intrigue in the Free French body which throws a great deal of light on the French Naval attitude. It is that, although we may have signed an agreement with de Gaulle, the French Navy never did and if they had been asked to sign it they would, I am sure, have insisted on certain modifications. Further, the French Navy had already settled down to work with us long before the agreement was signed. Admiral Muselier and a good many others do not look upon de Gaulle as Commander-in-Chief of the Navy, but merely as the more or less titular head of the movement. Had de Gaulle been wise enough not to interfere in Naval affairs, especially where no interference was necessary, he might have got away with it; but as he has gone out of his way to show at every turn that he is Commander-in-Chief, opposition has become stronger and

stronger. I am sure that as soon as we have patched up the affairs on our hands at the moment it will be wise to convene a small Committee to try to get to the roots of the trouble and propose new machinery, even if it means a drastic renunciation of the former agreement. But for heaven's sake a *small* Committee![33]

This was part of de Gaulle's problem as leader of the Free French. He may have been commander-in-chief of French forces in exile at least but the French Navy, quite simply did not trust or like him. De Gaulle certainly did not help matters with the French Navy when he imprisoned Admiral Muselier illegally to 'fort detention'. Muselier made it clear to the FO that he had never signed any form of agreement or engagement with de Gaulle and had quite simply lost all faith in him.[34]

On 14 December the War Cabinet, on the advice of Admiral Harwood, decided to continue as before on condition that Godfroy allowed officers and men from his squadron to join the Fighting French if they so wished. The term 'Fighting French' was first notified in September 1942 when the French National Committee informed the Soviet government that the French movement did not accept the French capitulation to Germany and would continue to fight for the liberation of France as 'Fighting France'.[35]

Meanwhile, Churchill noted that Godfroy was rapidly becoming an admiral in command of a fleet who did not recognise allegiance to any government. It was observed by the British that Godfroy and his men were being paid by the UK and giving nothing in return but that the situation would be allowed to continue until the end of 1942 when pressure would be applied to Godfroy in an attempt to make him comply with British wishes. Nevertheless, Godfroy held out for another five months despite all the evidence that French interests and liberty lay with the Allies and their success, and French collaboration was a requirement for this.[36] It was obvious that Godfroy's and the Vichy stances could not be maintained for much longer since the Allies were landing in North Africa. On 26 December Admiral Darlan was assassinated by a young French monarchist. However, by January 1943 a new name entered the frame – General Henri Giraud.

Chapter 7

1943

Firming Up Towards Victory

The last chapter dealt almost exclusively with the question of Vichy and mentioned de Gaulle only in passing. Why? There are several answers, the most obvious being that there was a French government in France, albeit a puppet government in the unoccupied zone governing a German vassal state and totally at the mercy of the Germans. The Americans recognised Vichy, something the British were able to take advantage of whilst trying to obtain imperial French territory at least cost. Via the Americans, the British were able to maintain some links with Vichy as well as dealing with those in French colonies, mainly in Africa and the Middle East. A major preoccupation for the British was to keep French warships out of German hands and deny the Germans the use of French colonies, especially for the re-supplying of U-boats. The episode with Godfroy is an example of the backdoor diplomacy going on in 1942 with Vichy. Godfroy, as we have seen, was typical of Vichy commanders, sitting on the fence and waiting to see who might win the war.

During 1941 the Germans, in the shape of Rommel and the DAK, arrived and quickly went onto the offensive. Later, during the same year, the British launched Operation CRUSADER which relieved the besieged port of Tobruk on the Libyan coast. CRUSADER drove the Italo-German forces back to Mersa el Brega. In late January 1942, another Axis counter-offensive pushed the Eighth Army back to the Gazala Line in Libya from where it prepared for a fresh offensive. This was pre-empted by Rommel a few days before that operation could begin. Rommel's offensive led to the fall of Tobruk and the advance of the *Panzerarmee* into Egypt where it was stopped along the line from El Alamein to the Qattara Depression. It was only some determined and skilled generalship by Claude Auchinleck and, later, Montgomery which stabilised the situation in North Africa in favour of the Allies; before then the campaign had swung back and forth with the critical factor being logistics to which Rommel had paid insufficient attention. The year 1943 was to be a better year.

In late 1942, an Anglo-American force landed in North Africa and a new front was opened. Vichy became irrelevant as the Germans occupied the remainder of France and so the Allied focus returned to de Gaulle. However, the Americans, especially Roosevelt, could not stand him and hence Giraud entered the frame, championed by Roosevelt. Giraud was considered to be a contender and an alternative to de Gaulle. In conversations between Roosevelt and Churchill it is also quite clear that the Anglo-American alliance had more to do with the complete defeat of Germany rather than simply the liberation of France, which would happen along the way to Germany. After the TORCH landings in French North Africa, Roosevelt telegraphed Churchill and stated that the situation in North Africa was an onslaught against the Germans and not an attempt to liberate France. Roosevelt was very concerned at what he considered to be de Gaulle's political ambitions, possibly on the backs of British and American endeavours on the battlefield, as he commented to Churchill:

> If you speak at a secret session of the House [of Commons] on Thursday I do wish you would give me any suggestion of what you propose to say. I still do not like the things that de Gaulle and his Headquarters are saying to the press. I understand that he intimated yesterday on some form of election in North Africa for a system of Central Government. In my judgement this would raise Jewish and Moslem trouble. I said to both Giraud and de Gaulle that elections should not be held.[1]

Roosevelt's hostility towards de Gaulle was such that when US and British forces landed in French territories in North Africa in November de Gaulle was kept in the dark. This was a personal decision by Roosevelt. Furthermore, Roosevelt was operating on two flawed premises: the first was that de Gaulle was a fraud and so despised him; the second was that the landings should initially be made by American troops as Roosevelt considered that, if British forces landed first, Vichy forces would resist the Allies with greater vigour.[2] Roosevelt was, of course, incorrect on both accounts and whatever he meant by de Gaulle being a 'phoney' is not clear. Historian William Mortimer Moore observes that de Gaulle, after learning from his then ADC Captain Pierre Billotte, who had been warned three hours before the operation had begun but decided to let de Gaulle sleep, that Allied forces had landed in North Africa was speechless at the British audacity before finally speaking saying that he hoped 'the Vichy people throw them back into the sea. You don't get into France *par effraction* – by breaking and entering'.[3] But it was proven that one could, even if Vichy forces fought for three days before understanding that the British and Americans meant business and were going to take the North

African coastline no matter what; they were not in the business of asking for permission to land on a foreign-held possession.

Roosevelt, typically as an American of his time, was against imperialism of any form despite the fact that the United States had been building an empire since the late nineteenth century: how the USA was settled at the expense of the Native American is yet another question. But in 1943 the USA was certainly against any further European empire building. This remained Roosevelt's grievance against de Gaulle – he feared that de Gaulle wanted to maintain the French Empire, which was true, but the Allies needed imperial French territory to strike back at Axis forces; the fightback on land began in Africa. Whether de Gaulle actually had political ambition is a difficult question. In 1940 he had destiny thrust upon him as leader of the Free French, but the war had morphed in many directions. In 1942 his role had become more political as he tried to keep his forces together and the question of France alive. Of course, he did become the greatest Frenchman of the twentieth century, but not a dictator as Roosevelt was to allege. De Gaulle never wanted to become a dictator and never did become one. Roosevelt's prejudices were the main reason for bringing Giraud into the picture as a rival to de Gaulle. The Americans held a weak hand in this matter. Yet who exactly was Giraud?

Quite frankly, he was a bit of a failure having been captured twice by the Germans – once in the First World War and again in 1940. He escaped both times. Nevertheless, this did not stop de Gaulle from taunting Giraud when they finally met in North Africa. In a FO report a conversation with a French officer, Captain Philippe Roy, was recorded. Roy said that on encountering Giraud; de Gaulle said, 'tell me is it true that when you were captured you and your officers didn't attempt to fight?'

It was noted that de Gaulle, when called on by the Germans to surrender, refused and he and his men and tanks fought their way out. In the opening of the conversation Giraud had taken a patronising air towards de Gaulle who had served as a colonel under him at Metz in 1940, calling him 'Mon Cher' but, by the end of the encounter, Giraud referred to de Gaulle as 'Mon General'. This first meeting of the two men as generals had shown increasing respect of each other but also of increasing frigidity. It should be noted that Captain Roy had little respect for Giraud's military value since he knew nothing of the advances made since 1940 in mechanised warfare.[4] Quite simply, the American backing of Giraud was foolish while Roy's observation of Giraud having been out of the loop since 1940 reflected Giraud's time in captivity since then and it was only with British aid that he managed to escape.[5]

There were several problems with the American selection of Giraud. The most obvious one was his support of the Pétain government or, quite simply, for that of Vichy, that treacherous body which betrayed its country and people at every turn. However, it must also be remembered that the USA continued to recognise that regime rather than accept de Gaulle. Giraud was the American alternative to de Gaulle, but as Jean Edward Smith observes, it was a poor choice since Giraud did not have the experience to replace de Gaulle. Furthermore, he knew nothing about the situation in North Africa. Eisenhower later said that Giraud 'wanted to be a big shot, a bright shining light, and the acclaimed saviour of France, but turned out to be a terrible blow to our expectations'.[6]

Black recounts the first meeting between Eisenhower and Giraud in Eisenhower's underground command room on the Gibraltar rock. Giraud was a pompous man who announced his own arrival in the command room with 'General Giraud has arrived. General Giraud is ready to assume command of the operation'. The operation being TORCH. Luckily for Giraud, Eisenhower did not understand French although he soon got the gist of what Giraud was saying. Giraud was hoping to assume command despite the fact that he stood before Eisenhower in civilian clothes which were mired by the waters of the Mediterranean owing to an almost fatal fall into the brine whilst being transferred between vessels. Not having had a chance to change his clothes, he stood before Eisenhower, full of his own importance in a sea-stained bedraggled civilian costume. He was a clown.

Over and over, Eisenhower tried to inform Giraud that he would not be commanding the operation since it probably involved Frenchmen fighting Frenchmen. Giraud had been promised by Murphy that he would be in command of the operation, but Eisenhower could see the flaws in a French commander ordering attacks against his own countrymen. Eisenhower had also been warned by political advisors that Giraud was seriously mistaken about his role in the forthcoming operation. Eventually, Eisenhower told Giraud bluntly that the operation was to proceed no matter what Giraud did and that he was about to waste his chance to play an important role in history. After seven hours Giraud left, announcing that 'General Giraud will be a spectator'.[7] Giraud's arrogance was quite staggering.

With Vichy forces resisting American forces in North Africa, the American government came up with a secondary plan and turned to Admiral Jean Darlan, Pétain's deputy, who was in Algiers on a family matter. The US High Command swiftly reached an agreement with Darlan. If he could persuade Vichy forces to cease fighting in Morocco and Algeria, he would be appointed high commissioner of North Africa as a token of American gratitude with Giraud commander of all French forces in the same area. De Gaulle, of course, was to be excluded.[8]

This was highly irregular and illustrated the attempts by Roosevelt who was driven by his own personal prejudice against de Gaulle whom he sought to undermine at every turn. In this case, however, the American president was setting himself up for a pratfall. His policies regarding de Gaulle and the Free French were those of utter failure, owing to his loathing of de Gaulle. As we shall see, Eisenhower understood and respected de Gaulle, with whom he got along with and worked with in more-or-less perfect harmony.

Nevertheless, Roosevelt's attitude towards de Gaulle caused anxiety to Churchill and his government. The British tried to make the Americans sweet whilst honouring pledges made to de Gaulle in 1940 when he and his forces had tried to stem the German invasion of France and later had stood with the British during the difficult days of 1940. During that trying period the Americans were remaining aloof from what they considered to be a purely European affair, albeit Roosevelt had been covertly aiding the British. Roosevelt tolerated Churchill but always sought to pick an argument with de Gaulle who, in turn, never seemed to try to duck a fight whenever he felt that he or France had been insulted. Both men were very difficult and prickly while Churchill, not the easiest of men, tried to referee some of the pointless jousting between them. It was fortunate that there were others who, even though they were subordinate to their political masters, were not afraid of them and so could unpick some of the foolishness which was masked as policy. For Churchill, there was his Foreign Secretary, Anthony Eden.

Eden was quite blunt in his assessment of the comparative qualities of de Gaulle, Darlan and Giraud. As Eden asserted, that there was no third party: he was instantly dismissing Giraud as a contender whom the British never saw as a runner.[9] The question of Darlan as an alternative French leader was vexing since he did hold great influence with the French, but it was dwindling. The British had been warned that Darlan could not be trusted because de Gaulle's senior representative in the Middle East, General Georges Catroux, had warned Eden on 26 November 1942 that 'Darlan is an utterly unreliable opportunist', 'opportunism' being a euphemism for treachery.[10]

Meanwhile, Darlan remained the problem that the Allies had to deal with in French North Africa, but he represented little in the eyes of the British. De Gaulle remained the most visible symbol of French resistance to the Germans and to Vichy. Ignoring the possibilities of de Gaulle's political ambitions, the British government supported him, especially as he was popular with the British public.[11] Something few Frenchmen have achieved!

Churchill remained faithful to de Gaulle and observed that the decision to isolate him was the fault of the Americans and the UK was forced to bow to American pressure. But Churchill pledged to de Gaulle that nothing had altered in his support for him and that no agreement between himself and the French leader had been revoked. As Churchill reminded de Gaulle, they had been through bad times together and, now that a corner was being turned, he would remain constant to him. Churchill also let his thoughts be known to Roosevelt, remarking in a cable to the US president:

> I ought to let you know that very deep currents of feeling are stirred by the arrangement with Darlan. The more I reflect upon it the more convinced I become that it can only be a temporary expedient, justifiable solely by the stress of battle.[12]

Churchill was letting Roosevelt down gently. Without doubt, he was aware that Roosevelt was prejudiced against the Frenchman. It was also obvious that Roosevelt was out of touch regarding the situation in North Africa, if not the entire war. As with Churchill and de Gaulle, Roosevelt was a product of his own family, class and country. He was a vain snob and instinctively distrusted Europeans, especially those he considered to be from the elite classes.

In his prejudice Roosevelt was missing the plank in his own eye since he was from a very privileged background. Even though it is true that he did a lot more than many American leaders to relieve poverty in the USA during the Depression, he had never experienced hardship himself, except his own physical disabilities. He suffered from polio. At the same time the USA was building an empire, something that Roosevelt and many Americans professed to despise. As already noted, the way in which the USA was colonised and settled during the nineteenth century is also questionable, and it certainly was not ethical. All three men, Churchill, de Gaulle and Roosevelt, were brilliant and at the same time quite foolish. Roosevelt's folly seemed to have been largely tied up with his attitude towards France and its leaders.

As Jean Edward Smith noted, the problem with Darlan was what Darlan represented. The American decision to install him probably did save American lives but not that many. However, the appointment of Darlan as high commissioner in North Africa was to accept aspects of the Vichy regime and, therefore, Nazi Germany – everything which Churchill and de Gaulle had been fighting against since 1939 and at great sacrifice to their respective countries and compatriots. Darlan represented the Vichy regime which maintained Pétain as leader, with Nazi sympathisers in office and Jews routinely persecuted while the de Gaullist symbol, the Cross of Lorraine, remained banned.[13] To say the least, it was not surprising that Churchill and de Gaulle were both astonished at American policy and what could only be perceived as reckless and lacking any understanding of the situation in France and within the French Empire. As Churchill said gently, perhaps it was due to the stress of battle, one which the Americans had only latterly joined. There is a further argument which suggests that American support for Darlan and then Giraud backfired.

However, the British received an early Christmas present as on Christmas Eve Darlan was assassinated. It is not clear who organised the killing; the White House claimed that it was de Gaullists, but there is significant evidence to lay the blame at the door of the Office of Strategic Services (OSS).[14] His assassin, Fernand Bonnier de la Chappelle, is credited with being a de Gaullist-Royalist, an interesting fusion of politics, but seen at the time as being of the left.[15] The OSS later became the Central Intelligence Agency (CIA) and, of course, both are and were the American intelligence networks responsible for the security of the USA.

Whoever was actually responsible for the murder of Darlan, it seemed that Bonnier was determined to take the rap and signed a confession, apparently without coercion. Bonnier implicated Henri d'Astier de la Vigerie, a royalist conspirator and brother of de Gaulle's recent emissary to Algiers had persuaded Bonnier to kill Darlan; de la Vigerie was never charged or officially connected with the slaying. François d'Astier de la Vigerie was one of de Gaulle's confidants whom Darlan had tried to have excluded from Algeria. In turn, the emissary had ignored Darlan when they met and then returned to London predicting that Darlan would soon vanish. The entire family seem to have had distinguished records of involvement in the Free French or the French Resistance. A further brother, Emmanuel, was a resistance hero and they were all nephews of a distinguished cardinal and members of a prominent family. The wretched Bonnier was court martialled and executed by firing squad at dawn on Boxing Day.[16] This was all very convenient for the Allies as an obvious thorn in their side had been dealt with very easily, in fact rather too easily.

Once Darlan had been assassinated, a problem had been removed. Roosevelt still supported Giraud and insisted that he replace Darlan – de Gaulle did not protest. It was clear that Giraud would be incapable of managing the political situation in Morocco and Algeria, something that de Gaulle sensed, but the tide was beginning to turn. It is claimed that the American support for Darlan and then Giraud provided stepping stones from Vichy to Free France and averted civil war in French North Africa.[17] Macmillan notes that, on the day of the Allied victory parade in Tunis on 20 May, there were two kinds of French troops – de Gaullists and Giraudists – and with Allied victory in North Africa, and no Germans left to shoot, there was a risk of civil war between the two groups unless Macmillan's diplomacy won through.[18]

This was the problem with Roosevelt's championing of Giraud: it had the potential to split the French command and to cause civil war within the French Empire. The former was not what Roosevelt wanted or desired. A little later Macmillan noted that the Americans who actually got to know de Gaulle discovered him to be very tiresome, yet he was the most intelligent of the French as well as being realistic and of 'a modern mind'.[19] Eisenhower was one of the Americans to make this discovery and was able fully to co-operate with de Gaulle in matters concerning the liberation of France and how it would be administrated by French civil authorities rather than falling under Allied military governance.

Within hours of the shooting of Darlan, de Gaulle symbols began to spring up all over Algiers, even if Giraud was still rounding up de Gaullists: de Gaulle could no longer be ignored. The British were delighted with the news of Darlan's death they could thus support the French resistance with every possible means. It was noted that, once Harold Macmillan arrived in North Africa, Giraud retreated into obscurity in British eyes.[20] It is interesting that Giraud was still waging war against de Gaulle. The assassination made life difficult for him in the long term. On 29 December, Giraud sent a message to de Gaulle which read:

> Great emotion had however been caused in civil and military circles in North Africa by the recent assassination. The atmosphere is therefore unfavourable at the moment for a personal meeting between us. In view of the rapid development now under way of the military situation here in North Africa, I believe it would be preferable for you to send me a representative qualified to arrange for the co-operation of French forces now engaged in battle against a common enemy.

On 25 December, de Gaulle had invited Giraud to meet him on French territory in either Algeria or Chad.[21]

The situation in Algiers after Darlan's assassination was certainly emotional and Giraud was on the wrong side of that emotion and of history. That he was continuing to arrest de Gaullists displayed his potential for treachery, but some Frenchmen saw their honour to be with the nation rather than de Gaulle or, in other words, their loyalty belonged to Vichy. But this was now in ruins as Darlan was dead and the Germans had occupied the previously unoccupied zone of France. Where was Giraud by the end of 1942? He needed time to gather his thoughts.

In January 1943, William Strang, at the FO, noted that Giraud had answered de Gaulle but did not want to see him before the end of January.

Giraud, however, would be happy to see de Gaulle in Algiers and requested that he send military representatives to Algiers to establish contact.[22] A further report to the FO from the diplomat Carrington-Bentinck stated that de Gaulle would only meet Giraud at Brazzaville, Lake Chad or in Syria, where he would only discuss the mechanism by which de Gaulle could assume French leadership. Carrington-Bentinck denied the latter half.[23] Clearly de Gaulle wanted home advantage but was he really angling for French political supremacy at that point of the war?

Meanwhile, the Allies had to sort out who their allies were amongst the French. General Charles Noguès, the Vichy Resident General in Morocco, was such an example. He was of a dubious quality to the Allies and had only been prevented from enacting Vichy anti-Semitic laws regarding the rounding up of Jews in Morocco and sending them to their deaths in Europe by the Sultan of Morocco who refused to ghettoise Jews in Morocco and have them sent to 'death factories in Europe'. The British representative in Morocco, Mr Bond, reported on Noguès in early January 1943. Bond considered that Noguès was widely said to be the principal obstacle to true co-operation with the Allies in Morocco. The assumption was based on the testimony of a number of 'prominent and patriotic French outside of official circles' who feared that Noguès would remain at his post and continue his policies.

Bond judged Noguès to be an ally in name only, and only as far as he was made to commit to the Allies. It was probable that he wanted the Axis forces defeated but with minimum French casualties and the maintenance of French interests, especially retaining Morocco for any future peace conference. Noguès was not convinced that the Axis were defeated and, therefore, sought to keep doors open, especially towards Vichy. Bond had also learned that Noguès was still in contact with Laval and receiving confidential messages from him. He was also constantly in touch with Vichy via the French Ambassador in Madrid. Furthermore, Noguès had no love for the USA and even less for the UK. After the Allied landings in French North Africa, Noguès discouraged close co-operation between the local French and the Allies but had been more cautious after the assassination of Darlan. Noguès was consistently hostile to de Gaulle and his followers; regarding them to be fighting a British war. Bond finished his assessment of Noguès with the warning that 'he has always been a trimmer and would be entirely unreliable in a crisis'.[24] It was quite clear that, despite what Roosevelt and his government thought, there was little in Vichy which was reliable. This boded ill for any meeting between de Gaulle and Giraud.

De Gaulle was constantly a source of concern regarding his behaviour and moods, as reported by Mr Peake, the British representative to the French National Committee (FNC). Peake met de Gaulle who was in a 'profound irritation of spirits from which he quickly worked himself into a rage'. The source of his rage was an undisclosed British press report. Peake reported that de Gaulle was refusing to meet Giraud or allowing any member of the FNC to do so. De Gaulle claimed that there had been two *moments psychologiques* when a single meeting might have settled everything regarding French North Africa. The first opportunity should have been within forty-eight hours of the Allied landings, the second within a week of Darlan's assassination. According to de Gaulle, despite what the British suggested, no third opportunity had presented itself and to suggest so spread confusion. It was noted that, on 14 January, the British newspaper, *News Chronicle*, had stated that de Gaulle was the UK's man while Giraud was the choice of the USA.[25]

This was to be a problem as both men were difficult, while sadly for Roosevelt, Giraud was the worse option and was to have little impact on exiled French circles. Nevertheless, the FO often commented on the difficulties encountered with de Gaulle, especially in relation with Giraud. Mack from the FO related a meeting between himself, de Gaulle and Giraud. Mack stated that de Gaulle was consistently unhelpful, had no interest in creating a good impression and affected complete indifference about the outcome of the meeting. The tone appeared to be that de Gaulle was determined not to allow Giraud to have any influence in the relationship between the British and French. In contrast, Mack considered that Giraud was friendlier but not forthcoming and had difficulties dealing with de Gaulle as an equal. Nevertheless, in the eyes of Mack, both generals wanted the meeting to be successful, especially as both Churchill and Roosevelt were pushing for some kind of agreement. Both Harold Macmillan and Mack were tireless in trying to bring de Gaulle and Giraud together. Any American documentation to suggest that Roosevelt wanted Giraud to protect French interests was absent.[26] For Giraud, who had been de Gaulle's senior officer in 1940, it was difficult to accept that de Gaulle was now his senior and that de Gaulle viewed him with contempt, mainly in relation to the circumstances of Giraud's capture in that year.

A couple of days earlier, Mack had written to Strang with an account of the meeting in which he stated:

> General de Gaulle started on a bad wicket. His first refusal to accept the Prime Minister's invitation created the worse impression. The Americans were particularly incensed and those of them who were anti-de Gaulle felt that this was a confirmation of the views they had always held of him. General de Gaulle did not do anything on his arrival to efface this bad impression. The language which he held enabled those who were not in sympathy with him to state that he thought nothing of the

prosecution of the war and was only concerned with political matters. If General de Gaulle had responded at once to the Prime Minister's invitation, he would probably have had a happier time. He would have at least been able to absorb the spirit of the historic conference which was taking place, and would have had opportunities for meeting the British and United States service leaders on terms from which formality and ceremony would have been completely absent. As it was, through his own fault entirely, he arrived when the conference was practically over. It is, however, something to be gained that the President was able to make his acquaintance and form an impression of his character.

It was clear that once General de Gaulle had arrived, he and General Giraud could not part without announcing an agreement of some kind. The announcement on which they agreed may not seem to amount to much. It is, however, the first step, and if satisfactory French liaison missions are established in London and Algiers with the right sort of person at the head, we can hope that in course of time two sets of Frenchmen will get together and come to an arrangement which may eventually lead to complete unity. If both sets can confine themselves to the points on which they are agreed and sink their differences, the talks should not be difficult. I am confident that if this first meeting between the two generals had not taken place under the aegis of the President of the United States and the Prime Minister, the results would have been less than was achieved at Anfa.[27]

There were further reports on de Gaulle's thinking and the future of France as Mack gave an account of the meeting at Anfa. De Gaulle considered that Giraud should be commander-in-chief and in control of all political and civil matters. De Gaulle also wanted all Vichy legislation abolished and a return to the laws of the French Republic as they existed in June 1940. He also wanted a complete sweeping out of all Vichy officials. In many ways this suited Roosevelt and Churchill who were anxious to split the authority of the Free French to prevent de Gaulle from dominating the movement.[28] G.S. Somers Locks provided a snapshot of de Gaulle's thinking in early February 1943, following a dinner provided by Eden in honour of René Massigli, recently rescued from France during January and, in February, serving as de Gaulle's commissioner of foreign affairs. Both de Gaulle and General Catroux were present.

Somers Locke stated that:

In the course of conversation General de Gaulle stated that the important thing in all French affairs was the mass of French opinion in France. That mass was at present with de Gaulle and it was his strength. It extended from the Communists to the right [political right]. It represented not only the resistance to the Axis but repudiation of Vichy and all that it stood for.

General de Gaulle went on to say that General Giraud, in the peculiar conditions of North Africa which had never been in the war and not suffered the humiliation of occupation, had found himself in the midst of opportunists who now, with the turn of the tide, were siding with the Allies with a view of returning to France under the cover of the Allied victory. There were two General Girauds, one the soldier, who was determined to fight the Axis, and the other, the Giraud, who by nature a reactionary, now surrounded and held by Vichy elements who had rallied to him in North Africa. General de Gaulle told the story of how he had drafted the joint communique and General Giraud had struck out the words 'democratic rights' which had to be changed to 'human rights'. Giraud alone represented nothing so far as the French people were concerned. But with those who surrounded him, he represented the continuation of the Vichy system and if he returned to France without having previously effected a union with de Gaulle, a civil war was inevitable. Only Communism could benefit from civil war. The repercussions of a civil war in France would be felt even in England.

Massigli confirmed that de Gaulle and Giraud had to work together to prevent civil war in France while nobody in France had respect for Vichy, while any future administration containing Vichy 'elements' would be resisted. Therefore, it was clear to the UK government that civil war had to be prevented; de Gaulle and Giraud had to agree and it was the duty of de Gaulle to work with Giraud.[29] De Gaulle certainly had the measure of Giraud, the situation in North Africa and the Vichy opportunists there. Without doubt, Massigli, who had to be spirted out of France as the Germans sought him, had nothing but contempt for Giraud and Vichy, but knew that, to avoid the horrors of civil war, there had to be unity and compromise as far as possible. However, Desmond Morton, Churchill's personal assistant, pointed out to Churchill after meeting Pannafieu, Giraud's temporary representative and a friend of Massigli, that, after paying tribute to de Gaulle, Pannafieu had said that Giraud did not understand politics and merely wanted to fight the enemy but even that had politics attached.[30]

Probably de Gaulle was of a similar mind to that of Giraud in 1940 but the intervening three years had taught him a lot about *Realpolitik*. Of de Gaulle, Macmillan once said that:

> I have never seen a man at once so ungracious and so sentimental ... the smallest act of courtesy or special kindness touches him with a deep emotion .... . The terrible mixture of inferiority complex and spiritual pride are characteristic of the sad situation into which France has fallen. I have often felt that the problems here could not be dealt with by politicians. They are rather problems for the professional psychiatrist.[31]

Macmillan, in a nutshell, analysed the condition of de Gaulle and all the exiled leaders. They had all lost their countries and had been traumatised. It did not help too much when they had to deal with the likes of Churchill who, as Harry Butcher noted, had an excess of confidence. Butcher's own president, despite his own physical problems, had a major sense of entitlement, owing to his own class and background. None of this was to feed well in a relationship with de Gaulle who was never overwhelmed by his situation but at times certainly behaved with less grace than he was bought up to display. Macmillan noted that Churchill, in his relationship with de Gaulle, was like the biblical father with the disobedient son. The father was quite capable of cutting off his errant son without a penny but equally killed the fatted calf once his son saw the error of his way.[32] Of course, both men were very emotional and had faced down the terror of Nazi invasion in 1940. Roosevelt had never felt such fear and could only read of it at a distance of several thousand miles.

The problem, however, in having two rivals for the possible leadership of the Fighting French was just who was loyal to whom. As we have seen, Giraud had only been bought into the picture owing to Roosevelt's prejudice against de Gaulle but had overlooked the latter's qualities while championing the dubious reputation of Giraud. This made it possible for the Americans to be able to claim that Churchill was on the cusp of dropping de Gaulle in favour of Giraud. Such talk was dangerous since it not only created a possible split within the Free French but it was also possible that Axis propaganda could take advantage of the situation to the disadvantage of the Allies as they sought to fight the war from French colonies in Africa.

Incredibly the American press gave concern to the FO as was reported on 1 March. Geoffrey Parsons at the *New York Tribune* had contacted Dupree to state that Wallace Carrol, head of the London Branch of the Office of War Information, had told him that the British government was almost certainly united in their desire to drop de Gaulle. It was further declared that Churchill was never going to speak to de Gaulle again and that only 'diehards' at the FO continued to support de Gaulle. Dupree considered that, perhaps, Carrol was trying 'to wean Mr Parsons away from his rather exaggerated pro-de Gaullism. Dupree stated that it had struck him that:

Mr Carrol was using a very dangerous and entirely misleading argument and I discussed the matter with Mr Carter of the M.O.I. [Ministry of Information] informally yesterday. Mr Carter sees a good deal of Mr Carrol but he thought it would be best if I were to discuss the French situation from a political point of view with Mr Carrol myself and he was very much in favour of it being done quickly as he too had the impression that American officials in London had been pursuing a similar line of talk.

Carrol was indeed spoken to on the morning of 1 March and requested to help 'scotch' the story which both American and British correspondents were spreading. Dupree told Carrol that, if the FO were forced to discuss the personalities of Giraud and de Gaulle, what must be avoided was the impression that de Gaulle was backed by the British and Giraud by the Americans. What concerned Dupree was that the press was threatening the unity between the British and American governments regarding support or otherwise of de Gaulle and Giraud. As ever, the problem was de Gaulle as he was 'sniping' at both Giraud and the American government, according to Carrol. The Americans were unbothered by de Gaulle's attacks on Giraud but felt compelled to retaliate whenever he attacked the US government. Dupree noted that, in the previous fortnight, de Gaulle had improved his attitude towards the Americans but he let it be known that the relationship between the two French generals needed to improve. Overall, it was quite clear in Dupree's message that the Americans were, beyond doubt, supporting Giraud and were determined that he would win in this matter while the British were 'subtly and under cover backing de Gaulle'.[33]

Quite simply, at this juncture of the war the Americans, acting with prejudice in addition to naivety and stubbornness, were determined to replace de Gaulle with Giraud. However, the US government did not understand that replacing de Gaulle would undermine unity within the ranks of the Fighting French as well as possibly split resistance fighters into at least two camps. The situation rumbled on, but the realities of the battlefield were to dominate events. On 1 April William Strang minuted a conversation with Cordell Hull, the US Secretary of State, regarding the French situation. Hull had been in talks with Anthony Eden, his British counterpart, where it was learned that the US government wanted a single French authority in order to make life easier. Eden agreed, but only if de Gaulle and Giraud could make an agreement over this matter.[34]

Clearly the Americans only wanted an agreement in which they could dominate French affairs; de Gaulle was too strong and therefore Giraud was vulnerable and suitable for American purposes. Eden, confident that de

Gaulle would win in any confrontation between the two French generals, gave his agreement. Nevertheless, the battlefield intervened as Churchill sent a personal minute to Sir Alexander Cadogan, the permanent undersecretary at the FO, stating that de Gaulle's visit to North Africa was to be delayed as 'the Armies are now approaching the crisis of a very great battle, and both Generals Eisenhower and Giraud must give their undivided attention to the movements of their troops'.[35] The fighting was the conclusion of the North Africa campaign as the Axis forces were forced into the remaining corner of Tunisia with the next stop being the Mediterranean.

As victory beckoned in North Africa, the poor relationship between de Gaulle and Giraud continued. Charles Peake informed Mack on 9 April that 'a friend of ours at Carlton Gardens (de Gaulle's London seat) tells us that he had a talk yesterday with M. de Pannafieu who said:

1. That General Giraud is becoming more and more irritated with General de Gaulle since he feels that his own attitude of sincerity and loyalty is being met with intrigue and disloyalty.
2. That General Giraud possessed a copy of a telegram which de Gaulle has sent to Captain Gayral in Washington [DC] instructing him to do as much underground propaganda work as he could among the sailors of 'RICHELIEU' and other Giraud ships.
3. That General Giraud had proof that General de Gaulle had given instructions that demonstrations should be organised on his arrival in Algiers.
4. That General Giraud receives every week a copy of the 'MARSEILLAISE'. Its effects on him can be imagined.
5. That three small demonstrations took place last Sunday at Marrakech, Rabat and Casablanca, in which shouts for de Gaulle were mingled with shouts for the Soviet [Union] and shouts for Germany.
6. That M. de Pannafieu is under the strong impression that the Americans are determined *not* to have de Gaulle in North Africa and that they would rather that the union between Generals Giraud and de Gaulle should fail rather than see the latter installed in Algiers.[36]

This attitude was the most obvious evidence of American or rather Roosevelt's antipathy towards de Gaulle: that the American president would rather see his work fail than see de Gaulle installed as the undisputed leader of the Free French.

The fact that Churchill had personally given his pledge of support to de Gaulle back in 1940 cut no ice with the Americans. Nevertheless, the British covertly pressed on with their support for him. It was quite clear that the British did not consider Giraud to be a winner, no matter the American hype. In a meeting with Eden, General Catroux told him that the progress in working towards reconciliation in France was progressing but was arduous and slow owing to the difficult personalities of those involved. Catroux noted that this was actually the only problem – the awkward characters of the players involved. It had been mooted that Giraud should be head of the French Army and de Gaulle the political head of a joint French authority. Giraud refused to co-operate in this matter.[37]

No doubt Giraud's head was some swollen by the support of Roosevelt. However, a memorandum from Harold Macmillan to Churchill on the same day stated that there had been a successful conclusion to the negotiations between de Gaulle and Giraud. Post-war, de Gaulle would be forced to declare his hand. Macmillan noted that part of de Gaulle's mystique tended towards a form of 'concealed fascism which will have to be abandoned'.[38]

This is a curious statement as de Gaulle was far from being a fascist. His actions between 1944 and 1946 reveal that he wanted France to be restored with dignity once it had been liberated. The American carping about de Gaulle being an imperialist was also wrong since he withdrew France from the Middle East and, after granting Algeria independence in 1962, there were several attempts on his life by his own countrymen. Basically, de Gaulle was a proud and patriotic Frenchman who sought to restore his homeland after the tyranny of Nazi occupation. He was not bothered who he offended as he, as leader of the Free French, defended French interests and prepared France for liberation and a post-war future under French rule rather than that of an Allied occupation government.

By 1943 the British had understood the need for pace and for maintaining it. The Germans had already learned that lesson by 1940 – stalling outside Dunkirk had probably cost them the chance of invading the UK; the Americans were yet to learn the lessons of pace and the need for continuity in prosecuting the war. Frenchmen of divided loyalties were also against pushing too hard as they were still trying to discover which horse to back since some people were deluded enough to consider that there was still a chance that the Germans might win the war in Europe at least – it was unlikely that by 1943 they might win in Africa. An example of this foot-dragging was the commander of the French Fleet in the Eastern Mediterranean, Admiral Godfroy, who, as we have seen, certainly did his best to avoid committing himself to the Allied cause as long as there was an outside change of a German victory in North Africa. By February 1943 it was clear that Godfroy was beginning to change his attitude towards the Allies but much of this was due to that fact that many of his officers wanted to fight for the Allies and had made several attempts to scuttle their vessels to prevent them falling into German hands, in addition to seeking asylum in neutral Turkey. It was admitted that it was unlikely that Giraud or Vice Admiral Felix Michelier, the Vichy commander who had been responsible for the defence of Casablanca during November 1942 when US forces attacked the area, would send an order or an emissary to intervene in the Godfroy episode since neither Giraud nor Michelier would recommend 'forcing the pace at the risk of losing other ships and of adverse effect on French North Africa crews'.

Richard Casey, who sent this intelligence to Churchill, was convinced that Godfroy would scuttle or attempt to leave Alexandria if the British took any measures such as cutting off pay and supplies to his ships. Casey noted that Godfroy still held sway with his commanders no matter how difficult the situation was becoming between his squadron and the British authorities in Egypt. Casey suggested that, if the present agreement between Godfroy and the local British authorities ended in Alexandria; Godfroy would be free to leave harbour unless the UK government warned him 'that we regard it as a hostile act'.

Casey further noted that Admiral Harwood

> has operational planned for dealing with Godfroy's Squadron in Alexandria harbour with artillery and MTB [motor torpedo boats] although this would be costly to the seventy supply ships loading and unloading in Alexandria harbour. Harwood had no naval force at Alexandria capable of dealing with Godfroy's squadron at sea without recalling ships from Malta and elsewhere.

Casey informed Churchill that Godfroy was willing to send an emissary to Algiers. Casey stated that the simplest thing was not to send any further pay or supplies to Godfroy's ships. The next payday was only two days away, 13 February, but Casey warned that the Allies needed to maintain some semblance of co-operation and understanding with the French as the main objective of the exercise was to obtain the French ships and crews with the intention of fighting alongside the Allies. Therefore, it was advisable that an emissary should be sent to Algiers. Nevertheless, it was considered advisable that any local anti-Allied propaganda should be countered and that the British should 'keep it up our sleeves for the present the final act of cutting off pay and supplies'. Overall, Casey considered that it was the likelihood of Godfroy's captains 'pulling themselves together and imposing a solution on Godfroy', adding that there was 'considerable ferment in the whole fleet'.[39]

Clearly there was such ferment as noted by Casey. The French officers were probably frustrated with Godfroy who seemed to be holding out for no apparent reason beyond fear – fear of backing the wrong side. As we have seen, the French Navy owed no loyalty to de Gaulle but by 1943 it was clear that Germany had lost the war and doubtless many young French naval officers, despite their loyalty and obedience to Godfroy, were becoming impatient and wanted a solution to their predicament – stuck in a British harbour since 1940. They simply wanted to get the war over with and go home. It was clear to them that the Allies, now consisting of the Soviet Union, the USA and the UK and many more nations, were undefeatable and that allegiance to the British was the only way forward. Even the temperamental de Gaulle could see that, but the problem was that he was an army and not a naval officer and the Americans did not back him. However, Churchill did not always agree with Roosevelt over France and its empire.

As we have already seen, Roosevelt, despite the USA clearly building up its contemporary empire, was an opponent of the European empires. In a telegram to Lord Halifax, the British Ambassador to the USA, Churchill asserted that he could not be against Roosevelt's message about the restoration of the French Empire because, as he remarked, if he failed to support Roosevelt it would be difficult to prevent the liquidation of the British Empire and urged Halifax not to get such assurances made by Roosevelt to France withdrawn.[40]

It is not clear why Roosevelt supported the restoration of the French Empire, but one can only think that he was operating under the restraints of war and needed French co-operation since it held the necessary territory to fight back against Germany and finally vanquish that nation. Empires and their futures could wait until after the war. Equally, there was a definite British need to co-operate with the Americans as illustrated in a telegram from Churchill to General Eisenhower. Churchill's telegram contained an extract from a speech which he made in the House of Commons on 11 February, which was an account of the changes in the North Africa campaign and the contemporary situation there.

Churchill made reference to the fact that Giraud commanded the French Army that fought on the Tunisian front. This army, noted Churchill, was supplied by the USA and would play its part in the eventual liberation of France together with the American army commanded by General Frank Andrews.[41] Andrews had succeeded Eisenhower as commander of all US forces in the European theatre of operations when the latter was appointed to command in the Mediterranean. It was quite clear that everything in the west would be dependent on American support and supply while the Red Army in the east was taking the fight to the Germans; even there the Red Army received large amounts of equipment from the USA.

Nevertheless, the British and American governments remained unhappy with their relationship with de Gaulle which the Americans had made worse by introducing Giraud into the equation. That had been an American attempt to inject an element of democracy into the politics of the Free French by trying to hold de Gaulle to account with elections to the Free French Committee, but the middle of a war is never a good time for such things, especially when France was occupied by its enemy.

Churchill revealed his thoughts to Roosevelt who was determined to prevent de Gaulle from taking complete power in Free French circles. Churchill also told Roosevelt that the British had finally stopped all money and supplies to Admiral Godfroy's squadron and made the first reference to de Gaulle and Giraud as being 'bride and groom'.[42] The fact that the British had gone for the 'nuclear option' was evidence that Churchill was acting tough with the Vichy French, who were supported by the US government. The idea that de Gaulle and Giraud were 'bride and groom' rather revealed a medieval concept of marriages of convenience made to get alliances sealed. Roosevelt referred to it as a 'shotgun wedding'.[43]

If de Gaulle was the groom and Giraud the bride, it was obvious in the mindset of 1943, especially of men born in the nineteenth century, who was the weaker in the marriage; de Gaulle was the man still supported by Churchill while Giraud was the unwilling bride and doomed, even if he had the support of Roosevelt. The 'shotgun wedding' took place at the Casablanca Conference, a meeting between Churchill and Roosevelt, held in January. De Gaulle came reluctantly and did not agree to put the Free French under Giraud's control. He agreed to photos with Giraud and the two Allied leaders but did not sign a document prepared by Churchill and Roosevelt which would have removed the Free French as the repository of French sovereignty. Churchill was furious. De Gaulle considered the attempt to relegate him and his movement to have been 'most ungracious'. He also saw Roosevelt who dealt with him correctly, but nothing else. Before leaving the conference, de Gaulle and Giraud signed a document in which it was stated that they had met and had spoken together. The document went further, affirming their common goal of victory for France and establishing a permanent liaison group. This was important for de Gaulle as the group paved the way to bring the Free French to North Africa.[44]

Much of the Godfroy activity was related to the de Gaulle-Giraud negotiations. Churchill was determined that Godfroy should be made to comply with British demands and join in the war against Germany and certainly not scuttle his ships or allow them to fall into enemy hands.

Churchill told Casey to forward the message informing Godfroy that the UK government was no longer willing to underwrite his squadron languishing in Alexandria harbour. Therefore, all monies were being stopped and any attempt to scuttle the French ships would lead to action in the Egyptian courts. Casey was not to see Godfroy. Churchill was relying on Casey to solve the matter and considered that the C-in-C of the Mediterranean area was responsible for the entire mess.[45] Meanwhile, Casey appraised Churchill of what had been occurring. He had done all possible propaganda work and reported that two of the French vessels were ready for action, the cruiser *Tourville* and the destroyer *Corbin*, as a result of direct action by junior officers who were rallying their ships to Giraud. Casey reported that he was trying to persuade a French admiral in Alexandria to represent Giraud. Casey considered that this was the way to get Godfroy onside.[46] As Churchill's man in situ it was obvious that Casey knew what was happening and used his judgement for the better. The main problem was that the French Navy had no allegiance to de Gaulle and made it clear that they were unlikely to accept his authority. But Giraud was a possibility for persuading the French Navy to join the Allies against Germany, but not necessarily under de Gaulle's command.

Casey further cabled Churchill with another report of the situation regarding Godfroy. It was observed that ships in 'Force X', Godfroy's squadron, had been used to assist the Axis powers. Therefore, Article XI of the Godfroy-Harwood Agreement of 2 June 1942 allowed for a reconsideration of the agreement since the vice admiral commanding the force did not agree to the terms. The UK government reiterated that it was not going to support the French ships any longer and that any attempt to leave harbour would be seen as a hostile act.[47]

Casey was certainly ratcheting up pressure on Godfroy and leaving him little room for manoeuvre. It should be noted that Force X had originally been raised to protect French interests against Italian hostility; it is not clear what point Casey was making in this extract of a note sent to Godfroy. Later Casey sent a further telegram to Churchill stating:

> Am keeping up pressure on Godfroy and his squadron by all possible means. There is considerable and growing uneasiness in squadron which we are promoting. Meanwhile, have been trying continuously to get visit from French naval representatives for North Africa and am not entirely without hope of this important link materialising even at this late date.[48]

However, prior to this message, there had been much movement in Alexandria, some of which was quite mysterious and puzzling. Nevertheless, Casey was not put off his stride as he began to sense that Godfroy was on the back foot and that events were beginning to conspire against the French admiral as the war progressed against the Axis powers. In another telegram to Churchill, Casey stated that he had seen Admiral Sir Henry Harwood, Naval C-in-C of the Eastern Mediterranean. Harwood told Casey that French ships were being used by the Axis powers against the Allies. Casey had also seen Godfroy, yet again, and told him of the British government attitude towards him. Casey still believed that Godfroy would neither scuttle his ships nor try to leave harbour and that a visit from a senior French naval officer would help the situation.[49] There were certainly strange things happening as, on 15 February, Casey reported to Churchill that 450 French sailors with suitcases, 33 officers in plain clothes and 11 others in uniform from Godfroy's squadron had landed in Alexandria. Casey was trying to discover what was happening.[50] It was all very puzzling and disconcerting. Later, Casey learned from Harwood that the French seamen had come ashore to collect their belongings. By this time, it was stated that 'It is not now believed that Force X is about to scuttle'.[51] This was quite a relief for the British authorities. Churchill told Harold Macmillan, the Minister Resident in the Mediterranean, 1942–1945, that he had been quite right not to attach too much attention or importance to French intrigues.[52]

The year 1943 was an important in the North Africa campaign as the Allies were beginning to sense victory on land for the first time. Nevertheless, Macmillan told Churchill that the Tunisian campaign had taken longer than anticipated. However, the Anfa conference which was to introduce de Gaulle and especially Giraud to the world was also held. Macmillan informed Churchill that the conference had improved matters as Giraud's position was supported. It was realised that the United Nations (UN), as the wartime alliance against Germany and its allies was becoming, had no intention of supporting a French army and there might be further definition of the policy. But, overall, a new joint approach could be made to de Gaulle and Giraud since unity in the French camp was sought.[53]

Meanwhile Casey continued maintaining pressure on Godfroy and reported to Churchill:

Am keeping up pressure on Godfroy and his squadron by all possible means. There are considerable and growing measures in the squadron which we are promoting. Meanwhile, have been trying continuously to get a visit from French naval representation for North Africa and am not entirely without hope of this important link materialising even at this late date.[54]

Casey continued his offensive against Giraud. In a further report to Churchill, he stated that he had sat with Godfroy who had told Casey that he was planning to sail his fleet to a North African port once Tunisia had been captured by the Allies. Casey believed that Godfroy and his men were receiving money from a source other than the British. Casey noted that Giraud had, in effect, accepted responsibility for Godfroy's squadron.[55] In a further telegram, Casey was able to report to Churchill that Godfroy had finally announced that he would join Giraud.[56]

Macmillan told Churchill that he hoped to persuade de Gaulle to accept Godfroy's offer to join Giraud since it would resolve the dispute between the two men. The British government feared that there might be yet another French leader, a 'third star', waiting in the wings which would have further watered down the Free French movement. Macmillan opined to Churchill that, given that the US government disliked de Gaulle, if de Gaulle failed to come to terms with the Americans, they would give up on him and give their full support to Giraud. Macmillan also observed that Catroux was de Gaulle's 'most valuable assistant' and, if the plan to reconcile de Gaulle and Giraud failed, Catroux would also give up on de Gaulle. Macmillan stated that de Gaulle should be able to win in the dispute as he was the stronger man, especially if he maintained the support of Massigli and Catroux, whom he judged as being more intelligent than Giraud's supporters. Macmillan said of de Gaulle that 'All the cards are in his hands. He has only to come in order to secure all that he can reasonably demand. But if he hesitates, I think he is lost'.[57] Later Churchill telegraphed Macmillan that there was no reason why the Alexandria squadron, Force X, or Godfroy's squadron, should not declare allegiance to Giraud.[58]

One should consider that Macmillan, like most senior British political actors, was aware that, no matter what the American government thought, de Gaulle was the founder of the Free French movement, remained at its helm and would do so for the immediate future. Giraud was somewhat second rate compared with him. US policy regarding the Free French stemmed mainly from Roosevelt's personal prejudice against de Gaulle. Churchill, meanwhile, had to deal with President Roosevelt's prejudice against the French and, in particular, de Gaulle.

Nevertheless, the British government seemed to agree with the concept that de Gaulle should not be allowed to rule everything within the Free French movement which had enlarged into a larger political body, the French National Committee for National Liberation (FNCNL). Even the British government sought to ensure that de Gaulle shared the leadership of the FNCNL with Giraud while continuing with its support of Giraud as commander of French forces as Macmillan re-affirmed to Churchill.[59] On the same day as Churchill received Macmillan's telegram, he received a furious cable from Roosevelt who stated bluntly that he was 'fed up with de Gaulle and that secret, personal and political machinations of that committee [FNCNL] as the last few days indicate that there is no possibility of our working with de Gaulle'.

Roosevelt considered that de Gaulle did not like either the USA or the UK and 'would double-cross us at the first opportunity'. This seems unfair as de Gaulle thus far had stuck by the UK, even in the dark days of 1940, and showed no sign of betraying the British. What de Gaulle did was defend France against British and American interests, something that an entitled person such as Roosevelt did not understand. Nevertheless, Roosevelt considered that de Gaulle was 'injuring the war effort' and was a 'dangerous threat to us' and argued that the US and UK 'must divorce ourselves from de Gaulle'. Roosevelt continued in his diatribe against the French leader with allegations that de Gaulle was unreliable, non-co-operative and 'disloyal to both our governments'. Roosevelt wanted the FNCNL to be focused totally on fighting the war and not thinking too much about politics.[60]

Perhaps Roosevelt was correct and that the French should focus more on the war rather than politics, but a liberated France was de Gaulle's sole aim and that could not happen in a vacuum. The FNCNL had to think of the future and how France was to return from the horror of occupation by an extremely violent occupant who revealed in anarchy. However, it will be seen that the US government did not see France as a country being liberated and waiting to return to the civilized world but as another country to be occupied and administered by US armed forces.

Churchill gave limited support to Roosevelt and his concept of the Free French in 1943. He agreed broadly with Roosevelt that de Gaulle should not be allowed to gain control of French armed forces in North Africa. However, he was not in favour of splitting up the FNCNL or putting de Gaulle in such a position that he had to submit totally to British and American demands or resign from the committee. Churchill also informed Roosevelt that, via Macmillan, Massigli had been informed that there would be no further payments from British funds directly to the French National Committee in London. Any further payments would be paid to the new French Committee of Seven acting in a majority. Overall, Churchill and Macmillan were seeking to keep de Gaulle in control of the Free French which was against Roosevelt's wishes. However, Churchill wanted de Gaulle to share power. De Gaulle could be in control of politics, Giraud head of the French armed forces and, perhaps, de Gaulle's portfolio as French minister of defence should be assigned to another.[61] Clearly, what Churchill was doing was continuing to champion de Gaulle while keeping the Americans happy in the face of their not really understanding what had happened in Europe in 1939 and 1940 and certainly not what been happening on the African continent since 1940. In effect the Americans were still playing catch up and many Americans were reluctant allies in the war against Germany.

Nevertheless, Churchill was not totally naïve in dealing with de Gaulle. He had been doing so since the summer of 1940 as well as having to work with another difficult European ally, the Polish general, Władysław Sikorski, who, though not as powerful as de Gaulle, was just as difficult. Churchill told Macmillan that it was important that the French Army in North Africa should be loyal and trustworthy, especially on the eve of a great operation, (the invasion of Sicily in July 1943). Churchill stated that no confidence should be placed in de Gaulle's friendship for the Allies. Nevertheless, Churchill was aware of the importance of the French committee of 'Seven' and did not want it broken up or forbidden to meet. However, the committee was to abide by Allied rules and, if de Gaulle should resign from it, it would be placed on the wrong side of public opinion; measures would have to be taken to prevent him being a nuisance. However, if de Gaulle submitted to Allied pressure, it would probably store up trouble for the future.[62] Basically, the problem with de Gaulle was that he was trouble inasmuch as he represented French interests only. As the Allies began to roll up the Axis powers from the south, it was clear that France could be reached relatively soon, and de Gaulle was determined that his country would not become an American satellite. Another side to de Gaulle to be considered was that he was winning public opinion which was strongly on his side in North Africa, France, the UK and even in the USA while Free French forces in the North African campaign had covered themselves in glory.[63] In June 1942, Free French forces at Bir Hakeim in Libya, commanded by General Koenig, numbering 5,500 men of the Light Division had held up Panzerarmee Afrika for almost two weeks, thus allowing the British Eighth Army time to regroup. This was impressive enough, but the fighting ability of the Free French was further illustrated as Koenig was also able to break out after the fighting and take his troops to safety. De Gaulle saw Bir Hakeim as the 'beginning of the recovery of France'. Churchill described it as 'one of the finest feats of arms in this war'.[64]

Furthermore, not only were things on the battlefield going well for de Gaulle but the various factions which comprised the French resistance were coming together. De Gaulle's representative in France, Jean Moulin, had worked hard on de Gaulle's political appeal to such an extent that groups as varied as the communists of the left and the monarchists on the right rallied to de Gaulle. On 15 May 1943 Moulin was able to inform de Gaulle that a National Council of the Resistance (CNR) had been formed and that it had endorsed de Gaulle as the 'unquestioned leader'. The CNR had sixteen members: eight from the Resistance movements in France, five from political parties (Socialist, Communist, Radical, Republican Federation and Democratic Alliance), two from trade unions (CGT and CFTC) and Moulin as chairman. The first meeting of the CNR was obviously clandestine and held in Paris on 27 May 1943. The most important result of the meeting was that the CNR recognised de Gaulle as the leader of the French Resistance and demanded that he be installed as president of a French provisional government.[65]

Quite simply, regarding the French of all political hues save Vichy, it was game, set and match to de Gaulle. Roosevelt could demand what he liked but, once de Gaulle set foot in France, he was going to be president of at least a provisional government there. Attempts by the Americans to govern France with some kind of Allied military government until elections were held were clearly going to be unpopular, if not impossible. De Gaulle held all the trump cards regarding the liberation of his country. Even Giraud recognised the success of de Gaulle and conceded. In late May Giraud bowed to the inevitable from Algeria and invited de Gaulle to come to Algiers and form a government with him. De Gaulle accepted Giraud's invitation.

On 30 May, de Gaulle landed in Algiers. This time, unlike Casablanca, Giraud met him at the airport while a French honour guard presented arms and a French band played *La Marseillaise*. Before the week was out, de Gaulle and Giraud had reached agreement. A French Committee of National Liberation (FCNL) had been formed with the two generals becoming co-presidents. The FCNL proclaimed itself 'the central French power. It directs the French war effort .... It exercises French sovereignty'.[66] This clearly was a blow to Roosevelt. It got worse for the American president as several Vichy office holders in North Africa retired and were replaced by Free French officials. Furthermore, de Gaulle was lionised in Algiers with a succession of popular demonstrations representing all classes and political colours. Roosevelt was appalled and was determined to break de Gaulle.[67]

It soon became obvious that Roosevelt was not going to get his own way, possibly because the British had worked with de Gaulle for longer and in harder times whilst Roosevelt and the US government were merely 'johnny come lately' full of anti-European prejudice. In June Churchill told Roosevelt that his War Cabinet did not agree with Roosevelt's view that it was time to break with de Gaulle.[68] A few days later Churchill mentioned to Macmillan that the consequences of losing de Gaulle might be severe. It was very possible that de Gaulle might resign from the French Committee of National Liberation and not accept a military post offered to him; it was suggested that de Gaulle might serve as a divisional commander of armour under Giraud's command. Churchill considered that it was necessary that de Gaulle should be prevented from resigning from the committee, even if it was only to keep him from stirring up trouble once free of any collective responsibilities.[69] It was quite clear that Roosevelt and the American authorities were doing their best to insult de Gaulle in their attempts to remove him from what they considered to be unparalleled power within the Free French movement.

The disagreement between the British and Americans regarding de Gaulle continued. Roosevelt expressed his continued fear that de Gaullists would dominate the French committee and jeopardise the military position in North Africa by 'an antagonistic element' and found the position unacceptable.[70] What Roosevelt meant was that it was unacceptable that he and his government could not micromanage de Gaulle. They struggled to replace him with Giraud who, as we have seen, was a second if not third rate once compared with de Gaulle and his achievements of holding the Free French and, indeed, France together. Churchill stated to Macmillan that he did not believe that Roosevelt and the US government would recognise any French National Committee dominated by de Gaulle and that the UK would probably follow that example.[71] A month earlier *The Economist* had noted that Giraud lacked appeal to the French military and was considered to be 'old school' in the manner of Pétain and Weygand,[72] hardly an endorsement to many French people or to many British.

There was a further element to the Allied recognition of a French Committee of National Liberation. It was made obvious in a telegram from Churchill to Stalin. Since the beginning of 1943 Stalin had been creating mischief throughout the Allied camp. Following the Soviet victory against Germany and its allies at Stalingrad, the Red Army had begun an advance westward which only ended in Berlin and the total defeat of Germany in May 1945. The Soviet march towards Germany was an opportunity to spread communism even if it was on the tips of the bayonets of the Red Army. As the Red Army advanced, it liberated Soviet territories and eventually annexed entire countries, notably Poland. In London, there was an internationally recognised Polish government in exile which opposed Stalin. The year 1943 was key in Polish-Soviet relations as, by April, diplomacy had broken down, leaving two allies no longer in communication and openly hostile to one another. Stalin, the stronger ally, began to set up his own vision of a post-war world, basically a Soviet world or one dominated by Russian hegemony.

To that end, he began to establish provisional governments or liberation committees in readiness for Soviet rule outside the Soviet Union. Those committees were formed of nationals of countries being liberated or annexed, depending on one's politics, and were Stalinists. Overall, Stalin was preparing puppet governments ready for Soviet rule. This was the very reason why Stalin was prepared to go against the will of the British and American governments and consider supporting the French Committee of National Liberation. Churchill told Stalin that both the US and UK governments had decided not to support the committee.[73] Stalin found later that he could not control de Gaulle when he came to Moscow after the liberation of France as he had little, if anything, to offer de Gaulle.

Macmillan finally began to make sense of the Free French situation after discussions with Jean Monnet (commissioner of arms and supplies for the French Committee of National Liberation). Monnet observed that, even though it seemed as if de Gaulle had been given a private army, that was not true. De Gaulle had no resources to finance the army if it was deprived of funds from the UK. Macmillan hoped that Churchill would support Monnet's view and solution and recommend it to Roosevelt. Macmillan also observed that any further intervention by the US and UK governments would only fuel further resentment amongst the Free French.[74] Nevertheless, the interference by the British and Americans continued as did purely French appointments and dismissals on French African territories.

Churchill continued to maintain his pro-de Gaulle stance in telegrams to Roosevelt as he informed the American president that he had seen the text of the decree of the French Committee of National Liberation (FCNL) and had considered that he did not believe that there was any need for Allied intervention at the time. Churchill's attitude was that military security in North-West Africa was safeguarded by the French Army there which remained in 'trustworthy hands'.[75] This exchange had much to do with the question of the political natures of French commanders in Africa. One such French general under question was General Pierre Boisson, the Vichy Governor General of French West Africa. Boisson's long-term future was in question. Churchill observed to Macmillan that if Boisson was ousted it would be a victory for de Gaulle and one bitterly resented by Roosevelt and the State Department. Overall, Churchill doubted that Boisson would be dismissed.[76]

Churchill also urged caution to Roosevelt regarding how he was promoting Giraud. Churchill's attitude was that it would be a mistake to allow Giraud to leave Algiers at the time as the trip was only a promotional visit. Churchill considered that Giraud's absence would provide de Gaulle the chance to act independently and stated plainly to Roosevelt that 'it is dangerous to leave the field open to de Gaulle especially while the position of Boisson is uncertain. While the mouse is away the cat will play'.[77] The American attitude towards the French continued to alarm Churchill who urged Macmillan to take note of Roosevelt's statement that, should Boisson be dismissed, he would send American troops and ships to Dakar.[78] It is not obvious why the US government and Roosevelt continued to support Vichy officials over de Gaulle; one can only think that again it was prejudice, principally on the part of Roosevelt.

Nevertheless, Roosevelt agreed with Churchill regarding Giraud and his travel plans and had asked Giraud to postpone his trip until the position of Boisson was settled.[79] The question of the French 'Committee of Seven' was also something that was not to really vex Allied planning because, as Macmillan reported to Churchill, de Gaulle had not been provided with a majority.[80] Stalin, meanwhile, maintained unity within the Allied camp over French matters at least. However, Stalin still continued in his line of refusing to understand why the British and the Americans were so concerned about de Gaulle and the FCNL but agreed to delay his recognition of the committee until it had been more or less established.[81] It should be remembered that Stalin, given his revolutionary background, never really sought unity with his natural enemies, capitalists and aristocrats such as Churchill and Roosevelt, unless he considered that he might profit from such an alliance. In Stalin's political world, distrust and anarchy were normal. At times it seemed that de Gaulle was of a similar disposition owing to his perpetual distrust of the British over the matter of the Levant.[82]

The question of Boisson remaining in place was one that needed to be secured totally as it was linked to so much and there was an existing requirement that de Gaulle conform with Roosevelt's wishes that Boisson should remain. Churchill supported Roosevelt in this matter and made it clear that, if de Gaulle retaliated by resigning from the FCNL, he would be refused future entry to the UK while support for Giraud would be total.[83] Churchill sent a further telegram to Macmillan which contained a message for de Gaulle and Giraud for Macmillan to deliver. Churchill wanted assurance from the two Frenchmen that Boisson was to remain in post. Churchill did not believe in French West Africa coming under de Gaulle's influence of owing to the uncertainty of his future; he also felt the French Army in North Africa should come under Giraud's control.[84]

The question of the French Committee and the French Army in North Africa vexed Churchill. Once more in contact with Macmillan, Churchill said that if de Gaulle obtained control of the FNCL he saw difficulties in the US-French relationship. Churchill would support the USA but worried that he would still be seen as supporting de Gaulle. Churchill stated a truism about France and de Gaulle when he told Macmillan that:

> De Gaulle will always try to win popularity for himself in France by showing how rough he is with Britain and the United States. But after all

it is only by British and American blood that France has any chance of liberation and regaining her position as a great European power.[85]

This statement was a prophecy as it was indeed only the sacrifices of British and US troops which liberated western Europe from Nazi occupation. Other armies were involved but nowhere in the numbers of the British and, especially, the Americans. Regarding de Gaulle, Churchill wanted a measure of truth as the FO informed Macmillan that Churchill had instructed it to send a note to the press concerning reporting on de Gaulle. Press reports from Algiers which were then printed in the UK press described de Gaulle as a fascist with dictatorial tendencies. Churchill requested a more measured approach towards de Gaulle and events in Algiers.[86] The press attitude towards de Gaulle no doubt suited Roosevelt and his government but Churchill knew de Gaulle and could see the larger picture – de Gaulle could carry the French even in the most difficult situations. Giraud could not. The French were very grateful for Churchill's support and said so, as Macmillan reported back to him.

Macmillan reported that he had passed on Churchill's message to his friends on the FCNL. It was well received. General Alphonse Georges, a minister from the FCNL placed importance on the recognition being given to the French committee and believed that it would give it confidence and help it to unite. However, de Gaulle took the position that the Allied plans for the FCNL to receive recognition might restrict its autonomy. Macmillan concluded his telegram by stating that he was seeing both General Catroux and Jean Monnet, the same day, 11 August.[87] This meeting went well.

After meeting with Georges and Monnet, Macmillan made his report to Churchill. Macmillan told him that:

Catroux and Monnet were most appreciative of your message. Catroux said that it was one more sign of the sympathy and understanding which you have always shown for France. He sincerely hoped that recognition would soon be generously accorded as Frenchmen were beginning to be seriously worried about delay. Monnet hoped that formula of recognition would take note of Committee's declared intention to hand over its powers to a legally constituted Provisional Government of France. Catroux spoke most optimistically about the future of the Committee which he said was shaping extremely well. Monnet was more cautious but thought it was now safely launched.[88]

This message was important, as the French needed their committee because as Monnet said, it was to provide the basis for the establishment of a provisional

French government once France was liberated. Furthermore, the Allies needed smooth co-operation with the French as France was to be the landing ground for the Allied invasion of western Europe; Churchill knew that only de Gaulle could really convince the French to co-operate in this venture while the presence of Monnet on the FCNL probably assured Roosevelt that de Gaulle was not trying to establish a dictatorship. Overall, Churchill's words were a good attempt to square a near impossible circle.

On the other hand, Roosevelt had ensured that de Gaulle would reign triumphant over all at the FNCL which, as we have seen, was never his intention. By pursuing his personal vendetta against de Gaulle and by inviting Giraud to the USA during July 1943 Roosevelt had shot himself in the foot. Giraud was not received well in the USA and, by the time he returned to Algiers, as Churchill had predicted de Gaulle had secured his position and was sole president of the FCNL which was by then the de facto French government in exile.

Churchill had warned Roosevelt against inviting Giraud to the USA as it was quite clear to him that de Gaulle would take full advantage of Giraud's absence. De Gaulle was warmly received by the remaining members of the FCNL. He later described his return to Casablanca during August 1943. He wrote, 'Six months before I had to reside on the city's outskirts, constrained to secrecy and surrounded by barbed wire and American sentry posts. Today my presence served as a symbol and a centre of French authority'.[89]

This was a clear case of Roosevelt undoing his own work. The FCNL was recognised at the First Quebec Conference, held in Canada during late August. Churchill had come to recognise that de Gaulle was definitely the French leader, no matter how much Roosevelt tried to tout Giraud, and that the FCNL was more-or-less the French government in exile. To make things even more awkward, as we have seen Stalin had already recognised the FCNL during July. It was becoming very obvious that the British and American governments needed to do the same, if only to preserve Allied unity. Stalin was skilled at dividing alliances as he looked towards a post-war Europe and possible Soviet domination of that continent. American and British recognition duly came about and statements were released at Quebec in recognition of the FCNL. The American statement was limited and read:

> The government of the United States recognizes the French National Committee of National Liberation as administrating the French overseas territories which acknowledge its authority. This statement does not constitute recognition of a government of France or the French Empire by the government of the United States.[90]

Roosevelt was beginning to lose the narrative regarding his feud with de Gaulle. Churchill probably saw what he had always seen in de Gaulle, despite their often fractious relationship: de Gaulle was France and France was de Gaulle. But then Roosevelt wasn't too fond of the French either. For de Gaulle it did not really matter what the two senior statesmen thought – he was the undisputed leader of the French government in exile. De Gaulle's fortunes continued to gather. On 12 September the FCNL created a Provisional Consultative Assembly, an embryonic genuinely representative government and, once more, de Gaulle was overwhelmingly endorsed.

By the end of 1943 de Gaulle had 400,000 men under his command. The French Resistance continued their support of de Gaulle and maintained unity in their struggle against the German occupation of France. Jean Moulin, the original resistance leader, had been captured by the Germans and tortured to death. De Gaulle appointed Alexandre Parodi as Moulin's successor and, shortly afterwards, named General Koenig, the commander at Bir Hakeim, to command the French Forces of the Interior (FFI) – simply the French Resistance. Koenig was based in London, but his command was comprehensive. The French communists continued in their support for the resistance movement and were rewarded with three seats on the FCNL.[91] The inclusion of communists on the FCNL undoubtedly alarmed Roosevelt but he was quite capable of making some very dodgy deals with Stalin, especially over Poland, while the creation of a Provisional Consultative Assembly pointed towards the fact that de Gaulle was not going to establish a dictatorship on his return to France but instead sought to re-establish democracy. However, we must now return to summer 1943 and North Africa to discuss the consequences of the Anglo-American recognition of the FNCL.

Macmillan was able to inform Churchill of the first reactions to the recognition of the FNCL, which were favourable. Macmillan doubted whether there would be any relapses concerning recognition of the French committee unless the British or American press started to lead people astray. Macmillan noted that the committee was beginning to settle down to important work. Most importantly, de Gaulle 'seemed pleased and relieved when informed by us'. Macmillan reported on the progress of the FNCL meetings; he told Churchill that 'real progress is being made with preparing an efficient modernised Army. Five first line and four second line divisions this year may prove invaluable'.[92] It was quite clear that, by this stage, the French were forming larger military formations to fight the enemy rather than an underground army. As the Allies had already invaded Italy and were beginning to move up the Italian mainland it was obvious that many troops would be needed to complete this operation.

By September 1943 Italy was negotiating its surrender to the Allies. Stalin, as awkward as ever, told Churchill that he was in favour of the presence of a representative from the FCNL in the Allied Commission negotiating with Italy.[93] Stalin loved to make the western powers uncomfortable, but he had a point since Italy had, in the dying days of the 1940 German invasion of France, invaded southern France and occupied the French Riviera. It was a cowardly act and, without doubt, the French would have wanted representation at any meeting with the Italians. But Stalin, as with many from the Soviet Union, saw the Italian campaign as a sideshow, once compared with the Russian Front and, of course, the negotiating Italians were not Italian fascists.

Despite what Stalin suggested, the French were kept out of negotiations with the Italians. Macmillan told Churchill that short armistice terms had just been signed (3 September 1943) but the French had not been informed. Macmillan added that the armistice would remain secret until after Operation AVALANCHE – the invasion of the Italian mainland.[94] The Allies began to sweep across the Mediterranean, crossing Sicily and landing in Italy, French territory was also liberated. Operation VESUVIUS saw the French island of Corsica liberated between 8 September and 4 October. Giraud stated that the liberation of Corsica was a prelude to the liberation of France.[95] The liberation of Corsica also delighted de Gaulle who sent a message to Churchill thanking him for his message of congratulations on the liberation of the island.[96] The liberation of Corsica by French forces, irregular and regular, was a fillip for French morale. The Allies were able to use it as a vast immobile aircraft carrier for aerial operations over Europe.

An atmosphere of harmony between the French and the Allies broke out temporarily. In November 1943 both de Gaulle and Giraud expressed their delight that Churchill was to visit the French Army.[97] The day before, however, Churchill had cabled Roosevelt expressing his dissatisfaction with changes in the FCNL which had left de Gaulle as president and suggested that 'we maintain an attitude of complete reserve until we can discuss the position together'.[98] Indeed, *The Economist* made the point that de Gaulle had acted very much like Napoleon who had removed his rivals of the French revolutionary directory on *Brumaire* 18 as calculated on the revolutionary calendar but 9 November 1799 to the rest of the world. This had been done shortly after Napoleon's return from Africa. *The Economist* noted that de Gaulle became president of the French Committee of National Liberation whilst still in Africa; Giraud, who was still commander-in-chief was removed from the Committee on *Brumaire* 18, 1943. So, too, were generals Georges and Legentilhomme and two civilian commissioners who held Giraudist views.[99]

A major flashpoint once more was Syria and the French attitude towards their mandate there compared with that of the British and Americans. Churchill began to take issue with how the French were beginning to treat the local populations in Syria and Lebanon, both of which had virtually been promised post-war independence by the French but now this seemed to be in doubt. Churchill contacted Richard Casey, Minister of State for the Middle East and told him that he believed that the Cabinet would take a very strong line against outrages in Syria, and against de Gaulle. He asked Casey what forces he had to overcome the French and asked 'Pray let me know urgently what forces you have to overawe and if necessary overpower the French, on the basis that the inhabitants are sympathetic to us'.[100] Churchill was anxious to ensure that the French treated local Syrians acceptably as well as place checks against de Gaulle which might not be in the interests of the Allies and their war aims. If necessary armed force was considered hence his questioning of Casey regarding British arms available in areas concerned.

Churchill was also having similar conversations with Roosevelt. He told the American president that he believed that the British and American governments should react strongly to the outrages in Syria committed by the French. Churchill suggested that the two governments demand the release of the Lebanese president and his ministers, who had been kidnapped by the French authorities. Churchill told Roosevelt that, if de Gaulle refused this, the British and American governments should withdraw recognition of the FCNL. There were other considerations regarding the French. There was a need to secure the Allied situation in North Africa as Churchill reminded Roosevelt 'for I assure you there is nothing this man will not do if he has armed forces at his disposal'.[101] It is clear that Churchill had the full measure of de Gaulle, having worked with him since 1940. Politically Churchill could see that de Gaulle was relatively reliable but failed to trust him with an army. The situation in the French Middle East mandates was rapidly becoming a disgrace and amplified American prejudices against European imperialism. And, of course, the most nagging problem was that French co-operation was necessary for the invasion of North-West Europe which was being planned; de Gaulle's co-operation would be essential.

Meanwhile, Casey reported that the situation in Lebanon was worsening and that he was flying to the capital, Beirut, with Major General Sir Edwards Spears (First Minister to the Republic of Syria and Lebanon) and would return to Cairo on 14 November.[102] Churchill later sent a telegram to General Sir Henry Wilson (C-in-C Middle East), Macmillan and Casey which asked three questions. Had the Lebanese hostages been released? Had the French replied to the message of Major General Spears? Were there enough British troops in the area? Churchill informed Casey that the government would not wait indefinitely for the release of the Lebanese government.[103] Casey replied swiftly, and it was not good news: the French had not replied to the British demands. Casey had spoken to General Catroux and pressed on him the urgency of replying to the UK government's demands.

Catroux blamed Jean Helleu, the Free French High Commissioner for the Levant, for everything. Catroux claimed that Helleu was acting without instructions from Algiers but Casey did not believe him and considered that the Free French were trying to scapegoat Catroux. If this was the case, Casey advised that it was of no concern to the UK. Catroux admitted that Helleu should be recalled and that the Lebanese government should be released but said that it would be difficult to do without the French losing face. Casey replied to Catroux 'that we had not created this situation and that this problem was their own affair'. Catroux was of a sombre attitude and told Casey that he thought that he should seriously advise the French Committee to evacuate the Levant entirely and leave their case for the world to judge. Casey, not taking any nonsense, made it clear to Catroux what the world thought when he replied, 'that public opinion generally and in Lebanon in particular would be unimpressed by legal niceties and would only remember that the French had promised the Lebanon independence and had then violently seized and imprisoned their legal government'. Casey left Catroux quite clear about where the British government stood regarding French actions in Lebanon and Syria and that the French needed to urgently respond to British inquiries on the situation in the Levant. Casey also reported that he had been in hourly contact with Spears by telephone as they assessed the situation in the Middle East.[104]

The situation in Syria and Lebanon was unsatisfactory as far as the British government was concerned. The French were behaving in a very highhanded manner and reneging on promises made earlier in the war concerning Syrian and Lebanese independence. The kidnapping of the Lebanese government was, for the British, the last straw and so Churchill began to rein in the French far more vigorously than before. He needed to prevent an Arab revolt against the French which would have had consequences for the Mediterranean area of operations. The French Army needed to be given worthwhile work and brought into the war properly at the earliest opportunity, thus reducing its abilities for mischief while idle. The British were not afraid to take all measures necessary to ensure that the French acquiesce to British demands regarding continued French rule in the Levant.

Casey contacted General Sir Henry Wilson to comment on the situation in the Levant from a military angle. Casey told Wilson that he had received a message from the FO which ordered him to fly to Beirut and that Catroux had not so far complied with the British demands. Therefore, Wilson was to declare martial law and free the Lebanese government whom the French continued to hold hostage. Overall, Casey was not happy with the situation and was contacting the FO.[105] Wilson informed Churchill of troop movements in the Middle East. In Tripoli, northern Lebanon, 9 Armoured Brigade were concentrated while 10th Indian Division, including 1st Royal Northumberland Fusiliers, were also in northern Lebanon. In Syria itself were 2nd Rifle Brigade, 4th/11th Sikhs, 2nd/7th Gurkha Rifles, supported by three medium regiments of the Royal Artillery based in the Syrian capital, Damascus, while three anti-tank regiments were stationed in Aleppo. To be moved into the area during the period of 18/19 November 1943 were 43rd (Gurkha) Lorried Infantry Brigade and 1st Household Cavalry Regiment. The 8th King's Own was to move to Palestine. There were a further two Indian infantry brigades ready to join 10th Indian Division. A single squadron from 1st Royal Tank Regiment was at six hours' notice to move into Palestine if necessary. All of these forces were under the command of Ninth Army.[106] The British had plenty of resources to deal with the situation in the Levant, but most of the forces detailed by Wilson were preparing for fighting in Europe, namely in Italy. In was therefore, quite galling for a situation to arise where some of this force might be depleted in order to restore a poor situation created unnecessarily by an ally in a theatre not really connected to the major operations of the war.

Macmillan consulted with General Georges on the situation. Georges suggested that the best way to solve the problem in the Levant was to start the French Army fighting the Germans as soon as possible. Georges outlined a plan for this. In his opinion Georges suggested that four French divisions from North Africa with II Polish Corps, all under French command, should form a third army in Italy under the Allied C-in-C and Theatre Commander. He was willing to compromise, suggesting that, if Allied strategy required it, the proposed army might operate in the Balkans, but it had to be under the Allied Theatre Commander to prevent interference by the French committee. Georges claimed that the result would at once deflect the interests of all Frenchmen away from the committee and from de Gaulle to the French Army in active operations under its own French general. A further advantage, according to Georges, was that his scheme would be insurance against the possibility of the Committee interfering with Allied communications to Africa by the withdrawal of French troops in the area. In Georges' opinion, Giraud should be the commander of his proposed army. This would forestall any attempt by the French Committee to dismiss him unilaterally as he was commanding an army in the field under a British or American commander.[107] Georges' plan seemed to have been the most sensible plan for the French for 1943 but it underestimated de Gaulle who remained popular in France while Giraud was seen as second rate.

Chapter 8

Preparing to Return to Europe

As with all the exiled European governments in London between 1940 and 1945, the French wanted to return home. It is the most natural thing to desire and to see a vile enemy driven from one's country can only be satisfying. De Gaulle wanted to return to France but was constantly plagued with thoughts of the sort of France to which he would return. Would he be welcome and what did the Americans, especially, want from the French in return for its liberty?

What was apparent to both Churchill and Roosevelt was that de Gaulle, the leader of the Free French, was the probable head of an immediate post-war France. That being the case, the two western leaders would have to work with him. Churchill had seen this in de Gaulle from their first meeting in 1940 but Roosevelt allowed blind prejudice to cloud his judgement and pressed for his man, Giraud, to be French leader. In April Roosevelt was still railing against de Gaulle, informing Churchill in a telegram Roosevelt said that he had no objection to de Gaulle visiting the USA but would not invite him. Roosevelt asked Churchill for his opinion on Giraud's dismissal and stated that he could not see any military advantage in informing the FNCL of anything of a confidential nature.[1] This was within six weeks of the Normandy landings, or operation OVERLORD to and Roosevelt's distain for de Gaulle remained obvious. However, this would be to ignore the sterling work that the Free French Intelligence service, *le Deuxiéme Bureau*, provided under 'Colonel Passy', the *nom-de-guerre* of André Dewavrin, a French officer with an engineering background. The French resistance was able to provide the Allies with detailed reports on the Atlantic Wall and other German defences which Allied troops would have to face in any landing in Northern France.[2]

However, it should be noted that Churchill had been making inroads towards making peace with de Gaulle as plans for the invasion of Normandy were taking shape. Even if Roosevelt seemed oblivious to the fact that, eventually, de Gaulle would have to be consulted on the matter, it had probably occurred to Churchill that, in time, de Gaulle would have to be informed. It could not be the case of the invasion of North Africa in November 1942 by Anglo-American forces when Roosevelt demanded that de Gaulle and the

Free French should not be informed until the landings were happening. In those days, Roosevelt was merely ignorant of how things should be – by 1944 he was just being bloody-minded. Churchill was of a different view. British historian Laurence Rees notes that Roosevelt's antipathy towards de Gaulle was partly personal. Just before D-Day, Roosevelt told Edward Stettinius, the undersecretary of state, that 'the only thing I am interested in is not having de Gaulle and the National Committee [provisional Free French government in exile] named as the government of France'. Roosevelt could not stand de Gaulle as a human being while, politically, he worried that de Gaulle might pursue colonial policies after the war.[3] In many ways, Roosevelt was typically American in his distrust of Europe and Europeans; de Gaulle was a convenient whipping boy.

After the Tehran Conference, held between 28 November and 1 December 1943, when Churchill, Stalin and Roosevelt met to discuss the progress of the war and its further prosecution, Churchill met with de Gaulle in Marrakesh, Morocco. As ever, the initial few minutes were cool before the two men began to warm to one another. Churchill expressed regret that friction had arisen between them and stated that France and the UK should work together. De Gaulle could only agree to that sentiment. Churchill inquired whether friendship between the UK and France would extend beyond the war. De Gaulle replied that 'France would be exhausted after this terrible ordeal and to recover she will need help from all quarters, especially the United States and Great Britain'. This response pleased Churchill, who said, 'if this is so, we should deal gently with each other'.[4] Despite these gentle words exchanged between de Gaulle and Churchill it was still not to be the smoothest of relationships during 1944.

Nevertheless, de Gaulle invited Churchill to join him in reviewing a military parade the next day and Churchill was happy to accept. This was a major success as the appearance of the two leaders together in Marrakesh illustrated that the two allies were working together and would jointly enjoy victory soon. On newsreels it looked especially good. De Gaulle was not only successful in working Churchill but had also made a good impression on General Eisenhower.

Throughout the Tunisian campaign Eisenhower had worked with both Darlan and Giraud. In the American general's opinion, both were no good since neither was capable of governing French North Africa, but de Gaulle and the FCNL had risen to the task and had done a good job. This convinced Eisenhower that de Gaulle was essential, especially with the pending invasion of Normandy. On 30 December 1943, just before leaving North Africa for Washington DC and London, where he would be appointed Supreme

Commander for the Allied invasion of Europe, Eisenhower requested an appointment with de Gaulle and then called in at de Gaulle's office.

Once with de Gaulle, Eisenhower told him that he had been described to him in a bad light and continued,

> today I recognise that that judgement was in error. For the coming battle, I shall need not only the co-operation of your forces, but still more the assistance of your officials and the moral support of the French people. I must have your assistance and I have come to ask for it.

Of course, de Gaulle was delighted and considered that Eisenhower was a true man for admitting and saying that he had been wrong. Then the meeting became a 'love feast'. De Gaulle raised the question of the liberation of Paris and said that the city must be liberated by French troops. Eisenhower agreed and it was decided that Leclerc's armoured division would be sent from North Africa to the UK as soon as possible. As he was about to leave de Gaulle, Eisenhower told him that he did not know what 'theoretical position' his political master might take but 'I can assure you that as far as I am concerned, I will recognise no French power in France other than your own'.[5] This was a great fillip for de Gaulle and the FCNL while it illustrated the fact that Eisenhower was a realist and not a bitter fantasist like Roosevelt. The reality was that, in a democratic and civilised country such as France, an invading army, even if its programme was one of liberation, still needed the support of the local people. Eisenhower, unlike Roosevelt, recognised that and saw that, despite the rhetoric coming out of Washington DC, de Gaulle was the man who would command the French people once they began to be liberated and even had a provisional government in his kick.

Eisenhower wanted to get on with the war and Germany; he did not want to be deeply involved in the administration of liberated territories when there were perfectly ordered organisations waiting, in the case of France, for the return of de Gaulle so that they could return to governing their country. Thus, Eisenhower had sought out de Gaulle in late 1943 – he had seen in him what Churchill had seen during the summer of 1940.

Eisenhower remained true to his word to de Gaulle. On arrival in London in January 1944, he was informed by his chief of staff, Brigadier General Walter Bedell Smith, that the State Department had given instructions that Allied headquarters were to have no dealings with de Gaulle or the FCNL in relation to civil affairs in France. The American government was following quite a different agenda, having established a School for Military Government at the University of Virginia in 1942. This was designed to train military officers to manage civil affairs in former enemy-occupied countries and was to produce the Allied Military Government in Occupied Territories (AMGOT). Roosevelt was determined to introduce this into liberated France.[6] But he was politically too short-sighted to recognise this would not be acceptable while his personal loathing of de Gaulle seemed completely to undo him and his plans for France. De Gaulle was aware of Roosevelt's intentions for France as is revealed in a conversation he had with one of General Leclerc's entourage, Captain Alain de Boissieu. De Gaulle told de Boissieu that the situation with the Allies was not good, with Roosevelt determined to impose AMGOT on France along with currency printed by the US treasury. This situation was totally unacceptable to de Gaulle who declared to the young officer that he would return to France at the first opportunity with or without the Allies' consent. He warned de Boissieu not to mention this to anyone save Leclerc.[7]

Eisenhower, on hearing of the State Department's instructions, was stunned. For him there was no alternative to de Gaulle and the FCNL. He recognised that Roosevelt's instructions had to be overturned and swung into action. On 15 January, Eisenhower cabled General George Marshal at the War Department with a message that read:

> It is essential that immediate crystallization of plans relating to civil affairs in Metropolitan France be accomplished. This requires conference with properly accredited French authorities. I assume, of course, that such authorities will be representatives of the Committee of National Liberation. I therefore request that General de Gaulle be asked to designate an individual or group of individuals with whom I can enter into immediate negotiations in London. The need for prompt action cannot be overemphasized, since we desire to turn over to French control at the earliest possible date those areas that are not essential for military operations.[8]

This was a clear assault on Roosevelt's policy and perhaps a step above Eisenhower's pay grade. He was a soldier, there to carry out his political masters' will, but he was also a realist who knew what lay before him and needed to demolish Roosevelt's personal campaign against de Gaulle in order to bring victory and peace to Europe. Eisenhower found support within the War Department and Assistant Secretary of State for War John J. McCloy was sent to see Roosevelt and persuade him to agree to Eisenhower's need for de Gaulle's aid once the liberation of France began. McCloy was a good choice since he was the former managing partner of a top New York law firm and a favourite of Roosevelt. After about thirty minutes of flannel, he had got Roosevelt to agree to Eisenhower's demands.

Roosevelt authorised McCloy to tell Eisenhower 'informally' that he should feel free in making decisions about French civil affairs 'even if it involved dealing with representatives of the French Committee'. McCloy continued to plague Roosevelt with Eisenhower's proposals. Two months later, Roosevelt approved a War Department directive that empowered Eisenhower to decide 'when, where, and how the Civil Administration in France' should be conducted. Eisenhower was given complete authority to work with the FCNL and to allow it to choose and install officers for civil affairs as long as that did not constitute official recognition of the FCNL as the government of France.[9]

Eisenhower was pleased with the results of McCloy's ventures, de Gaulle less so. Eisenhower had the authority to deal with those French authorities whom he chose to do so. De Gaulle's reaction was that of understanding – he could see clearly that Eisenhower had kept his word and had stuck by him in the face of his own powerful president, but it did not prevent de Gaulle from commenting,

> Actually, the President's intentions seemed to me on the order as Alice's Adventures in Wonderland. In North Africa, Roosevelt had already ventured on a political enterprise analogous to the one he was now contemplating for France. Yet of that attempt nothing remained.... That the failure of his policy in Africa had not been able to dispel Roosevelt's illusions was a situation I regretted for him and for our relations.[10]

And that was the problem for Roosevelt; his policies regarding de Gaulle and the FCNL were a bust. Roosevelt was not acting out of political skill or statesmanship; he was acting from prejudice, especially his spite against de Gaulle and all that he stood for. It should be seen that Roosevelt, as with many American presidents, before and since, are quite naïve when dealing with matters outside the USA. American politics tend to be isolationist, especially before 1945 while since then US foreign policy has been bound up in defeating the Soviet Union and, latterly, international terrorism. Since the beginning of the present century this has exploded into unfortunate examples of warfare in which the USA and its allies have been found wanting. Roosevelt was no different, he had little idea of foreigners and thought that he could bluster his way forward in France and ignore the wants and needs of the French. A more experienced man, such as Eisenhower, knew that Roosevelt's policy regarding the French was bankrupt and based on the American experience in Africa where Roosevelt seemed quite content to work with the collaborative

Vichy regime rather than de Gaulle. That did not work in North Africa and Eisenhower knew that it certainly would not work in France. Therefore he needed to have a correct regime in place which expressed the wishes of the French people and their support for de Gaulle rather than Roosevelt's bullying tactic of trying to subjugate France to the will of US military governors, not to mention that the AMGOT plan that treated France as a defeated former enemy. This was not the case and Roosevelt knew it in his heart, but his bile against de Gaulle was so great that it needed calmer heads to draw the poison from Roosevelt's more crackpot plans for liberated France and smooth the way to work with de Gaulle and the FCNL. Many had already accepted that the FNCL were to become the provisional government of France until such time that democratic elections were held in France for a government and president.

As late as 3 June 1944, Churchill was still trying to convince de Gaulle of the necessity of agreeing to Roosevelt's idea of French submission to AMGOT. That de Gaulle was so far unelected continued to vex Roosevelt and, to a lesser extent, troubled Churchill. It was clear that the Anglo-American leader did not understand the conditions that France and other occupied countries had operated under since 1940. De Gaulle asked Churchill why he thought that he should put himself 'up to Roosevelt as a candidate for power in France?' De Gaulle furthered his argument:

> the French Government exists. I have nothing to ask of the United States of America, any more than I have of Great Britain. That being understood, it is important for all the Allies that relations between the French administration and the military command be set in order. We have been proposing this for the last nine months. Since the armies are going to land tomorrow [*sic*] I quite see that you are in a hurry to have the question settled. We ourselves are ready. But for this settlement where is the American representative? Furthermore, I observe that the Washington and London governments have taken measures to dispense with any agreements with us. The troops who are preparing to land have been furnished with 'so called' French money which is absolutely unrecognised by the government of the Republic. Tomorrow General Eisenhower, in agreement with you, [will proclaim] that he is taking France under his authority. How do you expect us to negotiate on this basis?[11]

And here was the rub: it became quite clear that de Gaulle did not recognise the Vichy government, something that the American government had done. He also refused to acknowledge the fall of the Third Republic and, on reaching

Paris, proclaimed that it was the only legal authority in France at that time. On being requested to proclaim the Republic, De Gaulle replied:

> The Republic has never ceased to exist. Free France, Fighting France, the French Committee for National Liberation, have, in their turn, been part of it. Vichy always was and remains null and void. I myself am the President of the Government of the Republic. Why should I have to proclaim it?[12]

Nevertheless, Roosevelt, as D-Day approached, had tried to get his way once more and impose limitations on how Allied forces should work with the French as French territory was liberated by those forces. On 11 May Eisenhower was forced to write to the Combined Chiefs of Staff:

> The limitations under which we are operating in dealing with the French are becoming very embarrassing and are producing a situation that is becoming very dangerous. We began our military discussions with the French representatives here in the belief that, although we have no formal directive, we understood the policies of our government well enough to be able to reach a working way with any French body or organisation that can effectively assist us in the fight against Germany. For the present there is no such body represented here except the French Committee of National Liberation.[13]

Eisenhower expanded on his thoughts and made it quite clear that necessary arrangements had to be in place ready for when France was liberated and had to be administered, and not by the US military. To Eisenhower the only way forward was to invite de Gaulle to London to deal directly with him 'on the most pressing problems of the initial approach to the French people and their organised resistance groups'.[14] This was something Roosevelt was trying to ignore – the French people and, most importantly, the French Resistance, that all-encompassing group of people all sworn to de Gaulle and his ideals and to the liberation of France and damnation to Germany and the Germans. Both Eisenhower and Churchill knew that this could not be ignored. Indeed, resistance groups had been very much the brainchild of Churchill, who had sought to combine the spontaneous raising of men and women fighting clandestinely against the enemy in occupied Europe using the SOE. It seemed that, in Roosevelt's mind, nothing happened in Europe until the Americans arrived in early 1942. Of course, he was wrong while Churchill agreed with Eisenhower that de Gaulle should be invited to London.

As ever, Roosevelt disagreed that de Gaulle should be invited to London. Roosevelt's opinion was that there could be no discussion of French political matters with de Gaulle. Eisenhower was told by Roosevelt that he felt sure that he could understand that matters relating to the future government of France were political and not military. He also claimed that the French, owing to the trauma of being invaded and occupied by Germany, were 'shell-shocked' and would take time to resume normality. Roosevelt said, 'We as liberators have no "right" to colour their views or to give any group the sole right to impose one side of the case on them.'[15]

This was vintage patronising Roosevelt, especially the term liberators: it was true but to brag was tasteless, especially, being used by one who could only be seen as a parvenu to an ancient and honourable people. Roosevelt was supported in his anti-de Gaulle hostility by senior members of the State Department, who were still mesmerised by the failed Vichy regime while Admiral Leahy, the former ambassador to Vichy, launched anti-de Gaulle tirades virtually every day. By 1944 Leahy was chairing the Joint Chiefs of Staff with his office in the White House itself.

Eisenhower was quite taken aback by Roosevelt's stubbornness in his hatred for de Gaulle. Nevertheless, he was robust in his reply to his president. He told Roosevelt that his dealings with the FCNL would be confined to military matters and civil administration as and when called for. He also said that he understood Roosevelt's anxieties and would be careful to avoid anything that smacked of trying to influence the nature of a future French government. Eisenhower was blunt though in his assessment of the political situation in France as he wrote:

> However, I think I should tell you as far as I am able to determine from information given to me through agents and through escaped prisoners of war, there exists in France today only two major groups, of which one is the Vichy gang, and the other characterised by unreasoning admiration of de Gaulle.

Eisenhower informed Roosevelt that, once ashore, he was certain of 'a universal desire to adhere to the Gaullist group'.[16] It was clear that, in Eisenhower's opinion, Roosevelt and his political allies at the White House were trying to back the wrong French horse but could not be too open in their curious support for the failed traitor Vichy regime.

Eisenhower seemed to be more politically astute as, although he counted on Roosevelt ultimately being willing to defer to the commander in the field, he still decided on a belt-and-braces approach to what could become a problem once de Gaulle arrived in France. Therefore, he reminded Roosevelt that SHAEF (Supreme Headquarters Allied Expeditionary Force) was an Allied command, and not solely American. To this end, Eisenhower suggested that the British government needed to approve decisions relating to the future governing of France. Later, Eisenhower was to reflect that France needed de Gaulle and that he had already given him his promise of support. Eisenhower also knew that the invading Allies would be needing massive support from the French resistance while a major falling out with de Gaulle would hurt the Allies considerably. Eisenhower was very clear that Roosevelt was the problem regarding France, and de Gaulle, and the problem needed to be dealt with while de Gaulle was the only authority who could produce unity in France. But he put on notice that, once France was liberated, the French would determine their own government.

Unlike his president, Eisenhower maintained his charm offensive with de Gaulle. On 14 May General Juin's troops had broken through the Gustav Line in Italy but there was more to this than a bland message of victory. The *Corps Expéditionnaire Français* (CEF) – French Expeditionary Force –

had hardly covered itself in glory. It had gone through the Aurunci Mountains on the left (southern) flank of the Gustav Line and across the Liri Valley, committing savage war crimes en route, notably in Esperia. Juin was horrified when he learnt of the atrocities committed by a French force.

The CEF had not encountered the same resistance as the US II Corps, also in Fifth Army since the Germans had considered the Aurunci to be all but impassable. The CEF advance, combined with that of Eighth Army, was to prompt a German withdrawal to the Hitler Line. On 23 May Eisenhower sent de Gaulle his congratulations for this performance by Free French troops but, as we can see above, it was tarnished.

De Gaulle's reply was just what Eisenhower was looking for as it read:

> I assure you again that the French government is very happy to have a place in your army under your supreme command for operations in the Western theatre, and it had the fullest confidence that you will conduct your armies of liberation to a rapid and complete victory.

Less than two weeks before the Normandy landings the Committee of National Liberation in Algiers declared itself to be the Provisional Government of the French Republic with de Gaulle as head. Churchill cabled Roosevelt to point out the obvious: that it was going to be 'very difficult to cut the French out of the liberation of France.' He then asked the president to agree to an invitation to de Gaulle to visit London. Roosevelt agreed but was not happy and said that he hoped Churchill might be able to convince de Gaulle to contribute to the liberation of France but not impose his will on the French people.[17] Based on Eisenhower's evidence, it would seem that de Gaulle was pushing at an open door and did not need to impose his will. The French were waiting for liberation, and he was the man to bring it.

Both Churchill and Eisenhower knew that de Gaulle was the only French leader to unify his compatriots. It must be remembered that, in France, his name and symbolism had united communist and monarchist resistance fighters in the fight against the Germans. It was to this end that Churchill sent his own plane to Algiers to fetch de Gaulle who arrived in London on 4 June. This narrative has highlighted the poor relationship between de Gaulle and Roosevelt who alone of the three major Allied leaders, Stalin, Churchill and Roosevelt, hated de Gaulle beyond all reasoning. One can only wonder why Roosevelt clung so tightly to the Vichy regime which, by 1944, was totally dominated by Germany with the Vichy zone occupied by the German Army. Eisenhower was not the only peacemaker in the Franco-American relationship: the following evidence illustrates how the British tried to patch up the fractious relationship between de Gaulle and Roosevelt.

The British acted as intermediaries and began preparing for a possible visit by de Gaulle to the USA. Alfred Duff Cooper, always known as 'Duff' and the British representative to the FCNL, cabled Churchill with the information that he had informed de Gaulle that he should visit the USA. For his part, de Gaulle said that he would accept an invitation to visit at any time. Duff Cooper commented that de Gaulle considered that Churchill remained sympathetic to him and extended his personal gratitude to him.[18] Churchill had to reply swiftly and told Duff Cooper not to proceed with the proposal because, even if de Gaulle was welcome to go to the USA, Roosevelt was not issuing an invitation. Churchill was clear that this was Roosevelt's reaction to the dismissal of Giraud.[19]

Churchill and Duff Cooper began to work on the situation between the French and the Americans. Duff Cooper looked at the problem from Roosevelt's point of view and why he might be reluctant to invite de Gaulle to the USA. The most obvious problem was that it was an election year. Roosevelt had nailed his colours to Giraud's mast and' if he suddenly dropped him in favour of de Gaulle, it would look as if it was a case of 'off with the old and on with the new'. If that happened, Roosevelt's political enemies would make a lot of it. Duff Cooper considered that de Gaulle's visit should go ahead and that a solution should be found regarding the question of an invitation from Roosevelt. Duff Cooper told Churchill that 'I would add that de Gaulle being a soldier and not a politician was fortunately free from such embarrassments and that he was not I was sure a man to bother about formalities when the interests of France were at stake'.[20]

Duff Cooper might have been correct about a soldier's attitude and, while de Gaulle was a soldier, as a man he was quite touchy and knew when his honour was being besmirched and why. As he saw himself as the representation of France and of French liberty, he would have considered Roosevelt's attitude toward him as nothing less than disrespectful. Nevertheless, Churchill and Duff Cooper pressed in their support for de Gaulle's visit.

Churchill suggested to Duff Cooper that de Gaulle should contact his ambassador in the USA to enquire whether a visit would be welcome. Meanwhile, Churchill said that he would ensure that a meeting between de Gaulle and Roosevelt would be favourable.[21] Duff Cooper agreed with this plan but, when Churchill put it to Roosevelt, the American president suggested putting it back by a month citing 'accumulation of work here'.[22]

Churchill was disappointed with Roosevelt's response and said so: 'I had hoped you would go a little further with this.' After getting that off his chest, Churchill expanded on his thoughts and stated:

> After all this man, whom I trust as little as you do, commands considerable forces including naval forces and the *Richelieu* which are placed freely at our disposal and are in action or eager for action. He presides over a vast empire all the strategic points in which are at our disposal.

Churchill suggested a way out for Roosevelt. He proposed that Roosevelt continue with his claim of being busy but that after mid-May all might be possible, subject to unforeseeable events of the war. Churchill concluded his missive with the words 'I hope that you can go as far as this'.[23]

Churchill's exasperation with Roosevelt is obvious and what he said was true. From Churchill's point of view, de Gaulle was untrustworthy and capricious but so often he was doing what was necessary for France and not for his British allies. De Gaulle certainly had vast resources at his fingertips, including the *Richelieu*, a modern warship classed as a 'fast battleship', well-armed and well armoured. This class of ship served in the French Navy until 1970 such was its modernity. *Richelieu* had been kept out of German hands while imperial French resources had been used by the Allies to fight the Germans beginning in French North Africa, which had facilitated Allied landings in Sicily and Italy. The Allies were within weeks of landing in Normandy, something yet to be mentioned to the French, and Churchill was well aware that only de Gaulle could hold the French together as battles were about to be fought on the French mainland. French people were about to die as they, unfortunately, would be caught in the midst of the fighting while their property would also be destroyed as the war swept through France and beyond as the Allies liberated Europe. Only de Gaulle could stem French resentment and restore the country once it was liberated. This was what he wanted Roosevelt to understand and, further, to comprehend that the American favourite, Giraud, had nothing to offer the French. He was a mere general of the French Army; de Gaulle was the symbol that had kept the French in the war and their hopes of liberty alive.

Roosevelt was not welcoming but realised that he had to accept Churchill's criticism and accept that de Gaulle would be coming to the USA. After making a factually inaccurate statement that he did not consider that de Gaulle and the FCNL had made much contribution to the Allied war effort, and that all of the French war work had been before de Gaulle, Roosevelt conceded that he had no objection to de Gaulle being informed that he would receive him if he visited the USA.[24] Basically, Roosevelt loathed de Gaulle; this was quite clear. He knew that he was being foolish in his opinion about de Gaulle's and the French contribution to the war; the use of French North Africa is an obvious use of French assets while where did he think the Allies were landing in June 1944? North Carolina, Norfolk or Normandy?! Overall, Roosevelt, in spite of his personal antipathy for de Gaulle and the French, knew that he had to receive de Gaulle, albeit reluctantly but for show and Allied unity.

Churchill then began to look at the FCNL as he knew that as the liberation of France was at hand and that the FCNL was very likely to be at least the French provisional government until democratic elections could be held to restore the pre-war democratic status quo. Churchill told Duff Cooper to urge de Gaulle not to concern himself too much with French communists. He considered that de Gaulle had been wrong to include communists in the FCNL. For one, it prevented confidential information being shared with the French. Churchill noted that Russian and Yugoslav communists might be considered as heroes but French communists, prior to the German invasion of the Soviet Union in June 1941, had been traitors to France.[25]

Churchill had never liked communism since it was the antipathy of everything that he stood for – wealth and privilege – but he was right in his comments. He had met Stalin and knew not to trust him. Anything learned from the Allies would be squirreled away to be used by the Soviet regime. Churchill also knew that the Soviet regime was as murderous as that of the Nazis and that, after the war once the Nazis had been defeated, the world would have to face down its replacement, Stalin's regime with its agenda for world domination. Unlike Roosevelt, Churchill knew how to work with potential enemies. Roosevelt merely wanted his own way on a personal level but what Churchill knew was that, no matter their origin, were untrustworthy and certainly unacceptable to Roosevelt and Americans in general: hence his words of warning to de Gaulle regarding communists in the FCNL.

Roosevelt and the US government continued with its unhelpful attitude towards de Gaulle and the FCNL as Duff Cooper outlined to Churchill. Duff Cooper remarked on the effect that Roosevelt's and the American Secretary of State, Cordell Hull's speeches had had on the FCNL. The French committee saw themselves as the major authority in France. The fact that Eisenhower had been instructed not to deal with anything in France was viewed by the FCNL as an intentional snub. The FCNL issued a warning that if France was continually snubbed in favour of the Americans, it risked France returning to a policy of isolation.[26]

Churchill replied, informing Duff Cooper that neither he nor Roosevelt had recognised the FCNL as being France or as the heirs of the French government who had declared war on Germany in 1939. Churchill stated that there was a great deal in France which was represented by either the Vichy government or by the FCNL and that there was no chance of the American government altering its stance regarding its policy of Eisenhower more or less taking control of France once the Allies landed in that country.[27] It is interesting to learn that Churchill still considered that Vichy had any say in French matters since the Germans had occupied the vassal state since 1942. It was basically an extension of Nazi Germany but, overall, the question of who was France? rose quickly by 1944 and the American government failed to understand.

Churchill was faced with having to tell Roosevelt that the American view of France was out of step with that of the UK whose citizens were showing increasing support for the French. Churchill told Roosevelt that British people were aware that de Gaulle was difficult but felt that this had to be endured since it was not worth the lives which could be lost if the Allies did not have the support of the 'French national spirit'. Churchill stated that de Gaulle was showing signs of wanting to work with the Allies and that it would be very difficult 'to cut the French out of the liberation of France'.[28] Churchill was not wrong. He and Roosevelt knew that France was on the verge of invasion by the Allies and French co-operation was essential. However, as Churchill related to Duff Cooper, de Gaulle remained as graceless as ever. Churchill told Duff Cooper that, after contacting Roosevelt informing him that only a representative was needed for discussions with de Gaulle, he learned that this might be impossible as it had been reported that de Gaulle would not visit the UK unless an American official was present. Pithily, Churchill said to Duff Cooper 'this is just the sort of thing he always does to injure France at critical moments.'[29]

The question before them was when should de Gaulle be informed about the coming invasion of France? It was obviously going to happen, but when and where? Churchill told Roosevelt that he had no intention of inviting de Gaulle to the UK until D-Day. He suggested that Roosevelt send someone of the rank of Edward Stettinius (Undersecretary of State) to talks. Churchill continued to consider that the Allies should be in close contact with France.[30] Eventually, Roosevelt conceded that the French should be with the Allies regarding OVERLORD and hoped that talks with de Gaulle would help.[31] Finally, the penny had dropped. Roosevelt had to concede that de Gaulle was the single Frenchman with whom he and the Allies could do business. De Gaulle would be able to convince his compatriots that turning France into an invasion ground and a battlefield to gain liberty was the price that France had to pay. He had often supported the unsupportable beginning in 1940 when he had understood why the French fleet at Oran had been destroyed with 1,300 French sailors killed by the Royal Navy. In 1944, with the liberation of France at hand, he was hardly going to withdraw his co-operation. De Gaulle may have been challenging for the British and the Americans, but he wanted the same thing – the defeat of Germany and Europe liberated. De Gaulle, Churchill and Roosevelt had always been part of the same team, albeit with different approaches.

Churchill, after the apparent change of mind by Roosevelt, felt more comfortable to receive de Gaulle. Duff Cooper was notified that de Gaulle would be welcome to visit the UK as soon as it was convenient for him to travel. Churchill stated that he would send his own York transport aircraft to collect him, but the journey was subject to secrecy. Indeed, Churchill positively beseeched de Gaulle to come and wrote via Duff Cooper:

> Come please now with your colleagues at the earliest moment and in great secrecy. I give you my personal assurance that it is in the interests of France. I am sending you my own York [aeroplane] and another York for you starting tonight.[32]

Churchill also told Roosevelt that the War Cabinet believed that de Gaulle should be informed about OVERLORD before the landings took place. The safest way to tell de Gaulle was to speak to him once he was in the UK and, therefore, Churchill had requested de Gaulle's presence in the UK as soon as possible.[33] It was clear that Churchill considered it to be bad form if Normandy were to be invaded without the French being informed.[34]

There were still other matters relating to France and its pending liberation, as witnessed in an exchange between Averill Harriman, the US Ambassador to the Soviet Union, who was in Cairo and General Eisenhower. Harriman stated that it was widely believed that General Alphonse Juin (commander of the French corps in Italy) should command French forces during Operation ANVIL, the invasion of Southern France, but de Gaulle disapproved owing to Juin's association with Weygand.[35] This was a perennial problem for de Gaulle as he was aware that, once France was liberated, accounts would have to be settled and those who had collaborated with Vichy and the Nazis should face consequences. At all times, de Gaulle had to stand at arm's length from those associated with the Vichy regime so as not to compromise his standing in post-war France.

Duff Cooper had to tell Churchill that de Gaulle was not playing nicely. De Gaulle claimed that the Americans had no interest in his visit to London and so he would only visit the UK as a soldier visiting his troops. De Gaulle's attitude caused René Massigli, his foreign minister, to threaten to resign unless de Gaulle visited the UK in a co-operative spirit.[36] The next day Duff Cooper was able to deliver more promising news to Churchill as he reported that, after a meeting of the FCNL, it was decided that de Gaulle should go the UK on 5 August, irrespective of any guarantees. Massigli told Duff Cooper that, if de Gaulle continued to refuse to go to the UK, he and others from the FCNL would resign.[37]

The next day it was decided that, after all of the huffing and puffing, de Gaulle would visit the UK. Churchill told Roosevelt that Eisenhower would give de Gaulle a thirty-minute briefing on the military situation (OVERLORD) and that the next day Churchill would receive de Gaulle. He also told Roosevelt that he was uncertain just how far the Allies would actually advance on D-Day.[38] Given that this telegram is dated 4 June it was about time that de Gaulle was informed since the invasion force was about to be despatched to Normandy; indeed, it was within hours of going. One can only speculate how much longer the Allies were willing to keep de Gaulle out of the loop. De Gaulle actually arrived in London on 4 June.

Churchill immediately took him to Eisenhower's headquarters near Portsmouth. Churchill told Roosevelt that Generals Eisenhower and Bedell Smith went to their utmost limit in their endeavour to conciliate him, making it clear that, in practice, events would probably mean that the committee (FCNL) would be the natural authority with whom the supreme commander would deal.[39] Clearly, Churchill was preparing Roosevelt for the reality in France and not allowing him to continue with his deluded version of what should happen. As the Allies were invading France via Normandy, it was unlikely that Roosevelt might have found anybody from the Vichy authority there and, given four years of German occupation, it was unlikely that he would have found anyone with sympathy towards the Germans or to Vichy unless they were undiluted traitors. And how long might they have lasted during that incredible summer of 1944?

Even though Churchill had arranged for Eisenhower to give de Gaulle a thirty-minute briefing regarding D-Day, Eisenhower gave him the courtesy of a lengthy briefing, as would be expected when a senior ranking officer or, quite frankly, the leader of the country about to be invaded and turned into a battlefield is informed of an undertaking as serious as the Normandy landings were to be. A major agreement was made with the decision that General Koenig would place the FFI under the command of the French Army and from there on report to Eisenhower. Eisenhower confided to de Gaulle that he was concerned about the weather and had at best twenty-four hours to decide the actual date for the landings. He asked de Gaulle what he thought he should do. De Gaulle was flattered but insisted that Eisenhower should alone make the decision saying, 'Whatever decision you make, I approve in advance and without reservation. I will only tell you that in your place I should not delay.'

With the briefing over Eisenhower, with some embarrassment, gave de Gaulle a speech written by SHAEF speechwriters which they wanted de Gaulle to deliver once the landings had begun. Eisenhower knew de Gaulle well enough to know that he would decline. Instead, de Gaulle wrote his own.

> The supreme battle has been joined … . It is, of course, the Battle of France, and the battle for France! For the sons of France, wherever they are, whatever they are, the simple and sacred duty to fight the enemy by every means in their power … . The orders given by the French government and by the leaders it has recognised must be followed precisely … . From behind the cloud so heavy with our blood and our tears, the sun of our greatness is now reappearing.[40]

It was quite clear that the fighting in Normandy and across France was supported by France and the French. It could not be otherwise since it was obvious to de Gaulle at his briefing with Eisenhower that much of the fighting and indeed dying would be done by British and American troops supported by Canadians. De Gaulle's speech delighted Eisenhower as de Gaulle did not claim to be president of France and did not refer to Eisenhower as supreme commander, but it was clear that he saw him as such. This meant that Eisenhower was able to inform the Combined Chiefs that 'General de Gaulle and his chief of staff are anxious to assist in every possible way and to have the lodgements effected as soon as possible'.

Eisenhower, unlike his president, continued with his charm offensive and dealt with de Gaulle and the Free French with tact and consideration. He had previously, on 25 May, sent a directive to British and American commanders who were to land on D-Day which read: 'Military government will *not* be established in liberated France … . The French themselves will conduct all aspects of civil administration in their country, even in areas of military operations.'[41]

The idea that the French would be allowed to administer their own affairs, even in a military operational region, was quite a fillip to them. It was recognised by Eisenhower that the France and its people were to be treated correctly and with dignity and that they were genuinely in control of the liberated areas of their own land. Liberation was to be genuine, and Eisenhower was stamping his authority over this decision, more or less in defiance of his own president. The fuse was lit, and the invasion was at hand with the landing of 155,000 Allied troops on Norman beaches on 6 June 1944.

Nevertheless, the less than friendly attitude of Roosevelt towards de Gaulle continued. On D-Day itself Roosevelt cabled Churchill stating that de Gaulle had been invited to the USA for a visit at the end of June and the beginning of July. However, the next day Roosevelt wished Churchill good luck with talks with the 'Prima Donna' (de Gaulle). Roosevelt was anxious that de Gaulle was not to consider that the proposed visit to the USA as a friendly visit and that Roosevelt refused 'absolutely as Head of State to invite' de Gaulle to the USA.[42] Roosevelt's contempt for de Gaulle remained and it was a mixture of prejudice and pique as his choice of French leader had been outwitted and outmanoeuvred by de Gaulle. Churchill just about remained above Roosevelt's squalid attitude but was often cheering for Roosevelt from the side-lines, principally because the USA held all the trump cards regarding the war in western Europe, sending supplies and men.

On 8 June, Churchill wired Roosevelt regarding de Gaulle who had arrived in the UK alone; the French commissioners necessary for discussions had been left in Algiers. De Gaulle was not willing to discuss the civilian administration of France as it was being liberated without an American representative being present. There had been progress, however, as de Gaulle had modified his refusal to allow French liaison officers to join Allied forces in France until the question of the civil administration had been settled. Churchill told Roosevelt that, if de Gaulle continued to refuse to send for his commissionaires, it would be best that he returned to Algiers. He stated that, if de Gaulle were to accept an American presence at talks, it would be best that John Winant, the American Ambassador to the UK should be available. The tone of the telegram certainly suggests that Churchill was supporting Roosevelt over de Gaulle.[43]

However, a brief look at the diary of Sir Alexander Cadogan reveals his thoughts on the situation around D-Day as, on 7 June, he records that of the 'critical 72 hours' before and after D-Day, '40 have been occupied by all the High-Ups wrangling about purely imaginary and manufactured grievances against de Gaulle!'[44] Cadogan suspected that Roosevelt was still dealing with Vichy figures such as Pétain and Laval.[45] It remained clear to the FO that Roosevelt was doing anything to sabotage de Gaulle and his supporters from gaining any political credit in France as its liberation began and that the American president was wrong and foolish in his approach towards France.

However, as France was being liberated by the Allies it became obvious that de Gaulle's presence in his homeland was necessary, but Churchill was still flippant in his attitude towards de Gaulle. On 13 June Churchill cabled General Sir Bernard Montgomery, the legendary 'Monty'. In his telegram to Monty, Churchill said, 'I must inflict upon you a visit from de Gaulle tomorrow.' De Gaulle was to be at Allied HQ, probably in Bayeux, according to Churchill and added that, if the French wanted de Gaulle, Montgomery was to allow this as it could not be stopped,[46] a curious statement. The next day Monty reported that de Gaulle's visit had been a 'great success'.[47] On the same day, Montgomery sent a further telegram to Churchill when de Gaulle's visit had been concluded. De Gaulle had indeed been to Bayeux where his reception was lukewarm as had been the case in other small towns. Monty reported that de Gaulle had left behind a single civilian administration officer and three colonels. Montgomery had no idea why.[48]

Regarding de Gaulle's lukewarm reception in Bayeux and elsewhere, as claimed by Montgomery, this is denied by French historian Robert Aron who noted the enthusiasm by the newly liberated French as perhaps being slightly bewildered that de Gaulle was moving amongst them but received him warmly.[49] Jean Edward Smith writes that de Gaulle's visit to Bayeux and to two other towns had been successful and that he had departed that evening feeling in control. All American fears about de Gaulle's support in France should have been dispelled while Bayeux, the first French city liberated by the Allies, had in many ways become the temporary capital of liberated France.[50] Nevertheless, at least one Allied report claimed that even after the invasion 'the peasants still preferred to sell their butter to the retreating Germans than to our men who were considered suspect'. Whatever happened in Normandy, Roosevelt could not overlook de Gaulle's warm welcome in Bayeux and, as Rees notes, the Normans were not natural de Gaullists but there was something in his character and reputation which made them receive him with great enthusiasm. This contributed to Roosevelt's decision to acknowledge the de Gaullists as 'the working authority for civilian administration in the liberated areas of France'.[51] It was to be a great turn around by the American president.

President Roosevelt was to patronise de Gaulle visiting France. He told Churchill that he had no objection to de Gaulle visiting the British sector of northern France and said that such a visit would have a good effect on the French underground, over which de Gaulle had great influence and could obtain their will to continue to fight against the enemy.[52] De Gaulle, meanwhile, returned to Algiers on 16 June and there addressed the French Consultative Assembly, a temporary stand-in for the National Assembly. He informed his compatriots what had already been achieved in France and paid special tribute to Eisenhower. De Gaulle had recognised that Eisenhower's work raised him from being an outcast in the eyes of Washington DC to being the leader of France.

Eisenhower had seen the chaos of civil affairs in North Africa and was unwilling to endure that again.[53] North Africa, albeit the launchpad for the invasion of Italy and the Allied return to Europe, was still an outpost compared with France and Eisenhower could not afford inept civilian administration in liberated France as the Allies sought to advance across Europe to Germany. Poor planning risked prolonging the war; efficiency in France was found in de Gaulle and Eisenhower embraced him.

Roosevelt may have had his personal prejudice about de Gaulle, but the war was larger than the American presidency and events moved swifter than Roosevelt had anticipated. All too quickly for him, de Gaulle and Eisenhower were making local agreements, especially as the liberation of Paris was at hand. It was noted that these negotiations were not to involve the recognition of the FCNL as the provisional French government.[54]

Churchill was not only having to juggle and keep Roosevelt happy regarding de Gaulle, but he also had to hide further incidents of de Gaulle's inconsiderate behaviour. Churchill told Eden that he felt that 'the de Gaulle incident', de Gaulle's refusal to meet Churchill in Italy, should be kept from the French foreign minister, René Massigli, whether in formal or informal talks.[55] Since Massigli had previously threatened to resign and take several French ministers with him whenever de Gaulle had been difficult in his relations with Churchill, no doubt it was feared that he might do so again at a time when French unity was essential. The fighting in Normandy was reaching its climax and the Germans were beginning to show signs of withdrawing eastwards and out of France for the first time in over four years. Indeed, very quickly, the liberation of Paris was at hand. Churchill requested Eden to procure armour to be sent to Paris to support the French revolt in the capital.[56]

As Aron observed, by the time de Gaulle had reached Rambouillet, just before Paris, on 22 August, his position within the Allies had shifted for the better. The Provisional Government of the French Republic had been recognised by the Allies as the *de facto* French authority over those areas recently liberated. French troops were also on the move towards Paris. The French 2nd Armoured Division, commanded by General Leclerc was heading towards the French capital from Normandy. Furthermore, since being kept in the dark regarding the Normandy landings; things had improved for DRAGOON, the landings in southern France on 15 August as de Gaulle was kept fully in the loop and there was no question of AMGOT or American 'false money' in the south.[57]

Nevertheless, recognition of French sovereignty remained limited. France had not reached complete Allied status and de Gaulle was not invited to the major Allied conferences. On 23 August as de Gaulle, in Rambouillet, was waiting to go to Paris, Churchill, in a telegram to the American Secretary of State, suggested that a planned meeting of foreign ministers on future world organisation should exclude the French 'until they have broadened their government'.[58] The problem, according to the British and especially the American government, was that de Gaulle's provisional government was far too narrow. This attitude, coupled with Roosevelt's personal prejudice against de Gaulle, often hampered de Gaulle as he tried to retrieve his country from, firstly, the Germans and then, after 6 June, from the Allies. The latter initially tried to administer liberated France with military governance, despite the all too obvious French provisional government waiting in the wings.

As Aron observed, de Gaulle had been recognised 'with enthusiasm by all liberated France' while the setting up of his administration had been positive in those territories. Furthermore, the Allies, despite the distain some held for de Gaulle, could not provide a convincing rival to de Gaulle.[59] This was the setting as de Gaulle waited to enter Paris which he had previously demanded should be liberated by French troops. De Gaulle's authority was evident in the provinces already liberated as there was a lack of disorder there despite the legacy of defeat, occupation, fighting and bombing as northern France was liberated. All could have been chaos. It was very different in the south. There was a delay between the departure of German troops and the arrival of a de Gaulle administrative organisation. During the period of delay many excesses were committed.[60] There was another aspect to the improvement between de Gaulle and the Allies which was his diplomacy during June and July when de Gaulle made a trip to the Vatican where the Pope recognised him as the President of the Provisional Government of the Republic of France. He then made a trip to Washington DC where Roosevelt also recognised him as the same.[61]

That was a complete climbdown by the American president who, as we have seen, loathed de Gaulle. Aron noted that, even though de Gaulle and Roosevelt should take their share of the blame attached to Roosevelt's dislike of de Gaulle, it should also be considered that Roosevelt was badly advised by his own diplomats who seemed very determined to promote alternative French leaders. However, de Gaulle became increasingly irreplaceable as the head of the French government.[62] However, as is also pointed out, Roosevelt was the American chief of American diplomacy.[63] Therefore, we have to realise that, in the relationship between de Gaulle and Roosevelt, much of the blame has to be placed squarely on Roosevelt's shoulders, the more influential of the two men. As the more powerful, he should have been the more magnanimous.

It took almost all Churchill's powers of persuasion and friendship with Roosevelt to ensure that the Americans did not replace de Gaulle with an inferior substitute. De Gaulle had to be recognised by the American government as leader of the provisional French government since he was the only political leader recognised by the liberated French population and American troops were part of the liberation force.[64] Therefore, there could not be any thought of a schism between French leaders supported by the US government. Roosevelt eventually had to support de Gaulle, whether he wanted to or not, but he was a vain man and needed to save face regarding his previous anti-de Gaulle activities. Therefore, May and July saw some frantic diplomatic activity to preserve Roosevelt's reputation and ensure that de Gaulle was officially the head of any provisional French government once the Allies landed in France.

The need for Roosevelt to see sense over de Gaulle and to accord him his correct place in the pecking order within the Allies saw frantic activity throughout the spring by Churchill and his Chiefs of Staff as they sought to bring pressure on the White House to recognise de Gaulle and his 'group' as the provisional government of France. Roosevelt was quite stubborn and, at times, snobbish as was his nature; he was only willing to allow de Gaulle a lesser place in the rankings of the Allies and then only if he asked for this. This was never going to happen with de Gaulle who not only stood on his own honour, but also for the pride of France.

Churchill tried to smooth things over between the Americans and de Gaulle. Twice during April 1944 Duff Cooper, the British Ambassador to Algiers, gave de Gaulle messages from Churchill. The British prime minister, in an attempt to bring the CFLN and the American government together, had offered to communicate with Roosevelt a request from de Gaulle for a meeting with the president. De Gaulle was assured that any such application would be successful. De Gaulle objected to the word 'request'. He was not a supplicant. Aron observed that de Gaulle cared not for American recognition.

He only cared that he was recognised by the French nation, and he needed nobody to help him achieve that. Churchill's April mission failed.

In May 1944 another attempt was made. This time it was the Americans who tried their hand. Admiral Fénard, head of the French Naval Mission in the USA and well considered by the White House, arrived on 27 May with an unofficial message from Roosevelt. The president had asked Fénard to inquire unofficially if de Gaulle would accept unofficially an invitation to come to Washington DC. An official reception could be held through the usual diplomatic channels, and nobody would be aware of who had made the original approaches. This was quite daring for Roosevelt who was trying to save face after a period of trying to deny de Gaulle; he was now requesting his presence in the USA but at the same time desperate not to look as if he was altering his policy towards de Gaulle. De Gaulle was just as evasive and accepted the invitation in principle at least. He told Fénard 'to make a temporising reply'. De Gaulle acknowledged the invitation but said that, as he had to go to both the UK and France, he was not in a good position to make a firm commitment to travel to the USA.

De Gaulle then left Algiers for London. In London he discovered that the atmosphere was not too conducive for diplomatic projects which needed maturing. However, on 10 June as de Gaulle was still engaged in arguments with the British, he received a visit at his London headquarters, Carlton Gardens. Eisenhower had sent his Chief of Staff, Lieutenant General Bedell Smith, to call on the French leader. The timing of this meeting was critical as the Normandy landings and the subsequent campaign had begun only four days earlier. It was clear that the relationship between the Americans and de Gaulle was changing for the better. Bedell Smith requested that de Gaulle should visit Roosevelt. The situation had altered dramatically. It was critical that an agreement should be reached with de Gaulle as the only French political leader recognised by the French as Allied forces began the process of liberating their country.

De Gaulle agreed to go to Washington DC but with caveats. He was determined to maintain his proud demeanour and defend the integrity of France. After consulting with his government, de Gaulle accepted the invitation but let it be known that the visit was to be connected with the exchange of views of world problems that were important to both the USA and France. Furthermore, it was an acknowledgement by France of the American war effort and proof of an enduring friendship between the two countries. The question of recognition of his government by the USA was to be conducted using the usual diplomatic channels. It was clear that de Gaulle had been invited to the USA by the Americans and that he had not sought such an invitation.

On 6 July Roosevelt sent a special aeroplane to Algiers for de Gaulle's travel to the USA. De Gaulle spent 6–9 July in Washington DC, with 10 July being spent in New York. From New York, he flew to Canada for a relatively brief visit. He spent ninety minutes in Quebec, an evening in Montreal and a day in the capital, Ottawa. On the evening of 13 July, he returned to Algiers.

After some initial frostiness on the second day and his second meeting with Roosevelt, de Gaulle began to thaw out. At a dinner given by Forrestal, Secretary of State for National Defence, Forrestal announced, 'when we invited General de Gaulle to come here, we expected an ogre, but we have found a man'. In further talks with Roosevelt, the two men found that they had much in common and Roosevelt found that de Gaulle was as democratic as he was. De Gaulle also won over the American press who had tried to trip him up with awkward questioning. Even though de Gaulle understood English well, he asked for an interpreter, thus gaining time to answer questions. The main thing was that de Gaulle won over the American public. Even though Roosevelt told Churchill that he considered de Gaulle an egoist, it did not prevent him on, 7 July, ordering John J. McCloy, Assistant Secretary for War, and Daniel W. Bell, Assistant Secretary of the Treasury, to draw up an agreement recognising the French Committee of National Liberation as the *de facto* provisional government in France and even permitted the committee to issue currency. Everything moved rapidly as, before de Gaulle had left the USA, he was informed of the recognition.[65] De Gaulle appeared to be triumphant.

De Gaulle had worked hard with his collaborators to ensure that, when France was finally liberated, measures were already in place to prevent the chaos which, naturally, would follow as loyal French people took their revenge on those who had betrayed France by siding with the Vichy regime. The trip to the USA was the first of de Gaulle's eventual five trips to that country. He did well there. The former US Ambassador to Vichy, Admiral Leahy, acknowledged that de Gaulle has 'made a very good impression … including on myself. I had a better opinion of him after talking with him'. Black notes that this might have been better done when the US still recognised Vichy but, had he got to know de Gaulle earlier, perhaps Leahy might have been in a position to advise Roosevelt better than he had done in the four previous years. Nevertheless, Leahy said, 'I remained unconvinced that he and his Committee of Liberation necessarily represented the form of government that the people of France wished to have after their nation's liberation from the Nazis.'[66]

This was outrageous claptrap and from a closed mind. Leahy clearly only saw some extreme right-wing political entity as the only one capable of liberating France but, at the same time, refused to drop the notion that de Gaulle was some kind of closet Fascist. We know what de Gaulle thought of the American recognition of Vichy as, in 1942, he wrote to Adrien Tixier, Free French Ambassador to the United States, that the USA 'could have frankly supported Fighting France from the beginning', and dropped their embassy and consulates in Vichy. History, of course, has straightened the narrative. De Gaulle is known, Leahy not as well-known.

After the war and, especially after 1958, De Gaulle returned France to the world stage properly as President of the French Fifth Republic which he had established after being called back to power by the French people following the failure of the Fourth Republic and French de-colonisation. It took France nearly fifteen years to return to international prominence but at a cost. France lost its territories in Indochina, today's Vietnam, after a bloody war which saw France humiliated and foreshadowed the longer and more costly Vietnam war which saw the Americans driven from Vietnam. De Gaulle, in the face of widespread and at times bitter opposition from French colonists, saw fit to grant Algeria independence in 1962. This led to several unsuccessful attempts on de Gaulle's life by discontented French officers. De Gaulle was able to establish his credentials not only as the leader of the wartime Free French but as French leader and president after 1958. He removed himself from politics between 1946 and 1958; he never sought to use the army as a lever back into power as he had never tried to establish a dictatorship in France. True, he was an old-fashioned French conservative Catholic but never a dictator. Roosevelt and Leahy were wrong about de Gaulle. Churchill had assessed him correctly.

Chapter 9

De Gaulle Triumphant

August 1944 – Paris Liberated

The landings in Normandy had been successful; the Allies had not been pushed back into the sea, the Americans were advancing well and had also taken much of Brittany. The Germans were on the back foot and beginning the retreat on the long haul back to Germany. As an ally to Germany, Italy had been somewhat reduced since 1943, following the deposing of Mussolini and Italy largely going over to the Allies. Mussolini was rescued from Italian captivity by German commandos led by SS *Obersturmbannführer* (lieutenant colonel) Otto Skorzeny on 12 September 1943 in the Gran Sasso raid. He was taken to northern Italy to form and lead the Italian Social Republic based at Salo, on Lake Garda, where he remained an ally to the Germans. The last Axis combat sorties in the Italian theatre of operations were flown by Italian pilots.

The Red Army was in Poland where it was biding its time waiting for the destruction of the Polish Underground Army, the AK, along with the brutal killing by the Germans and their allies of hundreds of thousands of Polish citizens during the Warsaw Uprising. By June the Allies had liberated Rome and were grinding their way further up the boot of Italy, heading towards Austria which had been incorporated into the Reich in 1938. Allied armies had landed in both the north and the south of France, and the Germans had already lost mastery of the air and seas. In Normandy, the German Army was beginning to retreat during the third week of August 1944 but was showing all the signs of wanting to reach the far side of the river Seine and, once there, regroup and oppose an Allied eastern advance.

While this was happening, a revolt was beginning in Paris. Events in France were something that both de Gaulle and the Allies, especially the Americans, sought to control. It was known that the communists within the Paris Committee of Liberation (CPL) wanted the liberation of the French capital to be accomplished by insurrection. It was considered that, with the CPL being a key organisation of the Resistance; Stalin might be able to use a communist insurrection in Paris as leverage to try to establish a communist state in France, as he was to do across east-central Europe. In 1944, however, he was not in a position to do so owing to commitments to the Americans and British.[1]

The British had little interaction in this relationship while the Soviet Union was having more influence than perhaps one might have anticipated. It should be recognised that the Soviet government, or more accurately Stalin, was out to further the influence of communism and extend Russian hegemony. Before the outbreak of war in 1939 France had suffered civil strife and the Spanish Civil War of 1936 to 1939 had exasperated the situation. It seemed that anti-Semitism and the rise of Fascism was unstoppable. Sides had been drawn up before the war. After 1940, the right in France seemed to have won the argument when the Vichy regime was established and anti-Semites were given a free hand.

If the Vichy regime and its collaborators were enjoying a brief period of liberty, albeit under Germany control, the left of French politics, especially the communists, were struggling to exist. Naturally, French communists lived in fear of their lives and became part of the resistance. They also became the most successful and visible form of resistance. However, de Gaulle was concerned about the long-term plan of the communists in France. He understood that all planning for communists came from Moscow and that the Soviets were a valuable ally in the war. This meant that relations between the Soviet government and the British and American governments had to be kept harmonious. This was difficult for de Gaulle who wanted to keep Soviet interference in post-war France to a minimum or not at all, but he was aware that communism might well have a huge impact in France once the country was liberated. The other problem was the continuous sniping by Roosevelt and his government against de Gaulle. Equally, de Gaulle resented the highhanded manner in which the Americans wanted to treat France as the country was liberated; they saw France as just another European state to be liberated and occupied. This, of course, enraged de Gaulle as he sought to reclaim his homeland. Basically, there were two occupations in the offing, American or, possibly, Soviet. The Russians had been in Paris before, in 1814. Nobody alive remembered that, but if it had been possible then it was even more probable in 1944.

Meanwhile, the influence of communism was very persuasive, especially to the working classes and all those opposed to Fascism and Nazism. It has to be admitted that the evil of Stalinism was not widely known while the western allies had buried any evidence of Stalin's crimes. Only the Polish government-in-exile had tried to alert the world to Stalinist crimes but had been successfully closed down by the British and American governments. Therefore, as the Allied advance progressed the consideration of what to do with Paris became most urgent. There was already another European city in open revolt against the Germans: Warsaw, the Polish capital. The Warsaw Uprising was going badly. It had been poorly conceived and executed badly as Nationalist Poles wasted their underground army in a futile fight against the worst elements of the German armed forces. Polish civilians were systematically murdered by German police units while Warsaw was equally disposed of. The worst of the situation was that an Allied army was on hand, the Red Army, but was sunning itself on the banks of the river Vistula which divided Warsaw, east from west. Stalin had wanted the Nationalist Poles destroyed as they would have opposed Soviet rule in post-war Poland. The Allies in the west did not want a repeat of this in Paris and began to consider what might be done to liberate the city to prevent its destruction as well as limit any casualties which would occur as Parisians rose to drive the Germans out. Paris was also lucky as, unlike Warsaw, the German commander, General Dietrich von Choltitz, had little interest in defending the city against the Allies. Choltitz disobeyed Hitler's orders to destroy Paris. His motivation is uncertain, but he surrendered the city intact and was led into British captivity.

Many historians consider that it was only de Gaulle who considered seizing power at liberation, possibly once Paris was reached and freed. However, Jackson asserts that the communists were also planning to take control but more subtly with the fragmentation of power using local uprisings.[2] Anybody with knowledge of how the various communist groups achieved power in east-central Europe between 1944 and 1949 will be aware that power was taken not only by naked aggression but also by stealth and guile. While it is true that the advancing Red Army annexed rather than liberated territories – the menace of the Soviet armies was always in the background – political power was taken via the backdoor, using gangster methods such as intimidation, crooked elections and plebiscites, kidnapping and murder. The concept of French communists fragmenting power in an attempt to take control in France reflected method normally used by communists to achieve power with a very thin veneer of respectability.

In the summer of 1944, the Western Allies would not publicly admit how dishonest the Soviets were going to be and, probably, somewhat naively considered that the Soviet government would abide by terms of decency and allow 'liberated' territories to determine their own futures. The Soviet government did have every intention of doing so but on the terms of Soviet-friendly governments being established in east-central Europe. It should also be considered that the West did not really care as much about eastern Europe as about territory in the west taken by the Red Army including in Norway, Denmark and Finland, as well as Austria, were all reclaimed one way or another by the west. The Slavic lands were left to the tender mercies of the Soviet Union until 1989.

To return to France in 1944, where events were moving rapidly. By mid-August 1944, American forces had advanced halfway to Paris. Furthermore, a French force of four divisions, landed with American forces on the French southern coast on 15 August as part of Operation DRAGOON. It had already been agreed that a French division should participate in the liberation of Paris. The French 2nd Armoured Division, commanded by General Leclerc had been earmarked for this honour. Leclerc's division had been transported from North Africa to the UK during March. It should be noted that, as early as December 1943, de Gaulle had decided that Leclerc's armoured division would be tasked with the eventual liberation of Paris. However, he revealed this decision only to a select few to prevent the Americans finding out. De Gaulle considered that 'If the Americans know that I intend to use the 2e DB [2nd French Armoured Division, i.e., Leclerc's armoured division] to re-establish the French state in Paris, they won't transport you. Leclerc must keep this to himself.'[3] De Gaulle was well aware of American political shenanigans, especially those of Roosevelt, compared with de Gaulle's relationship with General Eisenhower. It was also quite clear that de Gaulle wanted to restore the French state and would do so. He never claimed that the French state of 1940 and before had been swept away by German occupation and Vichy rule: he considered instead that France had been ruled illegally between 1940 and 1944, which was clearly the truth.

On 1 August Leclerc's division disembarked in Normandy. Meanwhile, in July, strikes had begun to break out in Paris and the air was positively rebellious. De Gaulle was concerned with the consequences of a premature rebellion as witnessed with the Warsaw Uprising. Such premature action might benefit the communists or allow the Americans to take control.[4] The situation in Paris steadily ramped up against the Germans with increased strike action including, by 15 August, the police and fighting began to break out in the capital between the resistance and the Germans. Alexandre Pardi, de Gaulle's representative in Paris, sent an urgent message to London urging the rapid arrival of Allied troops to prevent a massacre.[5] Without doubt, Pardi feared another Warsaw. The Allies could not allow this to happen – two betrayed allies having their civilians killed by the enemy in failed uprisings would have been too shameful. Another side to de Gaulle's concerns in August was that he feared a repeat of the 1871 Commune.[6]

The revolutionary Paris Commune had been a far-left group that seized power in Paris on 18 March 1871, following the defeat of the French Army in the Franco-Prussian War, when Paris was besieged by the Prussian Army.

The Paris Commune was overthrown by French forces by 28 May 1871 but not before thousands of people had been executed or had died in the fighting as the French state restored order. Decades later, de Gaulle's son, Philippe, was asked if his father had really believed that a situation such as the Commune could have happened in Paris during the summer of 1944. Philippe de Gaulle asserted, that as the years passed, and especially after the publication of his memoirs, his father had moderated his claims, but asserted that in 1944 de Gaulle 'wanted, above all, to re-establish French sovereignty and impose his authority in the face of the Americans'.[7]

De Gaulle decided to return to France but needed permission from the Allies to do so. This was awkward as he had recently refused to meet Churchill who was travelling through Algiers where de Gaulle was still resident. Given that, on 3 August, Churchill had praised him and had included France amongst the four great powers to settle European affairs after the war, de Gaulle's snub seemed even ruder than usual. Indeed, his persistent undiplomatic behaviour, especially towards Churchill who had supported him through thick and thin since 1940, continued to exasperate Massigli, the French foreign minister, who noted to Duff Cooper that he hoped that de Gaulle would not last a year in power once back in France. The British did not object to de Gaulle's return but Duff Cooper noted that, as ever, de Gaulle started 'giving trouble about this as he does about everything'. De Gaulle said that he would only accept a French plane but would accept an American aircraft if it bore French livery.[8] Uppermost in de Gaulle's mind was probably symbolism – he wanted to be conveyed by a French craft as symbolic of French independence. He was willing to compromise however in an aeroplane which at least looked French. What he was determined to avoid was dependence on the USA.

On 20 August, de Gaulle landed near St-Lô in Normandy and immediately went to Eisenhower's HQ in Rennes. He wished to persuade Eisenhower to allow Leclerc, whose division had reached Argentan, about 150 kilometres west of Paris, to move immediately to Paris. What de Gaulle did not know was that Eisenhower wanted to go around the city since he feared that any operation against the French capital would slow the advance eastward. Therefore, he evasively told de Gaulle that the division would be sent to Paris 'soon'. De Gaulle was very suspicious of Eisenhower's motivation and considered that the Americans were trying to prevent him from gaining political power. As Jackson notes, it was de Gaulle who was politically motivated; Eisenhower was only operating from a military point of view.[9]

De Gaulle wanted to be in Paris before anyone else in order to take control. Perhaps not for personal gain, nor to establish a dictatorship, but to ensure that the French liberated their own capital. Events in Paris, as we have seen, were escalating. On 20 August, after a day of street battles between French Resistance fighters and the occupying German forces, the Swedish consul, Raoul Nordlings, negotiated a truce. The Germans agreed to allow French fighters to remain in buildings they had already occupied; in return the Resistance agreed not to fire on withdrawing German forces in Paris. The truce, which was denounced by the communists, lasted only for one day and on 21 August fighting resumed. De Gaulle heard of the true situation only on 23 August, by which time Eisenhower had given the order to Leclerc to move to Paris. De Gaulle, as Jackson notes, wanted Paris to liberate itself but wanted the Allies to be on hand; Eisenhower had received de Gaulle's letter on 22 August which meant that everything that de Gaulle desired regarding the military liberation of Paris was already in hand, but de Gaulle was not totally abreast of events regarding the imminent liberation of the city. Nevertheless, Eisenhower was concerned that he might be making a mistake in committing troops to Paris.

However, at 06.00 hours on 23 August, 400 vehicles of Leclerc's armoured division headed towards Paris. The first tanks arrived at the Hôtel de Ville during the evening of 24 August. Leclerc arrived in Paris with the bulk of his division on 25 August and made his headquarters in the Gare Montparnasse whence the German military commander was taken to sign the surrender of Paris. De Gaulle arrived the same day at 17.00 hours and didn't seem happy. He already wanted to stamp his authority on the liberated city.

On meeting Leclerc at Gare Montparnasse de Gaulle upbraided him for having allowed the communist leader of the FFI, Rol-Tanguy, to be a signatory of the surrender document. Next, de Gaulle, meeting Rol-Tanguy's military delegate, Chaban-Delmas, for the first time, was amazed at how young he was. De Gaulle was driven to the war ministry in the Rue Saint-Dominique where he had served for five days in 1940 as Undersecretary of State for Defence where he set up his HQ. Jackson notes that this was a deliberate political act as it demonstrated that the four years of Vichy rule (which had not been from Paris in the first place) was invalid and that de Gaulle's presence in London between 1940 and 1944 had illustrated the continuity of the French state. His presence and return to the Rue Saint-Dominique perhaps further illustrated this but Jackson does suggest an act of fiction.[10]

However, Jean Edward Smith notes that Eisenhower, unusually for an American, especially a general having had previous knowledge of Paris, knew that the city was not merely a capital city but was France. Whoever controlled Paris controlled France. Therefore, it became urgent that it fell into friendly hands. It was essential that Paris, and therefore France, did not collapse into civil war or experience the anarchy and horrors of a fresh Commune.[11] As we have already seen, Eisenhower and de Gaulle got along well and politically Eisenhower had thrown his weight behind de Gaulle in defiance of President Roosevelt's wishes.

Kissinger observes that, prior to the landings in Normandy, de Gaulle concentrated on the avoidance of civil war between his own forces and domestic political forces in France who claimed to represent the resistance. The British, but more so the American government, reluctantly accepted de Gaulle as head of the French Army but remained wary of accepting de Gaulle as a political equal. The American government remained convinced that de Gaulle would be shown to be of little importance once France was liberated. Indeed, the American Secretary of War, Henry L. Stimson stated, 'De Gaulle will crumble .... Other parties will spring up as the liberation goes on and de Gaulle will become a very little figure.'[12] De Gaulle swiftly proved this to be an erroneous assumption.

Preparations for entry into Paris had to be balanced. Eisenhower had considered bypassing the city but, as conditions in Paris deteriorated owing to local rebellion and strikes, de Gaulle urged Eisenhower to think again. After meeting Eisenhower on 20 August, de Gaulle wrote to him the next day; the letter was delivered personally by General Koenig. De Gaulle urged that Paris be occupied as soon as possible, using French and Allied forces. He reasoned that entry into the city might produce some disorder, and perhaps some damage to the city, but it would be better than if it were left and things were allowed to collapse; in de Gaulle's opinion that would hinder future military operations in France.

Eisenhower read de Gaulle's letter and listened to Koenig. It became clear that Paris was the centre of revolution and that another commune might be established. Therefore, the need to occupy Paris became very urgent but he could not act unilaterally and so he sent a long cable to the Combined Chiefs of Staff which spoke of tactics but only mentioned in passing the liberation of Paris. Writing that Paris had become 'a constant menace in our flank', his justification for entering the city, he declared that

> When Paris is entered, it is my intention to employ the French Division (Leclerc) for occupation. In entering the city, it will be accompanied by ten units of British and American forces. Some days thereafter, General DE GAULLE will be allowed to make his formal entry into the city. *I will not* personally go there until military considerations require.

One of Eisenhower's commanders, General Omar Bradley, was against the liberation of Paris but he, too, was finally convinced by other intelligence.

Eisenhower had already sent for Bradley to tell him of his decision but, in the intervening period, Roger Gallois of the Paris Resistance arrived at Bradley's HQ in Laval. Gallois did not see Bradley but spoke at length with Brigadier General Edwin Sibert, Twelfth Army Group's Intelligence Chief (G-2). Gallois was exhausted after three journeys by jeep that night but was able to make his case to Sibert and stated bluntly:

> The people of Paris wanted to liberate their capital themselves but cannot finish what they have started. You must come to our help, or there's going to be a terrible slaughter. Hundreds of thousands of Frenchmen are going to be killed.

This speech had the desired impact and, as they flew to see Eisenhower, Sibert briefed Bradley, telling that 'if we don't get to Paris in a couple of days, there's going to be an awful massacre'. Bradley knew then that Paris had to be liberated. The meeting with Eisenhower was brief with the French generals Koenig and Juin present. The decision was made. Eisenhower declared, 'What the hell, Brad, I guess we have to go in'. He then ordered Bradley to use Leclerc's 2nd Armoured Division as the vanguard as well as informing Bradley that he had ordered 23,000 tons of food and 3,000 tons of coal to be sent to Paris immediately. As Eisenhower remarked casually, 'No great battle is going to take place. The entry of one or two divisions would accomplish the liberation of the city.' Eisenhower had casually ordered the liberation of Paris – it was going to happen and, as Smith notes, the decision was breathtaking.[13]

The reason for American assistance in the liberation of Paris could be seen with an eye to history. Eisenhower had already given his word to de Gaulle that French troops would lead any entry into Paris, but one can be quite sure that, if any entry into the city hampered operations elsewhere, Eisenhower, ever the professional soldier, would have broken his oath to de Gaulle and justified it. However, there was another aspect of August 1944 and another capital city in revolt – Warsaw. As already narrated, the Poles had risen up against the Germans at the beginning of the month and were, by the third week of the uprising, being slaughtered. Predominantly, the victims of German mass murder were Polish civilians caught in the middle of the fighting while the Red Army sunbathed on the far side of the river Vistula which bisects Warsaw. The Poles had expected the Soviets to come to their aid but instead the Red Army was halted, thus allowing the Polish revolt to fail. How would it look if another revolt in an occupied city against the Germans went unaided by Allied armed forces and thousands died as predicted by Gallois? It would seem that the Allies, east or west, did not care. Whether Eisenhower knew much about

Warsaw is unclear, but he would have certainly been aware of the huge loss of civilian life and the reluctance of the Red Army to get involved. He was certainly aware of the situation in Paris, and he knew that, by bamboozling his own people, he could do something, which he did, and so paved the way for de Gaulle to enter his own capital in triumph.

Nevertheless, there were elements in the resistance and other oppositional groups who wanted de Gaulle to declare a new republic. De Gaulle sensed that he needed to act with caution but was also aware that he needed to push the Allies to accept a fait accompli. If a French general, de Gaulle of course being the most obvious choice, declared a new French republic or took control in Paris, without doubt it would be difficult for the Americans, especially, to remove him. The British government, even if they had not said it out loud, had always assumed that de Gaulle would form at least a provisional government in France on liberation and did not assume that he was going to establish a dictatorship.

However, the question originally posed was: is it true that, during the summer of 1944, France was on the cusp of a revolution in support of communism? The answer is probably not, but the communist movement had a history of knowing when to advance and when to withdraw. French historian Robert Aron wrote that the French Communist Party (FCP) after liberation either avoided or attempted to avoid 'a trial of strength'.[14] Aron quoted Paul Devinat, a French Radical-Socialist politician, who wrote in the *Manchester Guardian* at the end of 1948 that France had

> just passed through a profound revolution which had only recently and partially been bought under control …. If the action taken by the Provisional Government foiled the Communist Party's basic calculations, it is not less true that the Party succeeded in considerably widening its influence at the period. Numerous departments in the south were in fact for long months under its control. Under cover of the purge, it shook the official hierarchy of the country. Indeed, till April 1947, it had influential representatives within Government itself and was able to put into practice the methods applied with more success elsewhere, in Czechoslovakia and other countries.[15]

Aron noted that in August 1944 there was a 'great risk of revolution' in France.[16]

However, there was a major difference between those countries of east-central Europe and France, and that was the question of liberation. Even if Leclerc's armoured division were the first troops into Paris, and so French troops liberated their own capital, they were followed quickly by a division of

American infantry. Therefore overall, France was liberated by armies which came from western democracies who genuinely wanted to liberate territories which they encountered on the long march to Germany. However, east-central Europe was not liberated by the advancing Red Army but was instead annexed. In the wake of the advance of the Red Army came the Soviet security police and units necessary to ensure that 'liberated' territories such as Poland, Czechoslovakia, Hungary, and so on, were obliged to establish Soviet friendly regimes. Most of the Sovietisation of east-central Europe was completed by 1948 but involved bloodshed and, in the case of Poland, a little discussed civil war which ran roughly between 1944 and 1948. There were also insurrections in the Baltic republics as the Soviet Union sought to consolidate its rule over its gains, or rather war booty, with the Russian Empire being re-established.

In western Europe, notably France and Italy, it was different. France was a mature democracy and people knew it. There was no Red Army to enforce Soviet rule in France and so, if French communists wanted to obtain power; they had to do so via the ballot box. Of course, a political vacuum had developed in France, albeit briefly, once the Germans were driven out but this was filled swiftly as the Allies began to re-establish democratic French rule and law. It is true that the communist resistance movement helped fill the void left by the occupying Germans and Vichy, but de Gaulle and his provisional government were quick to establish the rule of law and thus thwarted any realistic chance of communism getting a grip between 1944 and 1947. Again, Aron observed that:

> de Gaulle had won. He and his men had prevented the Communist insurrection, not only by his overt action of replacing the administration and political cadres of the country, but by their necessarily concealed diplomatic activity. This was statesmanship on the grand scale, and it was able to be conducted at a critical moment and with few means due to the prestige of one man.[17]

The man being, of course, de Gaulle. De Gaulle not only prevented communism dominating France but was also able to render the Vichy regime null and void by linking the glory of France past with a fantastic future for France. He used Free France as the true continuity of France, even if this was from overseas in exile or on French imperial territory. Indeed, Algeria was considered to be part of Metropolitan France, despite being in North Africa with many French citizens being born there but considering France to be the motherland. Overall, few French citizens actively supported the Resistance, but it was the figure of de Gaulle which kept the symbolism of French freedom alive throughout the years of occupation. It was de Gaulle who was able to overcome the Vichy regime and reduce it to an act of betrayal and replace it with systems he had prepared previously in Algiers. De Gaulle was determined that anarchy would not take hold in newly liberated France.[18]

Aron notes that in 1944 Stalin still needed his Allies, principally the USA. He was willing to extend this further and accommodate minor allies such as France. In December de Gaulle, by then having seen Paris and most of France delivered from Nazi occupation, visited Stalin in Moscow. He was aware that France was not that important to Roosevelt and Churchill and so hoped that he might be able to convince Stalin that he was one of the two military powers in Europe able to chastise the Germans.

This failed, as was revealed in 1959 when minutes of the meeting between de Gaulle and Stalin were published by the Soviet Foreign Ministry; the record showed that Stalin considered him to be 'an arrogant Frenchman representing a weak, defeated nation'. De Gaulle also had a view of Stalin about which he was to write later. He said of Stalin that he was

> possessed by the will to power. Accustomed by a life of machination to disguise his features as well as his inmost soul, to dispense with illusions, pity, sincerity, to see in each man an obstacle or a threat, he was all strategy, suspicion and stubbornness … . As a communist disguised as a Marshal, a dictator preferring the tactics of guile, a conqueror with an affable smile, he was a past master of deception. But so fierce was his passion that it often gleamed through this armour, not without a kind of sinister charm.[19]

They had the measure of one another.

Stalin first tried to entice de Gaulle into accepting a representative of the Polish Committee of National Liberation or Polish Stalinists groomed by Stalin with the view of becoming the government of Poland once that country was liberated but was, in reality, a Soviet vassal; if de Gaulle accepted that request, Stalin offered to sign a Franco-Polish pact. On meeting the Stalinist Poles, de Gaulle declined to accept them. Nevertheless, the Soviets still signed an agreement with de Gaulle since it might be beneficial to French communists.[20] As we shall see this was very much the case.

From this rare visit to the Kremlin an apocryphal tale has grown. Stalin and de Gaulle discussed the return to France of the French communist leader Maurice Thorez from Moscow. Thorez, contrary to what the French had been led to believe, had spent most of his war in the Soviet Union and Stalin is reputed to have said to de Gaulle with a laugh 'Please wait a little before you shoot him'.[21] The American historian William Taubman notes that Stalin would have found a communist France or Italy far harder to control than a communist Romania or Bulgaria.[22]

In the Stalinist world Stalin's quip about Thorez may well have been fatal in time, but Thorez was to be returned to a civilised country where he was unlikely to be executed unlawfully or, to call a spade a spade, murdered. However, de Gaulle found it easy to accept Thorez who advocated union and loyalty to de Gaulle,[23] thus stifling a genuine communist uprising in France. Aron suggested that French communists were outplayed and outfoxed by the de Gaullists either from London and Algiers while the non-communist French resistance, the Maquis, had already prepared against any communist subversion in France. French military leaders knew who they could and could not trust in France. Once the occupying Germans left, even those Maquis groups cut off from the central power were able to take the necessary steps to protect towns and slowly begin to restore order in the countryside which at the time threatened to descend into anarchy. Aron also stated that the Communist Party in France might have been able to have anything as France was liberated but had not received any orders on how to proceed. The result was confusion and failure.[24]

This may have been true – if Stalin had issued orders to cause mayhem in France in preparation for the seizure of power by the communists in France – it would have happened. What the result might have been is uncertain. What is certain was that de Gaulle was able to absorb Thorez and his followers as well as satisfying Stalin. De Gaulle should be seen as acting shrewdly as, instead of vilifying Thorez and the French communists who had been branded rebels in 1939 (shortly before de Gaulle had been once France was overrun in 1940), de Gaulle included communists in the post-war French government. De Gaulle's visit to Moscow had consequences since, after the signing of the Franco-Soviet pact and de Gaulle's return to Paris, the Central Committee of the French Communist Party met on 21 January 1945. To the astonishment of the French communists Thorez stood down the communist resistance movement in favour of de Gaulle and his movement. Later, in 1947, the Yugoslav communist Marko-Ristitch considered that, as the war was coming to an end, Thorez was nothing but 'a super-patriot, a chauvinist, for whom, scandalously enough, the French Communist Party "was not under the thumb of Russia"'.[25]

Aron considered that de Gaulle, by allowing Thorez to return to France unhindered and signing the Franco-Soviet Pact, had calmly overcome the communist threat in France.[26] This would have been most satisfying to de Gaulle who, since 1940, had always expressed that he wished to avoid civil war in France or even the spectre of Frenchmen killing Frenchmen in the shape of Vichy forces and Free French forces clashing, especially in the Middle East where both sets of French forces had interests. It is interesting to note that even a staid British observer such as Sir Alan Lascelles did not fail to rule out the possibility of civil war in France as he confided to his diary in late 1944.[27]

Jackson, writing much later than Aron, points to the varied and many problems which de Gaulle encountered on receiving power following the liberation of Paris. The main one was communication since much of France was still unavailable to him owing to the continuing fighting in France. Even where areas had been liberated communications were often limited owing to either the fighting or because the retreating Germans, as might be expected, destroyed most things that could be useful to their enemy – a common tactic employed by any retreating army fighting a defensive action. Jackson also mentioned the nature of de Gaulle's provisional government established in September 1944. De Gaulle was cautious in how his first Cabinet was formed. It was relatively catholic unless one had been involved with the Vichy regime, thus blotting one's copybook, but he also isolated members of the French resistance. He had been quick to observe that there was only one army in France and that was the army of France.[28]

From discussions it was quite clear that de Gaulle wanted to draw a clear line under the resistance and the de Gaulle movement. As one resistance leader recalled, it was clear that de Gaulle meant to bring the Resistance to heel.[29] He wanted to close down the Resistance quickly and was willing to bring them into the provisional government following the liberation of Paris. However, within a week of the liberation, one former resistor began a comment with 'The Resistance' but was shut down by de Gaulle who responded by saying 'We have moved beyond the Resistance. The Resistance is finished. The Resistance must now be integrated into the Nation.'[30] Wise words, but quite a slap in the face for those who had risked all during the German occupation. However, once liberation was at hand many began to claim that they had served in the Resistance – something not uncommon across occupied Europe.

De Gaulle formed a new Cabinet on 9 September under his authority as president of the provisional government. It was a good mixture of Free French associates known to de Gaulle for a long time, experienced Third Republic politicians clean of Vichy collaboration, communists, Christian Democrats, former Resistance leaders and technocrats. All were encouraged to join this government of national unity. De Gaulle was very clear in his first Cabinet meeting that without a state there would be chaos. He was convinced that pre-war divisions had caused its decline and was determined that France would begin its post-war period unified.[31] There can be no arguing with this – de Gaulle's vision was not only clear, but it was also correct. Nevertheless, it should be remembered that, in the immediate period after liberation, de Gaulle struggled to have his government recognised by the Allies. This did not happen until 23 October.[32]

As might be surmised from the previous narrative the problem was the US government which, led by Roosevelt, had always taken a poor view of de Gaulle and the French in general. After the liberation of Paris, it was clear that the American position could not be maintained. France had been liberated and de Gaulle had cleverly taken control. He had not misused the forces available to him; he had not been vindictive towards those who had chosen to serve the Vichy regime – true he isolated them and allowed for French law to deal with the consequences for those who had betrayed France in its most extreme hour. De Gaulle was subtle in how he dealt with the new situation in France. He was determined to ensure that France returned to democracy and stability. He did not seek a return to the divisions of the Third Republic which he considered had destroyed France in 1940, but he did not want a radically altered country which was something that the communists would have ensured. Indeed, de Gaulle made his intentions quite clear once he finally stood amongst Parisians in August 1944. After meeting various dignitaries, he was welcomed to Paris by Georges Maranne, a communist, who spoke in the name of the Parisian Committee of Liberation. He was followed by others. Then de Gaulle was asked to speak.

He did so magnificently, beginning:

Paris! Paris outraged! Paris broken! Paris martyred! But Paris liberated! Liberated by itself, liberated by its people with the help of the French armies, with the support and the help of all France, of the France that fights, of the only France, of the real France, of the eternal France!

He continued in this vein, outlining the recent history of occupied France and its travails. He concluded:

This duty of war, all the men who are here and all those who hear us in France know that it demands national unity. We, who have lived the greatest hours of our history, we have nothing else to wish than to show ourselves, up to the end, worthy of France. *Vive la France!*[33]

Of course, de Gaulle's speech to Parisians and to those further away was hyperbole but it was magnificent and just what his compatriots needed to hear. It was also a definite call for unity. The main thing which he needed to avoid was civil war which he did. This speech certainly helped. Georges

Bidault, a senior resistance leader in Paris, with others, was in tears following de Gaulle's speech and, in the name of the National Council of Resistance and the Parisian Committee of Liberation, formally asked de Gaulle to proclaim the Republic before those gathered around him.

It was a moving request and quite a moment, but de Gaulle replied that the republic had never ceased to exist. De Gaulle stated quite clearly:

> Free France, Fighting France, the French Committee of National Liberation have successfully incorporated it. Vichy always was and still remains null and void. I myself am the President of the government of the Republic. Why should I proclaim it now?

De Gaulle was correct, but he cleverly made certain observations regarding the present and the years after 1940. He was head of state; Pétain's regime was and remained illegitimate and was a scar of the face of France; and he represented French legitimacy.[34]

However, one area which de Gaulle kept to himself was foreign policy. This probably made sense since the war was still on. France had largely been liberated but there were still provinces which had been annexed by Nazi Germany and those needed to be reached and returned to French rule. Furthermore, the war for France was not only against Germany but also with Japan since that country had seized French imperial territories in the Far East while, in the Middle East, the questions of Lebanon and Syria were yet to be solved.

Earlier during the war, de Gaulle had indicated that Lebanon and Syria would receive independence from France. By the autumn of 1944 this seemed less likely. As de Gaulle became surer of his place after the liberation of Paris, he continued to exasperate Churchill who by then had less influence over him. During the autumn of 1944, de Gaulle invited Churchill to Paris for Armistice Day, the celebration and commemoration of the ending of the First World War, held every 11 November. Churchill, despite his Cabinet advising not attending, went to France. Part of this was his love of France but he was also aware that France was an important component for a resurrected democratic Europe. With Churchill, went Mrs Churchill, Eden and Duff Cooper. De Gaulle was also in the mood for reconciliation and was determined to express his gratitude for all that Churchill and the British had done for him and for France since 1940. Black also notes that de Gaulle was on a charm offensive to try to wean the British away from American influence. The visit went well and de Gaulle certainly flattered the British party as he expressed his gratitude towards the British and their leader. At the end of a long lunch, de Gaulle proposed a toast to the British king, George VI, and the British people but he saved the best for last as he said, 'to a great statesman and a great man, whom I shall always be proud to call my comrade, my mentor, and my friend, the Right Honourable Winston Churchill'. This toast was well received and reduced Churchill to tears and it was several moments before he could compose and trust himself to reply to de Gaulle's gallant toast. When Churchill spoke, he recalled the difficult year of 1940 but knew that with the French people victory would prevail. Then he made his personal tribute to de Gaulle and said, 'I would be lacking in truthfulness and gratitude if I failed to pay tribute to the capital part that General de Gaulle has played in the transformation which had bought us ... to a new era of vision and greatness.' It was now de Gaulle's turn to be moved. He was not as demonstrative as the tearful Churchill, but he was quietly emotional. The two men stood together to receive a long and standing ovation from the company at table. Things had certainly moved on. Later Churchill and de Gaulle went to the starting point of the French offensive against the Germans in eastern France.[35]

Despite this bonhomie between de Gaulle and Churchill, de Gaulle had been following his own agenda for France and the future of Germany. In his meeting with Stalin, de Gaulle had not only discussed the future of Poland but the overall post-war settlement of Europe, making him the first western Allied leader to do so. De Gaulle avoided any difficulties over the future of Poland but put his vision of France to Stalin. He wanted German territories west of the Rhine ceded to France. This included the major coal-producing Saar region, along with parts of the Ruhr industrial region. Furthermore, in the new Germany, Prussia was to be dissolved, losing much of its territory to a new restructured province of Hanover. De Gaulle made no mention of speaking to the British and Americans about this while Stalin was without doubt astute enough to realise that they would never agree to de Gaulle's ideas which laid waste to 200 years of European history.

This time Stalin made his excuses and said that he would need to discuss the matter with the British, which implied that there might be a chance of settling the future of Europe without any input from the Americans.[36] The moment passed, but de Gaulle's attitude was fascinating for all the wrong reasons. However, this attitude was not new as the French attitude towards the Middle East was one which exasperated the British and, especially, the American government which, taking its lead from the prejudices of Roosevelt, considered that the French were trying to maintain their empire and probably trying to expand it further. There was also the question of how France was to be received as one of the major victors when the Yalta Conference took place at the beginning of 1945. De Gaulle was determined that France should have a place at that table and be credited as one of the powers which was to occupy Germany. He was not yet done, even if Paris had been liberated and had already stated that the 'traditional position' of France in the region had to be maintained.[37]

This of course was not quite what the Syrians and Lebanese had in mind whenever they considered independence. The lead from London was confusing since, in February 1945, Churchill told the Syrian president that France should be allowed to keep its 'privileged position' in the Levant. As Jackson notes, Churchill was trying to keep on good terms with de Gaulle while not alienating the Arab world and its goodwill towards the British at that time.[38] But, of course, it is never any good to try to please two people, especially those of studied differences of opinion. As the year 1945 advanced, anti-French unrest grew in Syria.

De Gaulle responded with tanks and more troops sent to the region. By the end of May, after French shelling of public buildings in the Syrian capital, Damascus, which resulted in 1,000 casualties, the British realised that it was not possible to stand by and do nothing. On 31 May 1945 Churchill issued an ultimation that either French troops in Syria withdrew to barracks or British forces in the region would intervene. By error, this was announced in the House of Commons, one hour before de Gaulle received notice of the British demand.[39] This was one of the last interactions between de Gaulle and Churchill in relation to the war. The war in Europe was over; Germany had been comprehensively defeated and was now occupied by the Allies. The war with Japan still had a few more months to run. The question which faced both the British and French was what to do with their overseas possessions. Both had been humiliated at one time or another in the war. The British may have been resolute on their home turf in 1940 but they temporarily lost their Far East empire to the Japanese who were only stopped at the eastern Indian frontier by British and Indian troops. The French had not lost too much of their empire to their enemies, but it was a close-run thing in the Middle East and had required British intervention in 1941; but France had been lost for four years. From this it was easily deduced by the local populations of overseas possessions that the European overlords were not all-powerful and were vulnerable.

Nevertheless, de Gaulle once more took a stiff turn towards the British as Duff Cooper related when de Gaulle received him on 4 June; it was as if de Gaulle was about to declare war on the UK. Indeed, de Gaulle had actually ordered a French cruiser, *Jeanne d'Arc*, to Beirut while French soldiers were ordered to fire on British troops if necessary. In the end de Gaulle backed down. He told Duff Cooper that France was in no position to wage war against the British. But he was outraged and fumed for years over this incident. At times he tried to blame the British for events and claimed that they were aware that the French had already restored order in Syria but even the French Ambassador to the UK later made it quite clear that could not have been true since he had heard nothing about it.[40]

Therefore, the relationship between Churchill and de Gaulle was forever one of disharmony and bluntness. They fought their war and defended their countries, often against one another. But together they triumphed. They may have both lost battles and had won a war, but their relationship remained awkward, although, as old men, it became better. Black notes that both de Gaulle and Churchill were brilliant writers, but de Gaulle often doomed himself with his prickly personality. He did not take lightly the liberation of France at the hands of the Allies, especially the Americans, and spent the remainder of his time trying to 'big up' France while chasing respect for himself. He is accused of trying to break up Canada by encouraging the French speakers to leave Canada. He blamed American isolation for the Fall of France in 1940 as well as accusing the British and Americans of being responsible for the division of Europe after 1945. He further blamed the Americans for unrest in France during 1968.[41]

This was grossly unfair. De Gaulle was often the author of his own misfortune. He would be negligent if he failed to try to return France to its pre-war status. He did this largely by shedding the French Empire and acquiring a European skin – today's EU or European Union. France joined NATO but later left its command structure although it has returned recently. The division of Europe was largely the result of Stalin and the Soviet Union trying to complete the 'revolution' and conquer the world. The British, particularly, indulged in pushback and restrained the mores of Stalin until his death in 1953. By then both the USA and the Soviet Union had nuclear arms and were wary about using them as mutual destruction was assured. When Stalin died, the Korean War, fought between North Korea, supported by China, aided and abetted by Stalin, against the UN, was at a stalemate. Within a few months of his death an armistice was agreed. The reality was that communism had lost in that arena, but nobody said so. There was to be another war in South-East Asia – Vietnam – which the USA lost. The French had lost in the same country in the 1950s. Since the collapse of communism in east-central Europe after 1989, Europe has become more united, largely in the guise of the European Union (EU). Only the British have seen fit to upset the applecart and voted in 2016 to leave the EU. During the 1960s de Gaulle denied the UK membership of the EU or Common Market as it was called at the time. De Gaulle would not have been surprised at the British withdrawal from the EU but he would have been shocked at German domination of this body.

The legacy of these two great men, Churchill and de Gaulle, is freedom. Even if some consider Churchill to be a racist, they act from a point of ignorance. At times Churchill's record is questionable but, like so much of the man, his critics are wrong. An often misquoted example was the Dardanelles Expedition in 1915 for the failure of which Churchill was largely blamed. He even served a period of penance in the trenches of the Western Front during 1916 as if he was indeed guilty of that failure. He and his critics were wrong. Churchill was let down.

Churchill stepped up to the plate in late spring 1940 and led the world. He had to endure what no British leader has had to do before or since – the threat of invasion, conquest and the ending of the British people. Churchill led the British people into facing down the Nazi threat, not only to Europe but to the entire world. At this difficult time, he found an ally in de Gaulle with whom he could work but it was a difficult relationship. Churchill had an equally vexing alliance with the Polish leader, General Władysław Sikorski. Sikorski died in 1943 and so perhaps Churchill's relationship with the exiled Poles died a little with Sikorski but that with de Gaulle persevered. De Gaulle had an advantage over Sikorski – territory in the French Empire, notably in North Africa, from where Churchill realised it would be possible to return to Europe, defeat Germany and liberate the continent.

In de Gaulle, Churchill recognised the single French leader who could inspire the French into working against the occupying Germans and the Vichy regime which did nothing except betray its own country. After the war was over and France was liberated, scores were settled and leading Vichy figures were imprisoned or executed for their betrayals. Post-war, de Gaulle remained controversial. He left politics in 1946 but was asked back in 1958 when the French Fourth Republic collapsed; he established the present-day Fifth Republic. He controversially granted Algeria independence and survived several assassination attempts by disgruntled French military officers opposed to this measure. In 1968 there was civil disorder, and it is claimed that France faced civil war. Only de Gaulle could get on top of that. Churchill died in 1965, de Gaulle in 1970. It should be always remembered that but for men such as Churchill and de Gaulle the world would be a far bleaker place. Some may look unfavorably upon the actions of the Allied wartime leaders. However, without these leaders Europe would not have its liberty. It comes from the leadership of men like de Gaulle and Churchill and the generation which they inspired to fight an obvious tyranny dedicated to the destruction of entire peoples, which is truly racist. Churchill and de Gaulle are two very good examples of genuine leadership and true courage.

Notes

Chapter 1

1. Jean Edward Smith, *The Liberation of Paris: How Eisenhower, De Gaulle and Von Choltitz Saved the City of Light*, New York, 2019, p.113.
2. Harold Macmillan, *War Diaries: The Mediterranean, 1943–1945*, London, Macmillan, 1984, p. xx.
3. Roy Jenkins, *Churchill*, London, Macmillan, 2001, p. 15.
4. Ibid, pp. 87–8. Violet Bonham Carter, *Winston Churchill as I knew him*, London, Weidenfeld & Nicolson, 1995, pp. 113–15.
5. Jenkins, p. 21.
6. Ibid, p. 23.
7. Ibid, p. 36.
8. Philip Warner, *Kitchener: The Man Behind the Legend*, London, Cassell, 2006, pp. 99–100.
9. Churchill Collection, Churchill College, University of Cambridge, CHAR 2/1/4, January 1899.
10. Churchill Collection, CHAR 2/1/6, 11 February 1899.
11. Churchill Collection, CHAR 2/1/5, 21 January 1899.
12. Evan McGilvray, *Hamilton & Gallipoli: British Command in an Age of Military Transformation*, Barnsley, Pen & Sword, 2015, pp. 3–4.
13. Jean Lacouture, *De Gaulle: The Rebel, 1890–1944*, Vol. 1, London, Harvill, Harper Collins, 1993, Translated by Patrick O'Brian, p. 38.
14. Ibid, p. 39. Aiden Crawley, *De Gaulle*, London, The Literary Guild, 1969, p. 13.
15. Ibid, pp. 34–5.
16. Brian Crozier, *De Gaulle: The Warrior*, London, Eyre Methuen, 1973, p. 31.
17. Lloyd George discussed this in his memoirs but only after the war. David Lloyd George, *War Memoirs*, Vol. 2, London, Odhams, 1938, pp. 1258–63.
18. Geoffrey Hoskings, *A History of the Soviet Union* (Revised Edition) London, Fontana, 1990, p. 43.
19. Major General Sir Edward Spears, *Two Men Who Saved France: Pétain 1917; De Gaulle 1940*, London, Eyre & Spottiswoode, 1966, pp. 43–7.
20. *Douglas Haig. War Diaries and Letters, 1914–1918*, (eds) Gary Sheffield & John Bourne, London, Phoenix, 2006, Diary entry, 2 June 1917, pp. 297–8.
21. Margaret Crosland, *Simone de Beauvoir: The woman and her work*, London, Heinemann, 1992, p. 216.
22. Crawley, pp. 36–9.
23. Ibid. p. 39.
24. Ibid. p. 67.
25. Julian Jackson, *A Certain Idea of France: The Life of Charles De Gaulle*, London, Penguin, 2019. Introduction, p.xxxvi.
26. Crawley. p. 70.
27. Ibid, p. 80.
28. Lacouture, p. 60.

29. Ibid, p. 126.
30. William Mortimer Moore, *Paris '44, The City of Light Redeemed*, Oxford, Casemate, 2015, p.2.
31. George A. Kelly, 'The French Army Re-enters Politics, 1940–1955' *Political Science Quarterly*, Vol. LXXVI, 1961, 367–92.
32. Moore, p. 2.
33. *The Diaries of Sir Alexander Cadogan, 1938–1945*, (ed) David Dilks, London, Cassell, 1971, p. 286, Diary entry, 19 May 1940. Hereafter referred to as *Cadogan*.
34. Ibid, p. 287, Diary entry, 21 May 1940.
35. Crozier, p. 97.
36. Julian Jackson, *A Certain Idea of France: The Life of Charles de Gaulle*, London, Penguin, 2019, p. 109.
37. Stanisław Mikołajczyk, *The Rape of Poland: Patterns of Soviet Aggression*, Westport, Connecticut, 1973, Second Greenwood Reprint, p. 9.
38. National Archives (UK) Kew, London, CAB 65/7, War Cabinet 132 (40) Minute 1, 21 May 1940.
39. *War Diaries 1939–1945. Field Marshal Lord Alanbrooke*, (eds) Alex Danchev & Daniel Todman, London, Weidenfeld & Nicolson, 2001, p. 80. Diary entry, 14 June 1940. Hereafter referred to as *Alanbrooke*.
40. TNA, CAB 65/1, War Cabinet 55 (39) Minute 9, 21 October 1939.
41. Major General Sir Edward Spears, *Fulfilment of a Mission: The Spears Mission to Syria and Lebanon, 1941–1944*, London, Leo Cooper, 1977, Introduction, John Terraine, pp. vii-viii. Churchill gives a more detailed account of de Gaulle's rescue inasmuch as that, on 17 June 1940, he went to his office as usual in Bordeaux and then drove with Spears to the airfield with Spears to see him off to the UK. The two men shook hands and said goodbye and then, as the plane began to move, de Gaulle stepped in and slammed the door. The aircraft took off leaving the French arrest party on the ground, shocked and open-mouthed. Winston S. Churchill, *The Second World War: Volume II. Their Finest Hour*, London, Cassell & Co, 1949, p. 192.
42. Paul-Marie De La Groce, *The French Army: A Military-Political History*, translated by Kenneth Douglas, London, Weidenfeld & Nicolson, 1963, p. 92.
43. Jackson, *France: The Dark Years, 1940–1944*, Oxford, Oxford University Press, 2001, p. 43.
44. Robert Aron, 'The Political Methods of General de Gaulle' *International Affairs*, 37, No. 1, January 1961, 19–28.
45. René Rémond, *Two Destinies: Pétain and de Gaulle*, in *De Gaulle and Twentieth Century France*, Hugh Gough & John Horne (eds), London, Edward Arnold, 1994, pp. 9–17.
46. Charles Williams, *Pétain*, London, Little, Brown, 2005, pp. 257, 267.
47. Martin S. Alexander, *The Republic in Danger: General Maurice Gamelin and the Politics of French Defence, 1933–1940*, Cambridge, Cambridge University Press, 1992, p. 1.
48. Ibid, pp. 37–8, 41.
49. William Mortimer Moore, *Paris '44: The City of Light Redeemed*, Oxford, Casemate, 2015, p. 2.
50. Ibid.
51. Lacouture, Vol. 1. p. 38.
52. *The Economist*, 20 January 1940.
53. Ibid, 18 May 1940.
54. Henry Kissinger, *Leadership. Six Studies in World Strategy*. London, Penguin, 2022, p. 63.
55. *The Economist*, 1 June 1940. *The Economist* confined its comments to naming the three men and their positions. I provided the additional comments and potted histories.
56. Mortimer Moore, p. 1.

Chapter 2

1. Map Room, Messages of President Roosevelt (1939–1945) Franklin D. Roosevelt, microfilm roll 1, Map Room Papers, September 1939–July 1942. T. 1622, Winston Churchill to Franklin Roosevelt, 12 June 1940. Brotherton Library, University of Leeds.
2. *Cadogan*, p. 302.
3. Ibid. p. 327, diary entry 17 September 1940.
4. Churchill, *Their Finest Hour*, p. 192.
5. Crozier, p. 109.
6. Pierre Galante with Jack Miller, *The General. A New & Revealing Portrait of the Man who is France*, London, Leslie Frewin, 1969, p. 86.
7. John Williams, *The Guns of Dakar, September 1940*, London, Heinemann, 1976, p. 7.
8. *Alanbrooke*, p. 101, added after diary entry, 19 August 1940.
9. TNA, CAB 65/7, War Cabinet 171 (40) Minute 11, 18 June 1940.
10. John Terraine, 'The Army in Modern France' *History Today*, XI, 11 November 1961, 733–43.
11. Jean Edward Smith, *The Liberation of Paris. How Eisenhower, De Gaulle, and Von Choltitz Saved the City of Light*, New York, Simon & Schuster, 2019, pp. 23–5.
12. Mortimer Moore, pp. 9–10.
13. Ibid. p. 10.
14. Ibid.
15. TNA, CAB 65/7, War Cabinet 175 (40), 22 June 1940 at noon; CAB 65/7, War Cabinet 176 (40) 09.30 hours, Minutes 1 & 2, 22 June 1940.
16. François Kersaudy, *Churchill and De Gaulle*, London, Collins, 1981, p. 78.
17. TNA, CAB 65/7, War Cabinet 177 (40), 23 June 1940.
18. Jean Edward Smith, p.8.
19. TNA, PREM 3 Prime Minister's Papers, PREM 3/186A/7, Review of the Situation in France and the French Colonies, 18 December 1940.
20. TNA, FO 371/24338/C13833, Campbell to Secretary of State, dated 14 August 1940, logged at Chancellery, 26 December 1940.
21. General de Gaulle, *War Memoirs. Unity, 1942–1944. Documents*, Translated by Joyce Murchie & Hamish Erskine, London, Weidenfeld & Nicolson, 1959, pp.29–30.
22. TNA, FO 371/24339/C7776/7328/17, Sir C. Bentinck (Santiago) to FO, 16 July 1940.
23. TNA, FO 371/24339/C7797/7328/17, Translated of propaganda directed against French Volunteer Forces, attributed to Capitaine de Vaisseau de Rivoyre, former naval attaché at French Embassy, 15 July 1940.
24. TNA, FO 371/24340/C8246/7328/17, Churchill to Foreign Secretary, 4 August 1940.
25. TNA, FO 371/24341/C9250/G, Major D. Morton, 23 August 1940.
26. Spears, p. 151.
27. Ibid.
28. TNA, CAB 65/7 War Cabinet 179 (40) Minute 5, 18.00 hours, 24 June 1940.
29. TNA, FO 371, Foreign Office Correspondence, FO 371/24340/C8246/7328/17, Churchill to Foreign Secretary, 4 August 1940.
30. TNA, CAB 65/7, War Cabinet 179 (40) Appendix, Minute 10, Communication from the French government.
31. Jean Edward Smith, p.9.
32. TNA, CAB 65/7, War Cabinet 180 (40) 10.30 hours, 24 June 1940.
33. TNA, CAB 65/7, War Cabinet 182 (40) 18.00 hours, Telegram from General Wavell, 3:25 pm, 25 June 1940.
34. Ibid, Telegram: Secretary of State to C-in-C of the Middle East Theatre, 74876 Cipher, 26 June 1940.

35. TNA, CAB 65/7, War Cabinet 183 (40) Minutes 8 & 10, 26 June 1940.
36. TNA, CAB 65/7, War Cabinet 184 (40)) Minute 9, 27 June 1940.
37. TNA, CAB 65/7, War Cabinet 185 (40) Minute 5, noon, 28 June 1940.
38. TNA, CAB 65/7, War Cabinet 186 (40) Minute 2, 17.30 hours, 28 June 1940.
39. TNA, CAB 65/8, War Cabinet 189 (40) 1 July 1940.
40. Churchill, *Their Finest Hour*, p. 450.
41. Jean Edward Smith, pp. 27–8.
42. PISM, PRM 20/40, letter to Churchill, 21 December 1940.
43. TNA, CAB 65/8 War Cabinet 191 (40) 2 July 1940.
44. TNA, CAB 65/8, War Cabinet 194 (40) Minute 6, 5 July 1940.
45. Kersaudy, pp. 85–6.
46. Kissinger, p. 65.
47. Ibid.
48. TNA, CAB 65/8, War Cabinet 196 (40) Minute 4, 7 July 1940.
49. TNA, CAB 65/8, War Cabinet 204 (40) Minute 8, 15 July 1940.
50. TNA, FO 371/24360/C8142, draft letter, Churchill to de Gaulle, August 1940.
51. TNA, CAB 66/9/227, Situation in Algeria and French Morocco. Memorandum by Minister of Information, 28 June 1940.
52. Ibid.
53. Jean Edward Smith, p. 28.
54. Ibid, p. 29.
55. *The Economist*, 7 September 1940.
56. Kissinger, pp. 65–6.
57. Crozier, p. 116.
58. Spears, pp. 136–7.
59. Ibid, pp. 139–40.
60. TNA, ADM 199/817, Operation MENACE, Telegrams, 18 August 1940–25 August 1940, naval attaché, Madrid, 13 September 1940.
61. Paul Preston, *Franco: A Biography*, London, Fontana Press, 1995, pp. 374 & 404.
62. Ibid.
63. TNA, PREM 3/174/3, Dillon (Algiers Military Mission) to Churchill, 26 June 1940.
64. Robert L. Melka, 'Darlan between Britain and Germany, 1940–41' *Journal of Contemporary History*, 8/1, April 1973, 57–80.
65. TNA, PREM 3/174/4, Churchill to Marshal Pétain and General Weygand, 17 June 1940.
66. TNA, CAB 66/9/231, Situation in Syria, Memorandum by Secretary of State for Foreign Affairs, 28 June 1940.
67. TNA, CAB 66/9/250, Weekly Resume (No. 44) of the Naval, Military and Air Situation, 27 June–4 July 1940.
68. TNA, CAB 66/9/252, Memorandum by the Secretary of State for the Colonies, 7 July 1940.
69. TNA, CAB 66/9/258, War Cabinet, 'French Equatorial and West Africa', Memorandum by the Secretary of State for the Colonies, 11 July 1940.
70. TNA, FO 371/24338/C13833, Campbell to Secretary of State, France: Necessity of action by General de Gaulle, dated 14 August 1940 but logged at Chancellery, 26 December 1940.
71. TNA, CAB 79, War Cabinet, Chiefs of Staff Sub-Committee, Minutes of Meetings, CAB 79/5 COS (40) 209th Meeting, Minute 2, French Hostilities, 5 July 1940.
72. TNA, CAB 80 War Cabinet, Chiefs of Staff Sub-Committee Memoranda, CAB 80/14 C.O.S, (40) 529 (J.P) Implications of French Hostilities, 4 July 1940.
73. *The Economist* (London) 7 September 1940. TNA, CAB 65/8 War Cabinet 236 (40) Minute 5, 29 August 1940; CAB 65/8 War Cabinet 238 (40) Minute 6, 30 August 1940.

Notes   215

74. TNA, CAB 70/6 C.O.S. (40) 275th Meeting, 20 August 1940. See also CAB 79/5 C.O.S. (40) 212th Meeting, 8 July 1940 in which the COS feared that unless something was done to rally French colonies in French West Africa they could fall under the influence of Pétain and therefore a force should be sent to Dakar.
75. TNA, CAB 80/15 C.O.S. (40) 569, 24 July 1940.
76. TNA, CAB 80/17 C.O.S. (40) 577, 27 July 1940.
77. TNA, CAB 80/17 C.O.S. (40) 672, 27 August 1940.
78. TNA, CAB 80/17 C.O.S. (40) 497, 2 September 1940.
79. TNA, CAB 80/18 C.O.S. (40) 704, Policy in Respect of French Colonial Possessions (draft) 4 September 1940.
80. *The Economist*, 21 September 1940.
81. TNA, CAB 80/18 C.O.S. (40) 718, 6 September 1940.
82. Williams, p. 20.
83. TNA, CAB 80/19 C.O.S. (40) 771, (J.P.) 25 September 1940.
84. Jackson, p. 149.
85. TNA, PREM 3/177/3 'OVERLORD' Security – Communications of Information to the French, 18 May 1944.
86. *The Duff Cooper Diaries, 1915–1951*, (ed) John Julius Norwich, London, Phoenix, 2006, p. 352, diary entry, 12 February 1945. Hereafter referred to as *Duff Cooper*.
87. TNA, FO 371/24351/C12138 No. 20 Military Mission Brazzaville to War Office, W.38 Cipher 29/10, 13 November 1940.
88. TNA, FO 371/24343/C10514, FO Minute (Mr Mack) 29 September 1940.
89. TNA, FO 371/24343/C10514, Nigel Law to W.H.B. Mack, 3 October 1940.
90. TNA, FO 371/24343/C10564, Minute by O.G. Sargent, 15 October 1940.
91. TNA, FO 371/24344/C11509, FO Minute by Mr Codrington, 24 October 1940.
92. TNA, FO 371/24344/C11509, D. Morton to R.L. Speaight, 1 November 1940.
93. TNA, FO 371/24345/C12367, 4 November 1940.
94. TNA, FO 371/24345/C12367, Letter W.82 B/G H. Farquhar to Lt Col Todd, Censorship, 14 November 1940.
95. TNA, FO 371/24361/C11442, Gascoigne, British Consulate General, Tangier, to William Strang, FO, 15 November 1940.
96. TNA, FO 371/24361/C13251, Minute by Mack, 11 December 1940 (W.H.B Mack, Head of the French Department, FO, 1940–42; British Civil Liaison Officer to Allied C-in-C, North Africa, 1942–43).
97. TNA, FO 371/24352/C13631/7389/17, de Gaulle to Sieyes (New York) No. 1396, FO received 19 December 1940.
98. Ibid. Sieyes to de Gaulle, FO received 26 December 1940.
99. Ibid. de Gaulle to General Catroux, 26 December 1940.

Chapter 3
1. TNA, CAB 65/9, War Cabinet 239 (40) Minute 6, 2 September 1940.
2. Ibid.
3. TNA, CAB 65/10, War Cabinet 285 (40) Minute 6, 8 November 1940.
4. Ibid.
5. TNA, CAB 80/22 C.O.S. (40) 948, Situation in French North Africa, Memorandum by Chief of Imperial General Staff (CIGS) 17 November 1940.
6. TNA, ADM 1/10799, HMAS AUSTRALIA, Reports of Proceedings, 1–30 September 1940, including War Diary and Report on Operation 'MENACE' General Description of Operation MENACE.
7. TNA, CAB 80/16 C.O.S. (40) 637 (J.I.C.) Possibility of a German or Italian Occupation of Dakar. Report by the Joint Intelligence Sub-Committee, 17 August 1940.

8. John Williams, *The Guns of Dakar, September 1940*, London, Heinemann, 1976, p. ix.
9. Ibid, pp. 96–7.
10. Conrad Black, *Franklin Delano Roosevelt: Champion of Freedom*, London, Phoenix, 2004, p. 777.
11. Williams, pp. x–xi.
12. TNA, CAB 80/106/3 C.O.S. (40) 3 (0) (J.P.) Implications of French Hostility Arising from OPERATION 'MENACE', 10 September 1940.
13. TNA, ADM 199/907 War History, OPERATION MENACE, Vol. 2, Enclosures to War History Case 7820 Volume 2. Williams, p. 25.
14. Ibid, p. 35.
15. TNA, CAB 84/18/37, J.P. (40) 434 (E) OPERATION MENACE, Note by Secretary A.T. Cornwall-Jones, 10 September 1940. (Churchill saw the letter on 29 August 1940).
16. TNA, CAB 84/19/11 Operation 'Menace' Security Arrangements. Note by Secretary Attaching Report by E.P.S. (40) 91, 21 September 1940.
17. TNA, ADM 199/907 War History OPERATION MENACE, Vol. 2. I.S.P. 77th Meeting, 9 August 1940, p. 4.
18. TNA, CAB 80/16/54 C.O.S. (40) 642 OPERATION 'MENACE' Note by the Vice Chief of Naval Staff, J.H.D. Cunningham, 17 August 1940.
19. TNA, CAB 80/17/27 OPERATION MENACE C.O.S. (40) 672, Memorandum by Maj. Gen. Irwin, 27 August 1940. Irwin cited C.O.S. (40) 628 (J.P.) 13 August 1940. He noted that there was no repetition of this in the latest directive regarding Dakar.
20. TNA, ADM 199/906, War History OPERATION 'MENACE' p. 12.
21. Ibid, p. 16.
22. TNA, ADM 1/100799 – HMAS AUSTRALIA: Report of Proceedings 1–30 September 1940, including War Diary and Report on Operation 'MENACE'.
23. TNA, WO 106/2119, Cipher Messages Spears Mission War Office, G.O.C. West Africa and C-in-C of the Middle East Theatre, Dakar (3 September–25 September 1940) WO to C-in-C of the Middle East; Governor and Commander-in-Chief, Gibraltar; Governor and Commander-in-Chief, Malta; repeated G.O.C. West Africa, 81899 Cipher (M.O.1) 14 September 1940.
24. Williams, p. 61.
25. *The Diaries of Sir Alexander Cadogan, 1938–1945*, (ed) David Dilks, London, Cassell, 1971, p. 327, diary entry 16 September 1940. Hereafter referred to as '*Cadogan*'.
26. Williams, pp. 63–4.
27. Cadogan, p. 327, diary entries, 17 & 18 September 1940.
28. TNA, ADM 1/10799 – General Description of MENACE.
29. https://ahoy.tk-jk.net/macslo/OperationMenace.September.html, accessed 11 September 2008.
30. *The Diaries of Evelyn Waugh*, (ed) Michael Davie, London, Penguin, 1979, pp. 482–3, diary entry, 29 September 1940.
31. Norman Sherry, *The Life of Graham Greene, Volume 2: 1939–1955*, London, Jonathan Cape, 1994, pp. 119–21.
32. Brett Bowles, 'Newsreels, Ideology and Public Opinion Under Vichy: The Case of *La France en Marche*', French Historical Studies, 27/2, 2004, 419–63.
33. TNA, FO 371/24339/C7776/7328/17, Sir C. Bentinck (Santiago) to FO, 16 July 1940.
34. TNA, CAB 80/19 C.O.S. (40) 781, Operations in West Africa Report, 26 September 1940.
35. TNA, Ibid, Annex 1, Telegram from General de Gaulle, no. 1909 N/24, 25 September 1940.
36. TNA, CAB 80/19 C.O.S. (40) 788, Minute 5, Operations in West Africa, Previous Reference C.O.S. (40) 326th Conclusion, Minute 2, Note by Secretary, 28 September 1940.

37. Andrew Roberts, *Masters and Commanders: How Roosevelt, Churchill, Marshall and Alanbrooke Won the War in the West*, London, Allen Lane, 2008, p. 430.
38. William Taubman, *Khrushchev – The Man – His Era*, London, Simon & Schuster, 2017, p. 404.
39. TNA, ADM1/19181, OPERATION MENACE, Responsibility for the interception of French Vessels. Vice Admiral Somerville, Flag Officer Commanding Force H to the Secretary of the Admiralty, No. 69/102, HMS *Renown*, 7 October 1940.
40. Ibid. M.019708/40 to Vice Admiral Sir James F. Somerville from R.H.A. Carter, 15 October 1940.
41. Jean Lacouture, *De Gaulle, the Rebel: 1890–1944*, Vol. 1, London, Harvill Collins, 1993, Translated by Patrick O'Brian, p. 247.
42. TNA, ADM1/19179, Report on Proceedings of Force H for the period 20 September 1940 to 28 September 1940, Vice Admiral J.F. Somerville, Flag Officer Commanding Force H No. 66/9. The Secretary of the Admiralty, HMS *Renown*, 29 September 1940.
43. Lacouture, p. 275.
44. TNA, WO 178/10, General Spears to Admiral Cunningham, 17:50 hours, 13 September 1940; Cunningham to Spears, 18:27 hours; Spears to Cunningham, 20:15 hours.
45. TNA, ADM 199/906, War History OPERATION 'MENACE', p. 11.
46. Ibid. p. 12.
47. TNA, WO 178/10, 20 Military Mission 'Spears' Military Mission, 1940, July-December, War Diary entry, 22 October 1940.
48. Pierre Galante, *The General. A New & Revealing Portrait of the Man Who is France*, London, Leslie Frewin, 1969, p. 91.
49. Ibid.
50. TNA, ADM 199/906 Appendix 1, p. 60. Minutes 18–23.
51. Gerhard L. Weinberg, *A World at Arms: A Global History of World War II*, Cambridge, Cambridge University Press, 1994, p. 160.
52. TNA, ADM 1/19197 Publication as a dispatch of Vice Admiral Sir John Cunningham's Report of Operations against Dakar, June 1946, John Hingham, Head of Military Branch I, 19 June 1946.
53. TNA, ADM 1/19197, 21 June 1946.
54. Ibid. J. Wilson (FO) to Allingham, Admiralty, 30 August 1946.
55. Churchill Papers, CHAR 2/398, Telegram from Harold [Esmil Cecil Rothermere] (Lord Rothermere) to Churchill, 1 October 1940.
56. Spears, p. 211.

Chapter 4

1. TNA, FO 371/24338/C13833, Campbell to Secretary of State, dated 14 August 1940 but logged at Chancellery, 26 December 1940.
2. TNA, FO 371/24338/C13855/7327/17, Mr A Stirling, Commonwealth of Australia, Department of External Affairs to Mr Mack, (FO) 21 December 1940.
3. TNA, FO 371/31959/Z2208, Record of a Discussion between Admiral Muselier and Mr Peake, 12 March 1942.
4. TNA, FO 371/31959/Z2206, Admiral Dickens to William Strang, 12 March 1942.
5. Spears, p. 174.
6. TNA, FO 371/31959/Z2087/G, R.H. Hoare (Political Intelligence Department) to Mack, 14 March 1942.
7. TNA, FO 371/C13858/7327/17, Scrivener, British Embassy at Lisbon, to Mack, FO, 18 December 1940.
8. *The Economist*, 4 January 1941.
9. Ibid.

10. Ibid, 8 February 1941.
11. Ibid, 15 February 1941.
12. Ibid, 26 April 1941.
13. Ibid, 17 May 1941.
14. Ibid, 24 May 1941.
15. Ibid.
16. TNA, PREM 3 Prime Minister's Papers, PREM 3/186A/5, General Spears to A. Bevir (10 Downing Street), 1 February 1941.
17. TNA, PREM 3/489/3, Copy of Cypher Telegram from the United Kingdom High Commissioner in the Union of South Africa, 5 June 1941, Smuts' comment.
18. *The Economist*, 7 June 1941.
19. TNA, PREM 3/486/2, Churchill to Roosevelt, 20 October 1941.
20. Crozier, pp. 151–2.
21. Sarah Farmer, 'The Communist Resistance in the Haute-Vienne' *French Historical Studies*, XIV/1, 1985, 89–116.
22. TNA, FO 371/24345/C12225, Sir R. Craigie (Tokyo) to Lord Halifax, Foreign Secretary, 11 November 1940.
23. Polish Institute and Sikorski Museum (PISM), Kensington, London, PRM 22 (Situation with the Soviet Union, 1940), Letter to Sikorski, 11 November 1940.
24. PISM, PRM 22, Gorka, London, 14 November 1940.
25. TNA, FO 371/24345/C12865, FO Minute, Mr Mack, General de Gaulle's Visit to London, 28 November 1940.
26. Ibid.
27. TNA, FO 371/24346/C12935, Speight to Foreign Secretary, 6 December 1940.
28. TNA, FO 371/124345/C12411, Churchill to Foreign Secretary, Prime Minister's Personal Minute, M.326, 20 November 1940.
29. *Cadogan*, p. 334. Diary entry, 5 November 1940.
30. Martin Gilbert, *Winston S. Churchill. Vol. 6. Finest Hour, 1939–1941*, London, Heinemann, 1983, pp. 867–8.
31. TNA, FO 371/24352/C13859/738/17, de Gaulle to General Catroux, FO received 26 December 1940. This information was obtained by British diplomatic channels and by emissaries sent by de Gaulle to Vichy and allowed to return. Vichy, as noted, accepted Free French authority in Equatorial Africa and claimed that they would only use propaganda to attack Free French soldiers there until February 1941.
32. TNA, FO 371/246361/C11442, Gascoigne, British Consulate General, Tangier to William Strang, FO, 15 November 1940.
33. Ibid.
34. TNA, CAB 65/9 War Cabinet 278 (40) Minute 5, 28 October 1940.
35. *Cadogan*, pp. 334–335, Diary entry, 8 November 1940.
36. TNA, CAB 65/10 War Cabinet 283 (40) Minutes 5 & 6, 6 November 1940.
37. TNA, PREM 3/186A/7, Review of the Situation in France and French Colonies, 18 December 1940.
38. TNA, CAB 65/10 War Cabinet 286 (40) Minute 7, 11 November 1940.
39. TNA, CAB 66/9/225, War Cabinet, Visit to French Morocco, Report by Minister of Information (Duff Cooper) 27 June 1940.
40. TNA, ADM 199817, Operation MENACE, Telegrams 18 August–25 October 1940, Admiralty to Naval Commanders Overseas, 14 September 1940.
41. TNA, CAB 80/21 C.O.S. 872 (JP) 27 October 1940.
42. TNA, CAB 80/22 C.O.S. (40) 948, Situation in French North Africa, Memorandum by CIGS, 17 November 1940.

43. TNA, PREM 3/186A/5, General Spears to A. Bevir (10 Downing Street) 1 February 1941.
44. TNA, CAB 80/26 C.O.S. (41) 121, 26 February 1941.
45. TNA, CAB 80/26 C.O.S. (41) 158, 12 March 1941.
46. TNA, PREM 3/186A/7, Sir H. Knatchbull-Hugessen (Angora) to FO, 24 December 1940.
47. *Cadogan*, p. 350, Diary entry, 18 January 1941.
48. TNA, CAB 79/10 C.O.S. (41) 116th Meeting, 31 March 1941.
49. TNA, PREM 3/186A/7, Morton to Churchill, Seen by de Gaulle. Morton appeared to agree with de Gaulle as he was also unhappy with British propaganda regarding France.

Chapter 5
1. TNA, PREM 3/120/A, Major Morton on British Relations with the Free French, 6 January 1940.
2. Ibid.
3. TNA, PREM 3/120/10A, Letter to V.G. Lawford at FO, 17 January 1942.
4. TNA, PREM 3/469, Former Naval Person (Churchill) to President (Roosevelt), Prime Minister's Personal Telegram T.174, 14 May 1941.
5. Martin S. Gilbert, *Winston S. Churchill, Vol. 6: Finest Hours, 1939–1941*, London, Heinemann, 1983, pp. 1089–90.
6. Crozier, pp. 152–3.
7. Evan McGilvray, *Field Marshal Claude Auchinleck*, Barnsley, Pen & Sword, 2020, p. 138.
8. Churchill Papers, CHAR 20/37/24, Telegram, Sir Miles Lampson to Churchill, 1 April 1941.
9. Churchill Papers, CHAR 20/37/69–70, Telegram, Sir Miles Lampson to Churchill, 8 April 1941.
10. Churchill Papers, CHAR 20/39/7, Telegram, Churchill to General Wavell, 21 May 1941.
11. Churchill Papers, CHAR 20/39/11–14, Telegram, General Wavell to Churchill, 22 May 1941.
12. Churchill Papers, CHAR 20/39/15, Telegram, Churchill to General Wavell, 23 May 1941.
13. Churchill Papers, CHAR 20/39/62, Telegram, Spears to General de Gaulle, 29 May 1941.
14. Churchill Papers, CHAR 20/39/67, Telegram, Churchill to General Wavell, 3 June 1941.
15. Churchill Papers, CHAR 20/39/81–83, Telegram, General Wavell to Churchill, 5 June 1941.
16. Churchill Papers, CHAR 20/39/87, Telegram, General Wavell to Churchill, 5 June 1941.
17. Churchill Papers, CHAR 20/39/88, Telegram, Churchill to General de Gaulle, 6 June 1941.
18. Churchill Papers, CHAR 20/39/89–90, Telegram, Spears to General de Gaulle and Churchill, 5 June 1941.
19. Churchill Papers, CHAR 20/39/91–92, Telegram, Spears to General de Gaulle and Churchill, 5 June 1941.
20. Churchill Papers, CHAR 20/39/93, Telegram, Churchill to General de Gaulle, 6 June 1941.
21. Churchill Papers, CHAR 20/39/95, Telegram, de Gaulle to Churchill, 6 June 1941.
22. Churchill Papers, CHAR 20/39/97, Telegram, Churchill to Robert Menzies, 7 June 1941.
23. Ibid.
24. Churchill Papers, CHAR 20/39/98, Telegram, Churchill to President Roosevelt, 7 June 1941.
25. Ibid.
26. Churchill Papers, CHAR 20/39/99, Telegram, de Gaulle to Churchill, 7 June 1941.

27. Churchill Papers, CHAR 20/39/100, Telegram, Spears to de Gaulle and Churchill, 7 June 1941.
28. Churchill Papers, CHAR 20/39/114–115, Telegram, Churchill to Menzies, 9 July, 1941.
29. Churchill Collection, CHAR 20/39/125, Telegram, de Gaulle to Churchill, 13 June 1941.
30. Churchill Collection, CHAR 20/39/127, Telegram, Churchill to Roosevelt, 15 June 1941.
31. Churchill Collection, CHAR 20/40/30, Telegram, Spears to de Gaulle and Churchill, 21 June 1941.
32. *The Economist*, 19 July 1941.
33. Churchill Collection, CHAR 20/40/81, Telegram, de Gaulle to Churchill, 29 June 1941.
34. Churchill Collection, CHAR 20/39/128, Telegram, Churchill to General Wavell, 16 June 1941.
35. Churchill Collection, CHAR 20/39/130, Telegram, General Blamey to Churchill, 17 June 1941.
36. Churchill Collection, CHAR 20/40/81, Telegram, de Gaulle to Churchill, 29 June 1941.
37. Churchill Collection, CHAR 20/41/10, Telegram, Churchill to de Gaulle, 15 July 1941.
38. Churchill Collection, CHAR 20/41/20, Telegram, Minister of State, Middle East to Churchill, 19 July 1941.
39. Churchill Collection, CHAR 20/41/33, Telegram, Churchill to Minister of State, Middle East, 22 July 1941.
40. Churchill Collection, CHAR 20/41/35–36, Telegram, Minister of State, Middle East to Churchill, 22 July 1941.
41. Churchill Collection, CHAR 20/41/43, Telegram, Churchill to Minister of State, Middle East, 24 July 1941.
42. Churchill Collection, CHAR 20/41/49, Telegram, de Gaulle to Churchill, 25 July 1941.
43. Churchill Collection, CHAR 20/41/57, Telegram, Minister of State, Middle East, to Churchill, 25 July 1941.
44. Churchill Collection, CHAR 20/41/76, Telegram, Churchill to Minister of State, Middle East, 2 August 1941.
45. Churchill Collection, CHAR 20/41/79, Telegram, Minister of State, Middle East, to Churchill, 3 August 1941.
46. Churchill Collection, CHAR 20/41/107, Telegram, Minister of State, Middle East, to Churchill, 12 August 1941.
47. Churchill Collection, CHAR 20/41/110, Telegram, Minister of State, Middle East, to Churchill, 15 August 1941.
48. Churchill Collection, CHAR 20/47/2, Telegram, Churchill to Spears, 12 December 1941.
49. Churchill Collection, CHAR 20/41/10, Telegram, Churchill to de Gaulle, 15 July 1941.
50. Churchill Collection, CHAR 20/41/20, Telegram, Minister of State, Middle East to Churchill, 19 July 1941.
51. Churchill Collection, CHAR 20/41/34, Telegram, de Gaulle to Churchill, 23 July 1941.
52. Churchill Collection, CHAR 20/41/49, Telegram, de Gaulle to Churchill, 25 July 1941.
53. Churchill Collection, CHAR 20/41/107, Telegram, Minister of State, Middle East to Churchill, 12 August 1941.
54. Ibid.
55. Ibid.
56. McGilvray, *Auchinleck*, Barnsley, pp. 64–72.

Chapter 6

1. Conrad Black, *Franklin Delano Roosevelt*, London, Phoenix, 2003, p. 686,
2. *King's Counsellor. Abdication and War: The Diaries of Sir Alan Lascelles*, Edited by Duff Hart-Davis, London, Phoenix, 2006, diary entry, 6 June 1942, p. 28. Hereafter referred to as *Lascelles*.

3. Ibid, diary entry, 4 January 1943, p. 91.
4. Churchill Collection, CHAR 20/69A/15–16, Telegram, Churchill to Roosevelt, 23 January 1942.
5. Churchill Collection, CHAR 20/47/122, Telegram, Churchill to de Gaulle, 30 December 1941.
6. Black, p. 707.
7. Ibid, p. 708.
8. Churchill Collection, CHAR 20/69A/67–69, Telegram, Roosevelt to Churchill, 29 January 1942.
9. *British Foreign Policy in the Second World War, Volume 3*, Sir Llewellyn Woodward, London, HMSO, 1971, p. 72. Hereafter referred to as *BFP3*.
10. *The Economist*, 27 September 1941.
11. *BFP3*, pp. 82–3.
12. Ibid. pp. 281–3.
13. *The Economist*, 14 February 1942
14. Marc Ferro, *Pétain*, Paris, Les Éditions de la Seine, 1987, *passim*.
15. *BFP3*, p. 284.
16. Ibid. pp. 284–8.
17. Ibid. pp. 290–3.
18. Ibid. p. 293.
19. Ibid. p. 297.
20. Ibid.
21. Jean Edward Smith, p. 17.
22. Mortimer Moore, p. 27–8.
23. *BFP3*. p. 300.
24. Mortimer Moore, p. 26.
25. *BFP3*. pp. 301–2.
26. *The Economist*, 6 June 1942.
27. *BFP3*, pp. 303–4.
28. Ibid. p. 307.
29. TNA, FO 371/31952, Paris, 14 November 1942.
30. Black, p. 779.
31. TNA, FO 371/31950/Z7371/G, From British Representative to Fighting French National Committee to FO, 28 September 1942.
32. TNA, FO 371/31959/Z2087/G, R.H. Hoare to Mack, Political Intelligence Department, 14 March 1942.
33. TNA, FO 371/31959/Z2206, Admiral Dickens to William Strang, 12 March 1942.
34. TNA, FO 371/31959/Z2208, Record of Discussion between Admiral Muselier and Mr Peake, 12 March 1942.
35. De Gaulle, *Unity: Documents*, 52. Text of Franco-Soviet Agreement of September 28th 1942, pp.55–6.
36. *BFP3*, pp. 308–312.

Chapter 7

1. Churchill Collection, CHAR 20/106/39, Telegram, Roosevelt to Churchill (T.133/3) 10 February 1943.
2. Jean Edward Smith, p. 35.
3. Mortimer Moore, p. 26.
4. TNA, FO 371/36171/Z1858/Z, Notes on a Conversation with Captain Phillippe Roy, 3 February 1943, Casablanca, A. Malcolm.

5. Anthony Verrier, *Assassination in Algiers. Churchill, Roosevelt, de Gaulle and the Murder of Admiral Darlan*, London, Macmillan, 1990, p. 110.
6. Jean Edward Smith, p. 35.
7. Black, p. 781.
8. Jean Edward Smith. pp. 35–6.
9. Verrier. p. 218.
10. Ibid. pp. 206–7.
11. Ibid. p. 232.
12. Jean Edward Smith, p. 36
13. Ibid.
14. Ibid.
15. Black, p. 791.
16. Ibid.
17. Jean Edward Smith, 36–7. Citing Antony Beevor.
18. Macmillan, diary entry 20 May 1943, p. 91.
19. Ibid, Diary entry 8 June 1943, p. 112.
20. Verrier. pp. 232–55.
21. TNA, FO 371/36170/Z30/G, From British Representative to French National Committee, to FO, 31 December 1942.
22. TNA, FO 371/36170/Z289/G, Note by William Strang, 6 January 1943.
23. TNA, FO 371/36170/Z538/G, V. Carrington-Bentinck to FO, 8 January 1943.
24. TNA, FO 371/36170/Z452/G, Mr Bond (Casablanca) to FO, 3 January 1943.
25. TNA, FO 371/36170. From British Representative to French National Committee to FO, Mr Peake, 14 January 1943.
26. TNA, FO 371/36171/Z11364/G, Minute by Speight discussing Mack's Account of Meeting Between de Gaulle and Giraud, 30 January 1943
27. TNA, FO 371/36171/Z1364/G, Mack to Strang, 28 January 1943.
28. Ibid.
29. TNA, FO 371/36171/Z1694/G, Report by G.S. Somers Locks, 5 February 1943. Dinner, Secretary of State in Honour of M. Massigli.
30. TNA, FO 371/36172/Z2559/Z, Morton to Churchill, 24 February 1943.
31. Black, p. 935.
32. Ibid.
33. TNA, FO 371/36173/Z3077/G, Dupree to Ridsdale, 1 March 1943.
34. TNA, FO 371/36174/Z/4044, Minute Mr Strang, conversation with Mr Hull regarding the French Situation, 1 April 1943.
35. TNA, FO 371/36174/Z4188, Prime Minister's Personal Minute, Serial No. M.232.3, to Sir Alexander Cadogan, 4 April 1943.
36. TNA, FO 371/36174/Z4616, Charles Peake to Mack, 9 April 1943.
37. TNA, FO 371/36174/Z 4644/5/G, Eden to Peake, 13 April 1943.
38. TNA, FO 371/36175, Harold Macmillan (Algiers) to Churchill, 13 April 1943.
39. Churchill Collection, CHAR 20/106/43–44, Telegram from Richard Casey to Churchill (T136/3) 11 February 1943.
40. Churchill Papers, CHAR 20/106/47, Telegram, Churchill to Lord Halifax, 10 February 1943.
41. Churchill Papers, CHAR 20/106/56–59, Telegram, Churchill to General Eisenhower (T.146/3) February 1943.
42. Churchill Papers, CHAR 20/106/60, Telegram, Churchill to Roosevelt, T,147/3, 9 February 1943.
43. Jean Edward Smith, p. 37.
44. Ibid.

45. Churchill Papers, CHAR 20/106/62, Telegram, Churchill to Casey (T.149/3) 12 February 1943.
46. Churchill Papers, CHAR 20/106/64–65, Telegram, Casey to Churchill (T.151/3) 12 February 1943.
47. Churchill Papers, CHAR 20/106/77, Telegram, Casey to Churchill (T.160/3) Extract of note sent to Godfroy, 13 February 1943.
48. Churchill Papers, CHAR 20/106/120, Telegram, Casey to Churchill (T.199/3) 19 February 1943.
49. Churchill Papers, CHAR 20/106/78, Telegram, Casey to Churchill (T.161/3) 13 February 1943.
50. Churchill Papers, CHAR 20/106/89, Telegram, Casey to Churchill (T.171/3) 15 February 1943.
51. Churchill Papers, CHAR 20/106/90, Telegram, Casey to Churchill, 15 February 1943.
52. Churchill Papers, CHAR 20/106/98, Telegram, Churchill to Macmillan (T.180/3) 17 February 1943.
53. Churchill Papers, CHAR 20/106/114–115, Telegram, Macmillan to Churchill (T.194/3) 18 February 1943.
54. Churchill Papers, CHAR 20/106/120, Telegram, Casey to Churchill (T.199/3) 19 February 1943.
55. Churchill Papers, CHAR 20/111/6, Telegram, Casey to Churchill (T.604/3) 28 April 1943.
56. Churchill Papers, CHAR 20/111/7, Telegram, Casey to Churchill (T.605/3) 28 April 1943.
57. Churchill Papers, CHAR 20/111/17–18, Telegram, Macmillan to Churchill (T.611/3) 29 April 1943.
58. Churchill Papers, CHAR 20/111/105, Telegram, Churchill to Macmillan (T.699/3) 13 May 1943.
59. Churchill Papers, CHAR 20/111/46, Telegram, Macmillan to Churchill, 17 June 1943.
60. Churchill Papers, CHAR 20/113/47–49, Telegram, Roosevelt to Churchill, 17 June 1943.
61. Churchill Papers, CHAR 20/113/52–53, Telegram, Churchill to Roosevelt, 18 June 1943.
62. Churchill Papers, CHAR 20/113/54, Telegram, Churchill to Macmillan for Roosevelt, 18 June 1943.
63. Jean Edward Smith, pp. 38–9
64. Ibid, p. 34.
65. Ibid, p. 39.
66. Ibid.
67. Ibid, pp. 39–40.
68. Churchill Papers, CHAR 20/113/57, Telegram, Churchill to Roosevelt, 18 June 1943.
69. Churchill Papers, CHAR 20/113/92, Telegram, Churchill to Macmillan, 21 June 1943.
70. Churchill Papers, CHAR 20/113/93, Telegram, Roosevelt to Churchill, 22 June 1943.
71. Churchill Papers, CHAR 20/113/96, Telegram, Churchill to Macmillan, 22 June 1943.
72. *The Economist*, 22 May 1943.
73. Churchill Papers, CHAR 20/113/108, Telegram, Churchill to Stalin, 23 June 1943.
74. Churchill Papers, CHAR 20/113/109, Telegram, Macmillan to Churchill, 23 June 1943.
75. Churchill Papers, CHAR 20/113/113, Telegram, Churchill to Roosevelt, 26 June 1943.
76. Churchill Papers, CHAR 20/113/115, Telegram, Churchill to Macmillan, 23 June 1943.
77. Churchill Papers, CHAR 20/113/123, Telegram, Churchill to Roosevelt, 25 June 1943.
78. Churchill Papers, CHAR 20/113/124, Telegram, Churchill to Macmillan, 25 June 1943.
79. Churchill Papers, CHAR 20/113/125, Telegram, Roosevelt to Churchill, 25 June 1943.
80. Churchill Papers, CHAR 20/113/130, Telegram, Macmillan to Churchill, 25 June 1943.

81. Churchill Papers, CHAR 20/113/134, Telegram, Stalin to Churchill, 26 June 1943.
82. *The Economist*, 3 July 1943.
83. Churchill Papers, CHAR 20/112/97, Telegram, Churchill to Macmillan, 11 June 1943.
84. Churchill Papers, CHAR 20/112/98, Telegram, Churchill to Macmillan, 11 June 1943.
85. Churchill Papers, CHAR 20/112/104–110, Telegram, Churchill to Macmillan, 12 June 1943.
86. Churchill Papers, CHAR 20/112/116, Telegram, FO to Macmillan, 12 June 1943.
87. Churchill Papers, CHAR 20/117/34, Telegram, Macmillan to Churchill, 11 August 1943.
88. Churchill Papers, CHAR 20/117/35, Telegram, Macmillan to Churchill, 12 August 1943.
89. Jean Edward Smith, pp. 40–1.
90. Ibid, p. 41.
91. Ibid, pp. 41–2.
92. Churchill Papers, CHAR 20/117/88, Telegram, Macmillan to Churchill, 27 August 1943.
93. Churchill Papers, CHAR 20/117/99, Telegram, Stalin to Churchill, 1 September 1943.
94. Churchill Papers, CHAR 20/117/114, Telegram, Macmillan to Churchill, 3 September 1943.
95. Churchill Papers, CHAR 20/120/23, Telegram, Giraud to Churchill, 6 October 1943.
96. Churchill Papers, CHAR 20/120/55, Telegram, de Gaulle to Churchill, 7 October 1943.
97. Churchill Papers, CHAR 20/124/22, Telegram, Macmillan to Churchill, 9 November 1943.
98. Churchill Papers, CHAR 20/124/24, Telegram, Churchill to de Gaulle, 10 November 1943.
99. *The Economist*, 13 November 1943.
100. Churchill Papers, CHAR 20/124/54, Telegram, Churchill to Richard Casey, 12 November 1943.
101. Churchill Papers, CHAR 20/124/56–57, Telegram, Churchill to Roosevelt, 13 November 1943.
102. Churchill Papers, CHAR 20/124/67, Telegram, Casey to Churchill, 13 November 1943.
103. Churchill Papers, CHAR 20/124/86, Telegram, Churchill to General Sir Henry Wilson (C-in-C of the Middle East Theatre); Macmillan; Richard Casey, 16 November 1943.
104. Churchill Papers, CHAR 20/124/93–94, Telegram, Casey to Churchill, 17 November 1943.
105. Churchill Papers, CHAR 20/124/95, Telegram, Casey to Churchill, 17 November 1943.
106. Churchill Papers, CHAR 20/124/96, Telegram, General Sir Henry Wilson to Churchill, 17 November 1943.
107. Churchill Papers, CHAR 20/124/108, Telegram, Macmillan to Churchill, 19 November 1943.

Chapter 8
1. Churchill Papers, CHAR 20/162/14, Telegram, Roosevelt to Churchill, 14 April 1944.
2. Nicholas Rankin, *Churchill's Wizards. The British Genius for Deception, 1914–1945*, London, Faber & Faber, 2008, pp. 566–7.
3. Laurence Rees, *Hitler and Stalin. The Tyrants and the Second World War*, London, Penguin, 2021, p. 342.
4. Jean Edward Smith, p. 42.
5. Ibid, pp. 42–3.
6. Ibid, p. 46.
7. Moore, *Paris '44*, pp. x-xi.

8. Jean Edward Smith, p. 46.
9. Ibid, p. 47.
10. Ibid.
11. Mortimer Moore, pp.58–9.
12. Ibid, pp. 430–1.
13. Jean Edward Smith, pp. 47–8.
14. Ibid, p. 48.
15. Ibid.
16. Ibid, p. 49.
17. Ibid. p. 50.
18. Churchill Papers, CHAR 20/162/22, Telegram, Duff Cooper to Churchill, 14 April 1944.
19. Churchill Papers, CHAR 20/162/24, Telegram, Churchill to Duff Cooper, 14 April – 15 April 1944.
20. Churchill Papers, CHAR 20/162/34, Telegram, Duff Cooper to Churchill, 15 April 1944.
21. Churchill Papers, CHAR 20/162/40, Telegram, Churchill to Duff Cooper, 16 April 1944.
22. Churchill Papers, CHAR 20/162/91, Telegram, Duff Cooper to Churchill, 18 April 1944–19 April 1944; CHAR 20/162/100, Telegram, Churchill to Roosevelt, 20 April 1944; CHAR 20/162/114, Telegram, Roosevelt to Churchill, 21 April 1944.
23. Churchill Papers, CHAR 20/163/16, Telegram, Churchill to Roosevelt, 22 April 1944.
24. Churchill Papers, CHAR 20/163/40, Telegram, Roosevelt to Churchill, 24 April 1944.
25. Churchill Papers, CHAR 20/163/42, Telegram, Churchill to Duff Cooper, 23 April 1944.
26. Churchill Papers, CHAR 20/163/67, Telegram, Duff Cooper to Churchill, 24 April 1944.
27. Churchill Papers, CHAR 20/163/93, Telegram, Churchill to Duff Cooper, 28 April 1944.
28. Churchill Papers, CHAR 20/165/32, Telegram, Churchill to Roosevelt, 26 May 1944.
29. Churchill Papers, CHAR 20/165/41, Telegram, Churchill to Duff Cooper, 27 May 1944–28 May 1944.
30. Churchill Papers, CHAR 20/165/44, Telegram, Churchill to Roosevelt, 27 May 1944.
31. Churchill Papers, CHAR 20/165/46, Telegram, Roosevelt to Churchill, 27 May 1944.
32. Churchill Papers, CHAR 20/165/69, Telegram, Churchill to Duff Cooper, 31 May 1944; CHAR 20/165/78, Telegram, Churchill to Duff Cooper, 1 June 1944.
33. Churchill Papers, CHAR 20/165/79–80, Telegram, Churchill to Roosevelt, 1 June 1944.
34. *British Foreign Policy in the Second World War, Volume 3*, Sir Llewellyn Woodward, London, HMSO, 1971, p. 51. Henceforth, *BFP3*.
35. Churchill Papers, CHAR 20/165/87–88, Telegram, Averill Harriman to Eisenhower, 1 June 1944.
36. Churchill Papers, CHAR 20/165/92, Telegram, Duff Cooper to Churchill, 2 June 1944.
37. Churchill Papers, CHAR 20/165/93, Telegram, Duff Cooper to Churchill, 3 June 1944.
38. Churchill Papers, CHAR 20/165/102–104, Telegram, Churchill to Roosevelt, 4 June 1944.
39. Jean Edward Smith, p. 51.
40. Ibid.
41. Ibid, p. 52.
42. Churchill Papers, CHAR 20/166/8, Telegram, Roosevelt to Churchill, 6 June 1944; CHAR 20/166/10–11, Telegram, Roosevelt to Churchill, 7 June 1944.
43. Churchill Papers, CHAR 20/166/19–21, Telegram, Churchill to Roosevelt, 8 June 1944.
44. *Cadogan*, p. 635, diary entry, 7 June 1944.
45. Ibid. p. 636, diary entry, 7 June 1944
46. Churchill Papers, CHAR 20/166/89, Telegram, Churchill to General Sir Bernard Montgomery, 13 June 1944.
47. Churchill Papers, CHAR 20/166/103, Telegram, Montgomery to Churchill, 14 June 1944.

48. Churchill Papers, CHAR 20/166/107, Telegram, Montgomery to Churchill, 14 June 1944.
49. Robert Aron, *De Gaulle Before Paris: The Liberation of France June–August 1944*, Translated by Humphrey Hare, London, Putnam, 1962, pp. 72–3.
50. Jean Edward Smith, p. 52.
51. Rees, p. 343.
52. Churchill Papers, CHAR 20/166/106, Telegram, Roosevelt to Churchill, 14 June 1944.
53. Jean Edward Smith, p. 53.
54. Churchill Papers, CHAR 20/180/20, Telegram, Churchill to Eden, 17 August 1944.
55. Churchill Papers, CHAR 20/180/24, Telegram, Churchill (Italy) to Eden, 18 August 1944.
56. Churchill Papers, CHAR 20/180/62, Telegram, Churchill (Italy) to Eden, 23 August 1944.
57. Aron, *De Gaulle Before Paris*, p. 284.
58. Ibid.
59. Ibid, p. 285.
60. Ibid. p. 291.
61. Ibid. pp. 291–3.
62. Ibid. p. 294.
63. Ibid. p. 295.
64. Ibid. p. 296.
65. Ibid. pp. 296–8.
66. Black, p. 963.

Chapter 9

1. Aron, *De Gaulle Triumphant*, p. 28.
2. Jackson, p. 324.
3. Mortimer Moore, p. xi.
4. Jackson. p. 325.
5. Ibid. p. 326.
6. Mortimer Moore, p. 358.
7. Ibid, pp. 358–9.
8. Jackson, p. 326.
9. Ibid. 126–7.
10. Ibid. p. 328.
11. Jean Edward Smith, p. 115.
12. Kissinger, p. 75.
13. Jean Edward Smith, pp. 120–3.
14. Robert Aron, *De Gaulle Triumphant: The Liberation of France August 1944–May 1945*, Translated by Humphrey Hare, London, Putnam, 1964, pp. 207–8.
15. Aron, *De Gaulle Triumphant*, p. 207.
16. Ibid, p. 208.
17. Ibid, p. 268.
18. Kissinger, p. 83. Regarding French attitudes towards Algeria see, Chantal Morelle, *Comment De Gaulle et le FLN ont mis fin à la Guerre D'Algérie*, Paris, Archipoche, 2020, p. 43.
19. Rees, p. 357.
20. *My Dear Mr Stalin: The Complete Correspondence Between Franklin D. Roosevelt and Joseph V. Stalin*, Edited, with Commentary by Susan Butler, London, Yale University Press, 2005, pp. 269–70.
21. Aron, *De Gaulle Triumphant*, p. 266.

22. Taubman, p. 331.
23. Aron, *De Gaulle Triumphant*, p. 266.
24. Ibid.
25. Ibid, p. 207.
26. Ibid, pp. 267–8.
27. *Lascelles*, diary entry, 28 November 1944, p. 273.
28. Jackson, p. 339.
29. Ibid.
30. Kissinger, p. 79.
31. Ibid.
32. Jackson, p. 351.
33. Jean Edward Smith, pp. 179–80.
34. Ibid, pp. 180–1.
35. Black, pp. 1023–5.
36. Kissinger, p. 81.
37. Jackson, p. 361.
38. Ibid.
39. Ibid.
40. Ibid. p. 362.
41. Black, p. 1132.

Bibliography

Unpublished Sources

Churchill Collection, Churchill Collection, University of Cambridge
CHAR
CHUR

Polish Institute and Sikorski Museum (PISM) Kensington, London
PRM – Office of the Prime Minister (Polish Government in Exile).

The National Archives (TNA) of the United Kingdom (Kew)
ADM 199 – The Admiralty.
CAB 65 – War Cabinet Minutes.
CAB 66 – War Cabinet Memoranda.
CAB 79 – Chiefs of Staff Minutes.
CAB 80 – Chiefs of Staff Memoranda.
FO 371 – Foreign Office Correspondence.
PREM 3 – Office of the Prime Minister.

Media
The Economist (London), 1939–1946.

Churchill
Bonham-Carter, Violet, *Winston Churchill As I Knew Him*, London, Weidenfeld & Nicholson, 1995.
Gilbert, Martin, *Winston S. Churchill. Volume 6. Finest Hour, 1939–1941*, London, Heineman, 1983.
Jenkins, Roy, *Churchill*, London, Macmillan, 2001.
Kersaudy, François, *Churchill and De Gaulle*, London, Collins, 1981.

De Gaulle
Aron, Robert, *De Gaulle. The Liberation of France, August 1944–May 1945*, translated by Humphrey Hare, London, Putnam, 1964.
——, *De Gaulle Before Paris. The Liberation of France, June–August 1944*, translated by Humphrey Hare, London, Putnam, 1962.
Crawley, Aiden, *De Gaulle*, London, The Literary Guild, 1969.
Crozier, Brian, *De Gaulle: The Warrior*, London, Eyre Methuen, 1973.
De Gaulle, Charles, *War Memoirs. Unity, 1942–1944. Documents.* Translated by Joyce Murchie and Hamish Erskine, London, Weidenfeld & Nicolson, 1959.
Galante, Pierre; Miller, Jack, *The General. A New and Revealing Portrait of the Man Who is France*, London, Leslie Frewin, 1969.
Jackson, Julian, *A Certain Idea of France. The Life of Charles de Gaulle*, London, Penguin, 2019.

Lacouture, Jean, *De Gaulle. The Rebel, 1890–1944, Volume 1*, London, Harvill, Harper Collins, 1993, Translated by Patrick O'Brian.
Morelle, Chantal, *Comment De Gaulle et le FLN ont mis fin à la Guerre D'Algérie*, Paris, Archipoche, 2020.
Rémond, René, 'Two Destinies: Pétain and de Gaulle' in *De Gaulle and Twentieth Century France*, (eds) Hugh Gough and John Horne, London, Edward Arnold, 1994.

Printed Primary Sources
British Foreign Policy in the Second World War, Volume 3, (ed) Sir Llewellyn Woodward, London, HMSO, 1971.
Douglas Haig, War Diaries and Letters, 1914–1918 (eds) Gary Sheffield and John Bourne, London, Phoenix, 2006.
King's Counsellor, Abdication and War: The Diaries of Sir Alan Lascelles (ed) Duff Hart-Davies, London, Phoenix, 2006.
My Dear Mr. Stalin. The Complete Correspondence Between Franklin D. Roosevelt and Joseph V. Stalin, (ed) Susan Butler, with commentary, London, Yale University Press, 2005.
The Diaries of Evelyn Waugh (ed) Michael Davie, London, Penguin, 1979.
The Diaries of Sir Alexander Cadogan, 1938–1945 (ed) David Dilks, London, Cassell, 1971.
The Duff Cooper Diaries, 1915–1951, (ed) John Julius Norwich, London, Phoenix, 2006.
War Diaries 1939–1945. Field Marshal Lord Alanbrooke (eds) Alex Danchev and Daniel Todman, London, Weidenfeld & Nicholson, 2001.

Printed Secondary Sources (Books and Monographs)
Alexander, Martin S., *The Republic in Danger. General Maurice Gamelin and the Politics of French Defence, 1933–1940*, Cambridge, Cambridge University Press, 1992.
Black, Conrad, *Franklin Delano Roosevelt: Champion of Freedom*, London, Phoenix, 2004.
Crosland, Margaret, *Simone de Beauvoir: The Woman and Her Work*, London, Heinemann, 1992.
De La Groce, Paul-Marie, *The French Army. A Military-Political History*, translated by Kenneth Douglas, London, Weidenfeld & Nicolson, 1963.
Fero, Marc, *Pétain*, Paris, Les Éditions de la Seine, 1987.
Hoskings, Geoffrey, *A History of the Soviet Union* (Revised Edition) London, Fontana, 1990.
Jackson, Julian, *France. The Dark Years, 1940–1944*, Oxford, Oxford University Press, 2001.
Kissinger, Henry, *Leadership. Six Studies in World Strategy*, London, Penguin, 2022.
Lloyd George, David, *War Memoirs*, Volume 2, London, Odhams, 1938.
Macmillan, Harold, *War Diaries: The Mediterranean, 1943–1945*, London, Macmillan, 1984.
McGilvray, Evan, *Field Marshal Claude Auchinleck*, Barnsley, Pen & Sword, 2020.
———, *Hamilton & Gallipoli: British Command in an Age of Transformation*, Barnsley, Pen & Sword, 2015.
Mikołajczyk, Stanisław, *The Rape of Poland: Patterns of Soviet Aggression*, Westport, Connecticut, 1973, Second Greenwood Reprint.
Moore, Mortimer William, *Paris '44. The City of Light Redeemed*, Oxford, Casemate, 2015.
Preston, Paul, *Franco: A Biography*, London, Fontana, 1995.
Rankin, Nicholas, *Churchill's Wizards. The British Genius for Deception, 1914–1945*, London, Faber & Faber, 2008.
Rees, Laurence, *Hitler and Stalin. The Tyrants and the Second World War*, London, Penguin, 2021.
Roberts, Andrew, *Masters and Commanders. How Roosevelt, Churchill, Marshall and Alanbrooke Won the War in the West*, London, Allen Lane, 2008.
Sherry, Norman, *The Life of Graham Greene, Volume 2: 1939–1955*, London, Jonathan Cape, 1994.
Smith, Jean Edward, *The Liberation of Paris. How Eisenhower, De Gaulle and Von Choltitz Saved the City of Light*, New York, Simon & Schuster, 2019.

Spears, Edward, Sir Maj-Gen, *Fulfilment of a Mission. The Spears Mission to Syria and Lebanon, 1941–1944*, London, Leo Cooper, 1977.
Spears, Edward, Sir, Maj-Gen, *Two Men Who Saved France. Pétain 1917; De Gaulle 1940*, London, Eyre & Spottiswode, 1966.
Taubman, William, *Khrushchev – The Man – His Era*, London, Simon & Schuster, 2017.
Vernier, Anthony, *Assassination in Algiers. Churchill, Roosevelt, de Gaulle and the Murder of Admiral Darlan*, London, Macmillan, 1990.
Weinburg, Gerhard L., *A World at Arms. A Global History of World War II*, Cambridge, Cambridge University Press, 1994.
Williams, Charles, *Pétain*, London, Little Brown, 2005.
Williams, John, *The Guns of Dakar, September 1940*, London, Heinemann, 1976.

Journals

Aron, Robert, 'The Political Methods of General de Gaulle' *International Affairs* 37, no. 1, January 1961, 19–28.
Bowlen, Brett, 'Newsreels, Ideology and Public Order Under Vichy: The Case of *La France en Marche*, *French Historical Studies*, 27/2, 2004, 419–63.
Farmer, Sarah, 'The Communist Resistance in the Haute-Vienne' *French Historical Studies*, XIV/1, 1985, 89–116.
Kelly, George A, 'The French Army Re-enters Politics, 1940–1955' *Political Quarterly*, Vol. LXXVI, 1961, 367–92.
Melka, Robert L., 'Darlan Between Britain and Germany, 1940–41' *Journal of Contemporary History*, 8/1, April 1973, 57–80.
Terraine, John, 'The Army in Modern France' *History Today*, X, 11, November 1961, 733–43.

Electronic Sources

http://ahoy.tk-jk.net/macslo/operationMenace.September.html, accessed 11 September 2008.

Index

Alexandria (Egypt), 42, 127–9, 149, 152–4
Algeria, 18, 38–9, 41–2, 44, 98, 111, 136, 139–40, 148, 157, 191, 201, 210
AMGOT, 52, 79, 85–6, 98, 165, 182
Andrews, Frank, General (1884–1943), 150
Anfa Conference, 143, 153
Asquith, Herbert, Prime Minister (1852–1928), 16
Auchinleck, Claude, General (1884–1981), 85, 99–100, 133

Bangalore, 3
Bedell Smith, Walter, General (1895–1961), 170, 182, 189
Beirut, 95, 165–6, 208
Belgian Congo, 39, 43, 64
Berlin, 64, 75, 93, 101–102, 115, 158
Billotte, Pierre, Captain, ADC to de Gaulle (1906–1992), 134
Bir Hakeim, 156–7
Bizerta, 105, 128–9
Boer, 5
Bombay, 3
Boud'hors, Franz, Lieutenant Colonel (1864–1956), 6–7
Bradley, Omer, General (1893–1981), 198–9
Brazzaville, 46, 77–8, 87, 97, 118, 122, 141
British Expeditionary Force (BEF), 13, 19
Brooke, Alan, General (1883–1963), 14, 23
BRUISER, Operation, 88

Cadogan, Sir Alexander, Permanent Undersecretary of State, Foreign Office (1884–1968), 14, 22, 57–8, 77–8, 81, 147, 185
Cairo, 52, 79, 85–6, 98, 165, 182
Calcutta, 3
Cameroons, 39, 42–4
Campbell, Sir Ronald (1883–1953), 27, 105
Canada, 68, 162, 190, 209
Casablanca, 57, 65, 74, 147, 149, 151, 157, 162

Casey, Richard, UK Minister Resident, Middle East (1890–1976), 129, 149–59, 152–4, 165–6
Catroux, Georges (1877–1969), 7
Chad, 39, 43, 64, 140–1
Chamberlain, Neville, Prime Minister (1869–1940), 17
Churchill, Jennie (1854–1921), 2
Churchill, Randolph (1849–1895), 2
Churchill, Winston (1874–1965), *passim*
Common Market, 1–2
Comte de Paris, Henri (1908–1999), 49, 77–8
Corps Expéditionnaire Français (CEF) French Expeditionary Force, 176–7
Crete, 72, 77–8
Cuba, 3
Cunningham, Andrew, Vice Admiral (1883–1963), 55, 65, 67–8, 88, 127–8
Cyprus, 88, 92
Cyrenaica, 106

Darlan, François, Admiral (1881–1942), 12, 18, 20, 23, 42, 45, 73–4, 77, 81, 85, 109–10, 112–13, 130–32, 139–42
Damascus, 87, 167, 208
Dentz, Henri, Vichy General (1881–1945) 94–5, 97, 99
De Gaulle, *pere*, 7
De Gaulle, Charles, General (1890–1970), *passim*
De Gaulle, Phillipe (1921–), 196
De Gaulle, Yvonne, née Vendroux (1900–1979), 10
Dickens, Gerald Louise Charles, Admiral (1879–1962), 70, 131
Douala, 46, 64
DRAGOON, Operation, Allied landings in southern France, 15 August 1944, 187, 195
Duff Cooper, Alfred, Minister of Information (1890–1954), 38, 40–1, 79, 177–8, 180–1, 196, 208

Eden, Anthony (1897–1977), 30, 32, 120, 123, 137, 186
Egypt, 39, 42, 74, 79, 82, 85–8, 98, 100, 121, 127, 133, 149
Eisenhower, Dwight D., General (1890–1969), 1, 136–7, 150, 169–72, 174–7, 182–4, 186, 189, 195–9

Fighting French (*La France Combattante*), 122–3, 132, 146
Force X, 152–4
Franco, Francisco, General (1892–1975), 40–1, 73, 75, 111
French Equatorial Africa, 28, 39, 42–4, 64, 94, 107
French 2nd Armoured Division, 2eDB, 187, 195, 199

Gallois, Roger (Roger Cocteau) Chief of Staff, Paris Resistance (1905–1995), 198–9
Germany, 6, 9, 11–20, 23–4, 27–9, 31, 33–4, 36–8, 40–3, 45–6, 48, 51, 53, 59, 62, 66, 69, 72, 74–6, 78, 80–1, 83, 85, 90, 98–101, 105–106, 109, 111–13, 115–16, 118–21, 125–6, 130, 132, 134, 138, 147, 150–3, 156, 158, 170, 174–5, 177, 180–1, 186, 192–3, 201, 206–208, 210
Gibraltar, 6, 29, 51–4, 57, 65–6, 91, 136
Giraud, Henri, General (1879–1949), 102–103, 124, 130–3, 136, 139, 140–4, 146–9, 151–4, 157–62, 164, 169, 179
Glubb, John, Lieutenant General, Commander of the Arab Legion, later Jordanian Royal Army (1897–1986), 96
Godfroy, Renè-Émile, Admiral (1888–1970), 127–30, 132, 148–54
Godfroy-Harwood Agreement, 152
Gorka, Olgierd, Professor, Polish Intelligence, 75–6
Gort, John, Lord (1886–1946), 40
Greece, 74, 78
Greene, Graham (1904–1991), 63
Gregory, Mackenzie J., Midshipman, Royal Australian Navy (1922–2014), 58–62

Halifax, Lord (1881–1959), 25, 27, 29, 31, 42, 51–2, 77, 79, 109, 113–15, 117, 150
Harriman, W. Averell (1891–1986), 90, 181–2
Harwood, Henry, Admiral (1888–1950), 128, 130, 132, 149, 152–3
Helleu, Jean (1885–1955), 166

Hitler, Adolf (1889–1945), 11–13, 15–19, 24, 26–7, 34, 39, 42, 51, 72–3, 75–6, 80–1, 99, 104–105, 119, 176, 194
Hoare, R.H., Political Intelligence Department, Foreign Office (1882–1954), 131
Hoare, Sir Samuel, British Ambassador to Spain (1880–1959), 51, 71, 80
Hull, Cordell, US Secretary of State (1871–1955), 104, 109, 146, 180

India, 3–4, 13, 30, 36, 39, 85, 88, 100
Indo-China (Vietnam), 7, 17, 105, 116
Iraq, 86–7, 100
Ironside, Edmund, General (CIGS) (1880–1959), 14
Italy, 20, 23, 29, 35, 39, 42, 50, 53, 64, 77, 81–2, 106, 111, 113, 163–4, 167, 176, 178, 182, 186, 192, 201, 203

Japan, 75, 81, 85, 90, 100, 102, 105–106, 109, 112–13, 124, 206, 208
Juin, Alphonse, General, Commander French Corps in Italy (1888–1967), 176, 182

Knatchbull-Hugessen, Sir Hughe, UK Ambassador to Turkey (1886–1971), 80
Koenig, Marie-Pierre, General (1898–1970), 156, 163, 183, 198–9
Koenigswater (de Koenig), 46
Kopański Brigade, 89
Kopański, Stefan, General (1895–1976), 89
Kowalewski, Jan, Lieutenant Colonel, Polish Intelligence (1892–1965), 75

Lampson, Sir Miles (1880–1964), 85–7
Lascelles, Sir Alan, Counsellor to King George VI (1897–1981), 103, 204
Leahy, William, Admiral (1875–1959), 104, 112–13, 121
Lebanon, 10, 36, 42, 84–5, 90, 92–4, 100, 165–7, 206
Leclerc, Philippe Leclerc de Hauteclocque, General (1902–1947), 67, 170–1, 195–200
Lille, 6
Lloyd George, David (1863–1945), 8, 16
Lyttelton, Oliver (1893–1972), 94–9

Mack, William Henry Bradshaw, Head of French Department, Foreign Office (1894–1974), 46, 71, 76, 131, 142–3, 147

Index 233

Macmillan, Harold (1894–1986), 1, 139–40, 142, 144–5, 148, 153–61, 163–5
Madagascar, 116, 120–1
Mahdi, 4
Mandel, Georges (1885–1944), 20, 26, 40
Marlborough, 2, 4, 6
Massigli, René (1888–1988), 142, 144
MENACE, Operation, 45–6, 52–4, 56–9, 61–5
Menzies, Robert (1894–1978), 90, 92
Michelier, Felix, Vice Admiral (Vichy Navy) (1887–1966), 149
Molotov, Vyacheslav Mikhaylovich (né Skryabin) (1890–1986), 75
Monnet, Jean (1888–1979), 25, 159, 161–2
Muselier, Émile, Admiral (1882–1965), 45–7, 70–1, 83–4, 132

Narvik, 19, 100
New Caledonia, 38, 43, 69
New Hebrides, 38, 69
Noguès, Augustine, General (C-in-C, French Armed Forces), 40, 141
Normandy, 19, 45, 64, 168–9, 176, 178–9, 181–3, 185–7, 189, 192, 195–6, 198
North-West Frontier, 3
Norway, 13, 19, 24, 31, 194

Omdurman, Battle of, 1898, 4
Oran, Mers-el-Kebir, 28–9, 36, 58, 63, 105, 120, 124–5, 127, 181
OVERLORD, Operation, 45, 168, 181–2

Palewski, Gaston (1901–1984), 47–8
Pétain, Philippe, Marshal (1856–1951), 20–1, 25–6, 31, 35, 43, 51, 67, 72–6, 105, 111–14, 125–6, 135–7, 185
Poland, 9–11, 13, 18, 35, 75, 89, 99, 158, 163, 192, 194, 201–202, 207

Rochat, Charles-Antoine, 112
Roosevelt, Franklin D. (1882–1945), 22, 90–2, 102–106, 108–17, 131, 134–5, 137–8, 140, 142, 145, 150–1, 154–5, 157–65, 168–82, 184–91, 195, 198, 205
Roy, Philippe, Captain, 135

Saint Pierre, 103–104, 107–109, 115
Salisbury-Jones, Colonel, 35–6
Sargent, Orme (1884–1962), 47
Ships,

Ark Royal, HMS, 57, 61
Australia, HMAS, 57–62
Barham, HMS, 58, 60–1
Cumberland, HMS, 59
Sikorski, Władysław, General, Polish Prime Minister in Exile (1881–1943), 8, 14, 17, 35, 70, 123, 156, 210
Smuts, Jan, Field Marshal, Prime Minister of South Africa (1870–1950), 74
Spears, Edward, Major General (1886–1974), 8–9, 15, 23, 30, 40, 57, 65, 78, 80, 85, 88–9, 97–8, 131, 165
Spears Mission, The, 66–7, 71
Speight, R.C., 77
Stalin, Joseph (1878–1953), 81–2, 99, 126, 158–60, 162–4, 169, 177, 179, 192–4, 202–203, 207, 209
Stettinius, Edward (1900–1949), 169, 181
Sudan, 3–4
Suez Canal, 36, 79, 87, 122
Syria, 32, 35–6, 42, 44–5, 52, 74, 80–1, 84–100, 108, 120, 127, 131, 141, 165–7, 206, 208–209

Thorez, Maurice (1900–1964), 202–203
TORCH, Operation, 119, 134, 136

USA, 37, 42, 53, 59, 63, 72–4, 81, 83, 90–1, 101–102, 104–109, 112–14, 118–20, 124, 128, 130, 135–6, 138–9, 141–2, 150–1, 155–6, 160, 162, 168, 172, 177–9, 184, 189–91, 196, 202, 209

Vichy, 17, 19, 23, 28–9, 31, 33–5, 37–8, 40, 43–6, 50–4, 57–63, 65–9, 72–4, 76–7, 79, 80–2, 84–6, 89–95, 96–101, 103–30, 132–4, 136–41, 143–4, 149, 151, 157, 159, 160, 173–5, 177, 180, 182–3, 185, 190–1, 193, 195, 197, 201, 204–206, 210

Waugh, Evelyn (1903–1966), 62–3
Wavell, A.P., General (1883–1950), 32, 36, 86–9, 93
Weygand, General (1867–1965), 10, 14, 20, 34–5, 42, 49–52, 69, 72–4, 76–81, 86, 91–2, 105–106, 124, 126, 158, 182
Wilson, Sir Henry Maitland, General (1881–1964), 94, 96–8, 165–7
Wilson, Woodrow (1856–1924), 10
Winant, John, US Ambassador to the UK (1889–1947), 105

Dear Reader,

We hope you have enjoyed this book, but why not share your views on social media? You can also follow our pages to see more about our other products: facebook.com/penandswordbooks or follow us on Twitter @penswordbooks

You can also view our products at www.pen-and-sword.co.uk (UK and ROW) or www.penandswordbooks.com (North America).

To keep up to date with our latest releases and online catalogues, please sign up to our newsletter at: www.pen-and-sword.co.uk/newsletter

If you would like a printed catalogue with our latest books, then please email: enquiries@pen-and-sword.co.uk or telephone: 01226 734555 (UK and ROW) or email: Uspen-and-sword@casematepublishers.com or telephone: (610) 853-9131 (North America).

We respect your privacy and we will only use personal information to send you information about our products.

Thank you!